SONG OF THE RAINBOW

A work on depiction of music through the medium of paintings in the Indian tradition

Song of the Rainbow

A Work on Depiction of Music through the Medium of Paintings in the Indian Tradition

DR. RICHA JAIN

KANISHKA PUBLISHERS, DISTRIBUTORS

NEW DELHI - 110 002

KANISHKA PUBLISHERS, DISTRIBUTORS
4697/5-21A, Ansari Road, Daryaganj
New Delhi-110 002
Phones : 327 0497, 328 8285
Fax : 011-328 8285

First Published 2002

ISBN 81-7391-496-6

Printed in India

Published by Madan Sachdeva for Kanishka Publishers, Distributors, 4697/5-21A, Ansari Road, Daryaganj, New Delhi-110 002. Typeset by Welcome Computers, New Delhi, and Printed at Nice Printing Press, Delhi.

Preface

A unique feature of the Indian tradition of miniature painting has been the visual interpretation of Rāgas and Rāginîs of traditional classical music. The Rāgas and Rāginîs were given an iconographic form of deities or the more secular Nāyaka and Nāyikās. Such a visualisation of music through paintings received great impetus from prayer formulas or 'dhyānas' given in various Sanskrit, Hindi and even dialect verses. These were given on top of the paintings. Thus, such paintings which were given the name, 'Rāgamalā' or a garland of Rāgas, constituted a confluence of music, painting as well as poetry. It was but obvious that they attracted attention from scholars not only from within the country, but also throughout the world. However, the musical aspect has been largely ignored until now, possibly because mostly painters have shown interest in the Rāgamalā series of paintings. Some work on this topic has been done in recent years, but the depiction of actual musical phrases in ascent or descent through paintings was so far deemed an impossibility. In the thesis titled 'Depiction of music through the medium of paintings in the Indian tradition', it has been an attempt to widen the musical horizon of Rāgamālā miniature paintings by actually depicting some characteristic phrases of chosen Rāgas. It is not being claimed that such a depiction is an actual translation of concert music in its total form. Only the framework of the tonal structure of the Rāgas or Rāginî has been inculcated in the paintings using colours along with the iconographic structure in order to create a link between practical music and the paintings. Such paintings can serve as an aid to the learning process in initial stages for students or connoisseurs of music, who can fathom the basic structure of the umpteen Rāgas through merely glancing at the paintings. These paintings serve as examples of the principle of assimilation of the fine arts and are of great significance for the study of Aesthetics.

The book has been divided into four chapters. The first chapter deals with art and the mutual relationship between the fine arts. Since the subject of the book is concerned with an assimilation of the fine arts of music, painting and poesis, a study of the basic elements of fine arts and the comparison of fine arts on their basis has been given in this chapter. The second chapter deals with the Indian tradition of classical music. The historical background of Indian classical music according to ancient canonical works and later authorities on music has been given in this chapter ranging from Vedic to Modern period. A brief description of various styles and Gharānās or schools of Indian classical music has also been given. In the third chapter, the tradition of painting in India has been taken up. The historical development of Indian painting on the basis of literary and archeological sources has been studied. The various schools of painting in Indian tradition, the materials and techniques of minature painting and description of Rāgamālā miniature paintings in these schools has been given in this chapter. The fourth chapter involves the actual depiction of musical phrases through paintings in which original work has been done by the author. Musical phrases have been depicted in three demonstrative paintings made by the author. The phrases depicted have been explained with the help of graphs. This is followed by conclusion and appendices etc. Care has been taken to complete the entire work scientifically, with the help of graphs and tables wherever required.

Dr. Richa Jain

Acknowledgements

I take this opportunity to express my sincere gratitude of all who have contibuted to the completion of this book. Most of all, I would like to express my deep sense of gratitude to Prof. Krishna Bisht for her inspiration and guidance. I will also take the opportunity to thank my brother and teacher Tilak Gitai, who took pains to appraise me with the intricacies of miniature painting. I would also like to thank the library staffs of Faculty of Music and Fine Arts, Lalit Kala Academy, Sangeet Natak Academy and the College of Art, New Delhi. I am particularly indebted to Ms. Shanta Jindal, Librarian-in-charge, College of Art and Mr. Mohammad Haroon, Librarian-in-charge, Faculty of Music and Fine Arts, who painstakingly provided me with assistance in consulting rare books.

I express my deep gratitude to my father-in-law, Prof. P.C. Jain, whose continuous support and keen interest has gone a long way towards the accomplishment of this work. I find no words to thank him for his valuable suggestions during the proof reading. I am particularly indebted to my brother-in-law, Ashish, for helping me bringout the graphs through computer, despite constraints of time.

Words are indeed inadequate to express the feelings of gratitude to my beloved husband, Maneesh, without whose support and constant cooperation, this book could not have seen the light of this day.

Dr. Richa Jain

Acknowledgements

I take this opportunity to express my sincere gratitude to all who have contributed to the completion of this book. Most of all, I would like to express my deep sense of gratitude to Prof. Krishna Bisht for her inspiration and guidance. I will also take the opportunity to thank my brother and teacher Shri K.C. Gupta who took pains to acquaint me with the intricacies of miniature painting. I would also like to thank the library staff of Faculty of Music and Fine Arts, Lalit Kala Academy, Sangeet Natak Academy and the College of Art, New Delhi. I am particularly indebted to Ms. Shanta Jain, Librarian-incharge, College of Art and Mr. Mohammad Hateem, Librarian-incharge, Faculty of Music and Fine Arts, who painstakingly provided me with assistance in consulting rare books.

I express my deep gratitude to my father-in-law, Prof. P.C. Jain, whose continuous support and keen interest has gone a long way towards the accomplishment of this work. I find no words to thank him for the valuable suggestions during the proof reading. I am particularly indebted to my brother-in-law, Ashish, for helping me through the graphics through computer, despite constraints of time.

Words are but inadequate to express the feelings of gratitude to my beloved husband, Mukesh, without whose support and constant cooperation this book could not have seen the light of this day.

—Dr. Richa Jain

Contents

List of Graphs

List of Plates

List of Tables

(i) Tables in Chapter 2

(ii) Tables in Appendix I

(iii) Table in Chapter 4

1
Art and the Mutual Relationship of the Fine Arts

INTRODUCTION

Rāgamālā Paintings are a pictorial interpretation of music in the Indian tradition. The paintings are a symbolic representation of the Rāgas and Rāginîs as prevalent in the medieval times. In their own unique way, the paintings convey to us the kind of music that was in vogue during the particular period.

The Rāgamālā miniature paintings are a beautiful amalgamation of music, painting and poetry. Due to this unique combination, these paintings are often held in awe the world over. The paintings are not only a classical example of traditional Indian art, but also prove the mutual relationship between the fine arts. Thus, they are of immense value for the study of various arts. It will therefore be feasible to discuss about art, its elements and the mutual relationship between the fine arts prior to the main subject.

ART

The word *Art* is so often used in day to day language, for instance, 'he has the art of making friends', and so on. We might say this is not a correct application of the term, but such usage is in the elementary sense. That is in the sense of a skill. According to Eric Gill, 'Art is skill, that is the first meaning of the word (art)'[1]. The Encyclopedia Britannica defines 'Art' thus.

> 'Art, in its most basic meaning, signifies a skill or ability. This definition holds true for its latin antecedent, ars, as well as its German equivalent, kunst (derived from könen 'to be able')'.[2]

It further states that 'while art continues to be associated with basic skills (e.g., the art of gardening, the art of warfare), the term more generally carries the connotation of non utilitarian activities, the art of painting, the art of poetry and the art of music.'[3]

The Indian equivalent of Art is 'Kalā', which has also been used in similar context since ancient time. This word has first been mentioned in the Rigveda.[4] The word 'Kalā' is derived from the root 'kal' of Sanskrit, meaning expression of the word in clear voice, contemplation, collection, meditation etc. Therefore, Kalā or art constitutes the collection of feelings or ideas upon which the artist contemplates and subsequently expresses.

Kalā is also known to be a derivative of the root 'lā', meaning to receive or to give. Accordingly, it can also be said that it gives pleasure. There are various theories about art in Indian as well as Western aesthetics. Let us first consider the various viewpoints regarding art before actually defining it.

Various Viewpoints on Art

(a) Indian Philosophers :

(*i*) Śukrācārya—'Learning (Vidyā) and art (Kalā) both are innumerable, yet number of learning has been counted as grossly thirty two and that of art as sixty four. Whatsoever is definable by words, that is learning, but what everybody, with an aesthetic taste, even a dumb, can do or explain, is an art.'[5]

(*ii*) Kshemarāj—'Art brings out the soul of materials or 'Pramātā' in a controlled manner, that is why it is called 'Kalā'.'[6]

(*iii*) K.C. Pandey—'Kalā (Art) means that human activity, the characteristic features of which are observation, calculation, contemplation and clear expression.'[7]

(*iv*) S.K. Saxena—'Art, I believe, is the creative invocation of (what is in principle) a presence.'[8]

(*v*) H.L. Sharma—'Art in the simplest form, means to create, to do, to express. Man creates a form, or does something clever, or he expresses his meaning and motive. This calls for skill and a mastery over his muscle and mind. If what he creates, does and builds has a lasting value of joy for many men, it becomes a work of art. This work we call beautiful.'[9]

(*vi*) Dr. Syamala Gupta—'To give a definite form to one's imagination is the true objective of art.'[10]

(b) Western Philosophers :

(*i*) Kant (18th century)—'Art is not pure beauty wholly detached from concept, it is adherent beauty which presupposes and attaches itself to a concept'. Art may represent natural ugliness, artistic beauty 'is not a beautiful thing but a beautiful representation of a thing.'[11]

(*ii*) Benedetto Croce (1866-1952 AD)—'Art is intuition ... intuition is expression of impressions.'[12]

(*iii*) S.K. Langer (mid twentieth century)—Art is a 'creation of forms symbolic of human feeling'[13] ... works of art are 'images of the forms of feelings' and there purpose is to 'express its creator's ideas of immediate felt life'.

Evaluation of the Viewpoints on Art

The old Platonian view of considering art as merely an imitation of nature has given way to the 'expression theory' of art. A meeting ground of these two theories can be found in Kant's philosophy, when he uses the term 'representation'. The great Italian philosopher Benedetto Croce in his idealistic philosophy of art used the word 'expression' to explain art in his *Aesthetic.* This approach received the most vocal support from Susanne K. Langer. The expression theory of art that Langer advocates, arose with the Romanticism of the 19th century Europe. Many poets and artists of the period drew inspiration from Wordsworth's famous dictum 'Poetry is the spontaneous overflow of powerful feelings'.

The expression theory of art appears in a somewhat modified form in Leo Tolstoy's *What is Art* (1896 AD). Instead of the term 'expression', he uses 'communication' or 'transmission' of the feelings. Tolstoy believes art to be a means of communication in which the artist transmits via his art work, his own feeling. Langer differs from this opinion in that, art expresses human feeling, not the actual present feeling of the artist himself. According to Langer,

(*i*) Art is the creation of forms.

(*ii*) Art expresses human feeling. That is, not the actual

present feeling of the artist himself, but his 'knowledge of human feeling'.[14]

(*iii*) Artistic expression is symbolic. It is symbolic in the sense that it expresses the artists 'knowledge of the life of feeling'. This knowledge is 'articulated' in such a manner, so as to enable the beholder to 'contemplate life as it feels'.

Dr. H.L. Sharma has also elaborated the same view point. He endorses the Indian philosophy of a work of art giving joy. Kshemarāj follows the hedonistic moral viewpoint that believes art to enlighten the soul. Dr. Syamala Gupta also conforms to Langer's treatment of an art work as a 'form'. Dr. S.K. Saxena refers to art as a 'creative invocation of a presence'. In creation, he includes :

(*i*) The 'emergent' quality and unity (or form) of art; and

(*ii*) The interplay of process and the product.

By 'presence', he means a 'felt influence' in a manner similar to Marcel as he himself says. To invoke is 'to call up a being or an influence that is higher or benevolent', suggesting a transcendental quality of art. The presence that is invoked is 'received, felt or gathered to oneself ... 'whatever be the precise form of this activity, a passage from words to feeling imagery or the indrawn sweetness of intense musicality, it is always a disinterested self subjugation to the other.'[15] He refers to it as a communion rather than communication.

K.C. Pandey has given the Indian perspective of art. According to him, the definition of art (Kalā) is complete in the meaning of the word 'Kalā' itself. The *activity* involves observation (of surrounding environment and life in general), calculation, contemplation (of the ideas thus collected) and their clear expression in that order.

An artist creates a form using his imagination. He brings into being something which was not there before, in the form of an illusion. This illusion is virtual space in visual arts, virtual time in auditory arts, kinetic volume in sculpture, virtual domain in architecture and virtual life in poesis. By careful selection of images and symbols, he derives relationships within a virtual realm. To deliver his ideas, he requires a medium. That medium is his particular artistic skill. Art, thus, becomes an *expressive form in images and symbols created by the artist's imagination.* This 'form' conveys his ideas and interpretations of human feeling cultured throughout his life *symbolically*. The effect that the expressive form produces on its beholder is that of aesthetic rapture. The factor responsible for this experience is called 'Rasa' in Indian tradition, which is manifest within the *Significant or expressive form.* Rasa lies latent within this form, which results in aesthetic experience upon receiving external stimuli.[16] The factor of human feeling is conveyed through Rasa which becomes the significance of the art form. This can be described as 'that living or dynamic quality of the form resulting in the aesthetic experience referred to as 'Rasa nishpatti' in Indian Aesthetics, culminating, into a feeling akin to that of the absolute (*Brahmānanda Sahodara*' or twin brother of *Brahmānanda*) at the highest level. Thus, Rasa is the soul or essence of an art form.

THE FINE AND UTILITARIAN ARTS

The term 'fine arts' is a translation of the French 'beaux-arts', meaning the arts concerned only with the beautiful. In other words, those arts which are cultivated more for their own sake rather than for some ulterior purpose, are fine arts. They afford an intrinsic pleasure to those who experience them. K.C. Pandey relates this pleasure to the feeling of 'the absolute in sensuous garb, and aesthetical relation as distinct from the utilitarian, with a work of which gives rise or leads to the experience of the absolute.'[17]

In Western aesthetics, Hegel recognises five fine arts, namely, architecture, music, poetry (Langer uses the term *poesis* which is more closer to the Indian equivalent *Kāvya*), sculpture and painting. He has distinguished them into three categories viz, *symbolic,* in which he includes architecture, *classical,* which includes sculpture and *romantic*,. which consists of music, painting and poetry. For poetry he keeps an open boundary saying it can be included in any category, because it is based mainly on imagination. This perspective seems to have fault, because we can say the same for music and painting, particularly in the Indian context. In Indian aesthetics, there was no classification uptil the vedic period. Then Pancāl classified the arts into *Mula* and *Antara.* He enumerated sixty four Mula and five hundred and eighteen Antara arts. Later, the sage Bharata classified them as *Mukhya* and *Gauna.* Finally, the Indian authorities on aesthetics accepted three arts as absolute or independent, which correspond to the fine arts. They are poetics (Kāvya) , music and architecture. These were known respectively as Rasa-Brahmavāda, Nada-Brahmavāda and Vastu-Brahmavāda. Painting and sculpture were included with architecture for theoretical purposes. Similarly music consisted of dance as well. Thus,

***Gïtam vādyam tathâ nrittam trayam samgitam ucyate*[18]**

Utilitarian arts are usually analogous to craft. They have the ability to give pleasure to the beholder and also require a certain level of creativity and skill. For example cookery, pottery, flower arrangement, hair dressing etc. Yet, they don't lead us to experience the absolute. As compared to the fine arts, they have a specific purpose to achieve. Whereas for pure or fine arts, Stanislavsky says 'the very least utilitarian purpose or tendency, brought into the realm of pure art kills art instantly'.[19] For utilitarian art or craft, Collingwood says 'craft envisages preconceived ends, dinstinct from the means there to which are discarded when the end is achieved ... distinctions between matter and form, raw material and artifact are clear in craft, not in the case of pure art'.[20] Also, the level of complexity varies in both that is, the fine arts are much more complex than utilitarian arts.

There are other systems of classification of art also, such as auditory, visual and audio visual arts, arts of time and arts of space, moving and stationary, performing and non-performing, decorative and expressive and the like. Here it ought to be noted that philosophers such as Croce, were against the very idea of classifying the arts in a manner that set aesthetic limits to each art. He believed that the 'so called arts have no aesthetic limit, because in order to have them they would also need to have aesthetic existence in their particularity and we have demonstrated the altogether empirical genesis of these partitions (by defining art). Consequently, any attempt at an aesthetic classification of the arts is absurd. If they be without limits they are not exactly determinable and consequently cannot be philosophically classified'.[21]

THE BASIC ELEMENTS OF FINE ARTS

According to Aristotle, arts differ in their subject, medium and style. Dr. Kumar Vimal points out that though the arts may differ in their style, technique, mode of expression and communication, there is an elementary relationship between the arts. All fine arts have the basic elements of imagination, images, symbols and of course beauty of form. The difference is in their combination and proportion. Though peculiar to its nature also, these basic elements are present in all probability. Before going into the details of these elements, let us first discuss what exactly is meant by the word 'element'. An element is a factor or unit that contributes to the creation of the 'presence' or 'semblance' that is art. Elements are actual components of the total form. They differ from the materials like the colours on the palette and the strings of the instrument. These same colours become elements of a painting when they become part of the 'significant form'. Similarly, when the strings of an instrument are plucked, they become notes, which are elements of music. These individual elements take up the role of embodiment of basic elements for their respective art form. The basic elements are discussed below :

Beauty (Form or Rupa)

According to Richard Payne Knight 'the word beauty is a general term of approbation of the most vague and extensive meaning, applied indiscriminately to almost everything that is pleasing, either to the sense, the imagination, or the understanding, whatever the nature of it be, whether a material substance, a moral excellence, or an intellectual theorem'.[22]

F.E. Sparshott uses the phrase 'that delights perception'[23] for beauty, but also says that 'it is not only things perceptible by the senses that are called beautiful'.[24]

The word 'beauty' is derived by addition of the suffix 'ty' to the word 'beau'. The word 'beau' stands for girl's admirer, lover or suitor. Thus, beauty in the literal sense means the quality of the beloved. Beauty in the context of art is often used synonymously to the sublime. Sparshott calls it the extreme form of beauty. In the Indian context also this usage is more appropriate. The Hindi equivalent for beauty is 'saundarya' derived from sundara = su + und-valedane + arah, which means that which makes the soul sublime.[25]

Dr. H.L. Sharma in '*Aesthetic Education and the Grammar of Art* speaks of beauty as 'a whole consisting of parts related to each other'.[26] According to him, beauty is 'an aesthetic creation of forms, which differ from the ugly in that, the parts are not just put together, but are organised and vitally connected with each other'. Such a concept of beauty holds true in the case of art. Even if ugliness is shown in a work of art, it is shown in a beautiful manner. As Kant says, art is 'a beautiful representation of a thing'. Plotinus (204-269 AD) distinguished the beautiful from the ugly in that there is predominance of matter over form in the ugly.

In Indian Aesthetics, a single term for beauty or form has been used—'Rupa'. This seems analogous to the term 'significant form' coined by Clive Bell, that Langer has so forcefully advocated. According to Langer 'significant form is the essence of every art'.[27] Langer has used the term to include all art, whereas Bell uses it initially only for visual art, thus ... 'lines and colours combined in a particular way, certain forms and relation of forms, stir our aesthetic emotions. These relations and combinations of lines and colours, these aesthetically moving forms, I call 'significant form' and it is the one quality common to all works of visual art'.[28]

Certain factors contribute to the achievement of beauty such as purity of medium, balance, rhythm, and harmony. The Indian tradition identifies ten ways in which parts combine to form aesthetically pleasing wholes. These are Slesa[29], Madhurya, Udarata, Samadhi etc. Rasa is an essential part of Rupa, which leads to the experience of the absolute. Without Rasa, Rupa is like a body without soul.

Imagination

The faculty of the mind to create images is of utmost importance for an artist. According to Natal's standard dictionary, imagination is,

(*i*) The strictly poetic or creative faculty as exhibited in the vivid conceptions and combination, more specially of the fine arts;
(*ii*) Image in the mind;
(*iii*) Idea;
(*iv*) Contrivance or device;
(*v*) A unsolid or fanciful opinion.

The last explanation seems to be in the context of colloquial usage. Dr. Ramlakhan Shukla clearly differentiates between fancy and imagination. He refers to fancy as an uncontrolled mental faculty, whereas imagination is more controlled.

Plotinus differentiates between memory and imagination by relating memory to recording of actual facts by the mind whereas in the latter there is 'no idea of truth or falsity with reference to external object and implies no relation to any past time, in which its contents were first experienced'.[30]

According to De.E. Litre, ParA.Beaujeau, Dictionnaire de La Langue Francaise, there are two meanings of imagination,

(*i*) 'A faculty that we have of recalling vividly, and of seeing, so to speak, objects that are no longer before our eyes; and

(*ii*) Particularly in literature and the fine arts, the faculty of inventing, of conceiving, joined to the talent of rendering conceptions in a lively manner'.

The second type, Litre calls *creative imagination.* Plotinus gives two types of imagination—sensible and intellectual. Sensible imagination consists of impact from outside on the irrational soul. It is the final stage of perceptual operation, when a percept becomes a purely mental representation. As an image making faculty, related to perception, sensible imagination is the summit of the perceptual faculty. Intellectual imagination is attached to the rational soul. It gives form to intellectual and spiritual conceptions. It can also spiritualise what is visible and corporeal, filling it with a higher meaning. Plotinus has linked art to intellectual imagination.

'Kalpanā' is the Hindi equivalent for imagination. It is the derivative of the root 'klripa + lyut'[31], with its meaning ranging from forming, arranging, invention, imagination to an idea, fancy or image (conceived in the mind), the power of forming ideas.

Images

The Encyclopedia Britannica quotes C.W. Bray as—'images are conscious memories which reproduce a previous perception in whole or in part, in the absence of the original stimulus to the perception'.[32] It further, 'possibly every sense can produce its own type of image, the visual being the commonest and the most stirring, though it has been claimed that the organic sensations, including pain, and the muscular or kinesthetic sense may not call up conscious memories but actually, if faintly, reinstate immanet experience'.[33]

The concept of synaesthesia is also associated with imagery, where 'a percept (example the sound of a violin) may evoke an image not of the instrument but of a colour or texture, so a timbre, a pitch, a voice quality, even a musical key, may conjure up images of colour ... there may also be associations between images of the different senses, or, if the auditory image (say of a voice) cannot be evoked, a visual image (example of gray velvet) may symbolise the voice'[34]. The concept of *Dhyān* in Indian Classical Music in which different images symbolise different Rāgas, is an extension of this principle.

According to Dr. Kumar Vimal, 'imagery is the practical aspect of art, that arises from imagination. It is a step towards the development of imagination. Imagination gives rise to images and images form symbols. When imagination takes a visual/ iconographic form, then images are created and when images are formulated to depict a particular concept then symbols come into being. Thus, from the analytical point of view of aesthetics, image is the meeting point of imagination and symbol'.[35]

Symbols and Symbolisation

S.K. Langer has called all art a *symbolic activity*. She refers to symbolisation as an 'act essential to thought' and prior to it. Symbolisation is the starting point of all intellection in the human sense and is more general than thinking, fancying, or taking action'.[36] Further she says, 'the fact that the human brain is constantly carrying on a process of *symbolic transformation of experiential data* that come to it *causes* it to be a veritable fountain of more or less spontaneous ideas'.[37] When artistic expression is called symbolic, it is the artist's, 'knowledge of the life of feeling' that is expressed . This knowledge is conveyed in such a way, so as to enable the beholder to 'contemplate life as it feels'. The function of symbols is the 'articulation and presentation of concepts for contemplation'.[38] A symbol is meant to represent something. In language for instance, words represent or stand for thought. Thus, words are verbal symbols of thought. According to Langer, 'A signal is comprehended if it serves to make us notice the object or situation it bespeaks. A symbol is understood when we conceive the idea it presents'.[39]

According to R.K. Ghosh 'the symbol leads to a conception that fits a certain object'.[40] For example the colour white is symbolic of purity. Whereas smoke signifies the presence of fire. Langer distinguishes two types of symbols—Presentational and Discursive. In the case of the former, the various units contribute to the total meaning without a separate entity, such as in art. In the latter, the units contribute to the whole meaning, without losing their set individual meanings, such as in words.

THE FINE ARTS

The five fine arts, namely-music, painting, sculpture, architecture and poesis are being discussed in this section. As given earlier, the basic elements of the fine arts are beauty (form or rupa), images, imagination and symbols (symbolisation). These elements are incorporated in each fine art through the unique elements of the particular fine art. In this section, the infusion of basic as well as particular elements in relation to the fine arts is being discussed taking each fine art individually. It will be appropriate to start with music, since it is the main subject of this thesis.

Music

Among the fine arts, music is a performing or occurent art. It is the closest to being a living form, particularly in the case of vocal music, since the medium is also organic. According to S.K. Langer the essence of music is 'the creation of virtual time, and its complete determination by the movement of audible forms'.[41] She refers to music as 'a tonal analogue of emotive life'.[42]

In his lecture on 'Hindustāni Music—Some Basic Reflections'[43], S.K. Saxena throws light on fundamental facts of music. According to him the elements of music are notes and rhythm. Further, he elaborates on how the virtual realm in music is created by the opening line of the composition (Sthayi). In artistic jargon, it is referred to as *zameen kāyam karnā.* For Rāga, the essential feature of Hindustāni music, he says, 'an intimate unity of accents that make for musical experience..,'[44] and quotes Ustad Rahimuddin Dagar, who said of a Raga as being 'like a living entity and that it is to be handled with care and love which a living organism demands'.

The basic elements of art find full place in the musical matrix. In fact, S.K. Langer has propounded the theory of expressive form for all arts, with music as the basis. The reason that she gives for this is that it exhibits pure form not as an embellishment, but as its very essence ... 'purely artistic meaning should be most accessible through musical works.'[45]

Classical music, whether Indian or Western is nothing but pure expressive form consistent in the dynamic tonal structures. The basic elements, such as beauty, imagination etc., find embodiment through the unique elements of music, the notes, rhythms and words (in case of vocal) as discussed below (with particular reference to Indian style of classical music) :

(a) Basic Elements :

1. *Beauty*—Beauty of form emanates form the 'presence' as a whole that the musician creates. The complete significant form depends on many factors such as purity of sounds, the increase or decrease of volume and pause at appropriate places and the most important factor being the artist's talent in organising the matrix of audible forms with a proper balance and sense of rhythm. When words are used in vocal music, the manner in which weight is given to the letters determines the beauty of the form. Various embellishments also contributes to the element of beauty in music. For instance, the slight use of adjacent note(kaṇ) in the renditions of a note, through 'meenḍ'[46] at once enhances the beauty, however, only a correct proportion of such embellishments creates beauty.

2. *Imagination*—The *upaj* in Dhrupad or *bol banāv* in Khyāl and Thumri styles of Indian classical music are pure imagination. The word 'khyāl' itself means imagination .What the artist calls *baḍat* in technical jargon or the elaboration of the Rāga, is nothing but imagination. The artist innovates ex tempore in the Indian classical forms of music. The same may not be applied to Western classical music, but even there, the original piece of composition is the composer's imagination.

3. *Symbols*—The symbols here are the notes and rhythm (non-discursive) and in case of vocal, we have words also (discursive). The notes and rhythm do not have their separate individuality, but merge to give a single presence of a common idea. Certain feelings or processes of the mind, which cannot find expression through discursive means are communicated through these symbols.

4. *Images*—Each Rāga has its own image or 'Dhyāna' which will be discussed at length. The image can be of a particular idol associated with a certain feeling or symbolic of some human emotion. Therefore, indirectly, the notes and rhythm signify certain feelings. Certain factors contribute to the expression of certain human emotions (Rasas), such as slow tempo, along with the notes komal ṛshabha and madhyam prominent gives the impression of Raudra (Śiva), with komal nisāda—Karuṇa, with śuddha notes —Ṣānta (a sage or Brahma), fast tempos—erotic (Śrngāra)—Krishna and Rādha.

Certain beats or tāla as well as type of instrument also determines the type of feeling expressed such as Kaḥarwa tāla —Śrngāra, Pakhāwaj instrument—Raudra etc.

(b) Particular Elements:

1. *Notes*—The most fundamental audible unit of music is the note. There are seven basic notes in the *Saptaka* of Indian classical music which takes the name of an octave in Western classical music by the repetition of the first note in the end. The notes are essentially the same except for a slight difference in the frequency of one note.

Table 1(a)

S.No.	*Indian Notes*	*Freq. of Notes*	*Western Notes*	*Freq. of Notes*
1.	Ṣadja (Sa)	240	Do (C)	240
2.	Ṛshabh (Re)	270	Re (D)	270
3.	Gandhār (Ga)	300	Me (E)	300
4.	Madhyama (Ma)	320	Fa (F)	320
5.	Pancama (Pa)	360	So (G)	360
6.	Dhaivata (Dha)	405	La (A)	400
7.	Niṣāda (Ni)	450	Si (B)	450
8.	Saḍja (Sa)	480	Do (C)	480

Details of the note are given in the Chapter 2.

2. *Rhythm*—Rhythm is a measure of time. Music is essentially a fine art of time, the primary illusion being that of virtual time. In Indian classical music, a composition is set in a particular 'tāla'. There are innumerable tālas or beats with definite intervals. Owing to these beats, which signify rhythm, the musical form gets a

semblance of motion, or in a way, becomes a semblance of *living form*[47]. There is an inherent rhythm in all life forms. The heart beat and breathing signify rhythm in life processes. Hence, the basic requirement for symbolic transformation, a common analogy of form, is met with between music and life.

According to S.K. Langer, 'the essence of rhythm is the preparation of a new event by the ending of the previous one'[48] ...Rhythm is the setting up of new tensions by the resolution of the former ones. They need not be of equal duration at all; but the situation that begets the new crisis must be inherent in the denouement of its fore runner ... Rhythm is the building up of a new dynamic Gestalt in the very process of a former one's passing away'[49].

3. *Words*—A constituent of vocal music, words enhance the 'bhāva' or feeling as well as meaning which is the content of the form. As has earlier been said, they also contribute to the beautification of the form, when used aesthetically according to the artist's talent. Even though, it is possible to convey the musical import without words, the use of words makes music more far reaching and touches the soul of the layman as well.

Painting

Painting and other plastic arts involve creation of virtual space and its organisation by visible forms. Virtual space is 'the primary illusion in which all harmonious forms exist as secondary illusions, created symbols for the expression of feelings and emotion... whether it be two dimensional or three, it is continuous in all its possible directions, and infinitely plastic'.[50]

Visual space in painting provides the frame work for the actual symbolic form in the same way as virtual time in the case of music. Just like in music, where the primary illusion of virtual time comes with the first line of the composition, in painting, the primary illusion of virtual space comes with the first stroke of brush or pencil.

The basic elements of art are asserted in painting through colourful motifs as follows :

1. *Beauty of Form*—Through a proper composition of motifs having a balanced proportion of colours, the form is created. Its beauty depends on the purity of colour and motifs, a harmony of

colours and a certain rhythm that is conveyed through the right postures of the figure depicted in the painting. In the traditional Indian painting, this element is divided into several parts which come under the six elements peculiar to painting. This will be explained later.

2. *Imagination*—The element of imagination is very much present in case of painting, though is a lesser proportion than in music and poetry. Here also abstract painting is based purely on imagination, whereas figurative painting has some amount of symbolic representation, either if nature or the artist's notions about life and ideals.

3. *Symbols (Symbolisation)*—In case of painting, there is more of symbolisation than imagination. Symbols in the form of colours as well as motifs can express their importance with great clarity. For e.g., the colour white symbolises purity, red-courage and anger. In case of motifs—a circle denotes completeness, a bird denotes freedom etc., the sun conveys a spirituality and so on.

4. *Images*—Images are an important element of pictorial art. As compared to other forms of art, this element is directly expressed within the significant form. Owing to the visual character of this art, the motifs directly transmit the artist's visual imagery. For e.g., if the artist want to express the image of a Hindu God in a particular state of emotion—Raudra, Shanta or Śṛngāric, he can reproduce it as it is. Whereas in music or poetry, he would have to use notes or words for the same representation.

In the Indian tradition, sculpture and painting have been included in architecture. Hence, we find the evaluation of painting in the canons of architecture, such as:

Viṣṇudharmottaram, Samarāñgaṇa sūtradhāra, Vāstusāstram, Mānasollās, Śilparatnam etc.

Apart from that, the *Kāmasutra* also gives some important information about painting. In the commentary by Yaśodhara, six elements unique to the art of painting have been identified. They are—Rūpabheda[51], Pramāṇa, Bhāva, Lāvaṇyayojanaṁ, Sādrāśya and Varnikābhaṅga.

1. *Rūpabheda*—Defining of the form. 'Rūpabheda' is the differentiation of various forms by showing their characteristics. To achieve the distinction of form, *Rekhā* or line is of paramount

importance As is said in *Viṣ ṇudharmottrama,—Rekhām praśañsañtyācaryāh* ... i.e., the master artists praise the line.

2. *Pramāṇa*—Pramāṇa sets a standard for correct proportion and balance of the form. This element is very important for the composition of the significant form, since even a slight loss of proportion or balance can disturb the inherent 'rhythm' or overall impact of the 'presence'.

3. *Bhāva*—Rūpabheda and Pramāṇa help in the evolution of the form. Bhāva is the content of the form. This element is of special significance in the Indian tradition of painting, since it conveys the feeling essential for the manifestation of 'Rasa'. Even in Western tradition we come across this element quite often e.g., an exquisite painting that shows the burial of Christ after crucification. (Plate l(a) in App. II)

4. *Lāvaṇyayojanaṁ*—This involves the infusion of a certain freshness, brightness (aujjvalya), softness and a waving movement in the form. As a result, the form gets a semblance of 'livingness'. Nihar Ranjan Ray relates the word 'Lāvaṇya' to a Sanskrit word 'Navāni' (Lāvṇi or Loni in prakrit) meaning fresh and soft butter as opposed to the ordinary usage in the sense of 'salty'. He uses the simile of 'melting butter' with reference to Indian literature for the word.[52] This element plays a major role in the determination of beauty of form. Lāvaṇya is enhanced by the proper usage of curves and colours in adequate amount.

5. *Sādrśya*—A likeness to reality. Even if some imaginary scene or person is depicted in a painting, the appearance should be close to life. In case of portraiture, certain aspects of the actual person should be chosen in such a way, so as to reflect the true nature as well. Also, to enhance this element, a three dimensional effect is produced in a two dimensional space by the proper use of line, light and shade.

6. *Varṇikābhaṅga* — The colour composition in the painting. A certain balance in the use of colour is required. Care has to be taken to achieve a harmony of colours by using mutually compatible colours.

Sculpture

Whereas the domain of painting comprises of two-dimensional space, a work of sculpture is the center of three-dimensional space. Therefore, sculpture creates the abstraction of 'virtual kinetic volume'. An illusion of movement is created within the virtual framework of a static three-dimensional space. The work creates a visual semblance of tactual (of touch and contact) space as opposed to a space of direct vision as in case of painting.

According to S.K. Langer—'there is nothing actually organic about a work of sculpture. Even carved wood is dead matter. Only its form is the form of life and the space it makes visible is vitalised as it would be by organic activity at its center. It is 'virtual kinetic volume' created by and with the semblance of living form'.[53]

This is very much relevant for the other art forms also. The semblance of living form is found in the basis of the 'significant form' about which Langer has frequently talked.

The basic elements of art as imbibed in the art of sculpture are as follows :

1. Beauty (Form)—In sculpture also, the beauty of form conforms to the laws of purity of medium, balance rhythm and harmony. The medium used here varies from the traditional stone, wood and metal to modern glass, papier mache and any number of materials. Purity of the medium would depend on the texture and mouldability of these materials. Balance is of great importance in sculpture. A prerequisite for a work of Sculpture is that the created form must stay firmly in position. For this it has to achieve a state of equilibrium of forces, such as the gravitational force and also the linear movement of the figure itself. Apart from that, balance is also needed in the structural organisation of the form. The postures depicted in the figure of a sculpture give an impression of motion, which in turn gives the semblance of living form. The rhythm is inherent in this semblance of living form. The different units of the figure have to be in harmony with each other and also with the immediate environment. The factor of human feeling should also be given full expression. Only then, true beauty of form can be achieved.

2. *Images*—Just like in case of painting, imagery can be directly expressed in sculpture also. In fact, sculpture can give a more realistic depiction of imagery because of its tactual three-dimensional space.

3. *Symbols*—In sculpture, the element of symbolisation is perhaps even greater than in painting. Particularly in the case of religious iconography there is an abundance of this element. The

wheel of prosperity, the various idols of Buddha and Mahāvira symbolic of their ideologies, idol of Goddess Durgā symbolic of power and courage. Apart from this, human feelings of pathos, joy, fear etc., are also symbolised through various works of sculpture. An experience of the absolute can be had by perceiving the sculpture of Lord Buddha from Gandhār depicting him as an ascetic with a parched body (Plate l (b) in App. II).

4. *Imagination*—Similar to that of painting.

The six elements of painting can be applicable to sculpture also to a certain extent, since they basically involve the visual enhancement of the beauty of form. Particularly *Lāvaṇyayojanaṁ* is of special importance in the figures of sculpture, as it induces a semblance of life in the form. Owing to the tactual three dimensional space that sculpture creates, the softness and freshness of the texture can actually be felt.

Architecture

Like the other plastic arts, architecture also creates the illusion of virtual space, but the virtuality is often missed due to the use of an actual place. According to Langer, the illusion is effected by a basic abstraction of 'an ethnic domain'. Thus, 'As scene is the basic abstraction of pictorial art and kinetic volume of sculpture, that of architecture is an ethnic domain ... 'Painting creates ... place'.[54] This illusion can be established by a boundary wall, a hedge, an array of stones or even the foundation stone in case of a monument. In Indian aesthetics, architecture is the basis for the theory of plastic arts, viz.—painting sculpture and architecture. The Hindi equivalent for the word architecture is 'Vāstu'. 'Vāstu' is a Sanskrit word derived from the root 'vas' meaning 'to live in'. 'Vāstu' has been used in a much broader sense by Cānakya in his 'Arthaśāstra'. According to him, house, field, garden, dam, bridge, lake and tank come under 'Vāstu'.[55]

The basic elements of fine art are present in architecture also. Even though a philosopher of Aristotle's stature has not included architecture in fine art owing to its functional aspect. Still, if we see the monuments and temples, the functional aspect is absent. So, we cannot view it as purely utilitarian. The least that can be done is to treat the utilitarian housing apartments as a separate division. This would be in a similar way just like in sculpture and painting, the ones for commercial purpose are treated as utilitarian like decorative pens etc.

The basic elements of fine art are incorporated in architecture as follows:

1. *Beauty*—The laws of beauty are fully adhered to in case of architecture. There is a balance of structure as well as a rhythm and harmony within the constituents. The medium used is brick, cement, stone, wood, granite etc. The beauty of form can be apprehended from the composition of various arched walls, curved windows combined with floral motifs and intricate inlay work. Particularly in the case of monuments and religious architecture, the dome shape and cylindrical minarets play an important role in the enhancement of this element. Of course, the more imaginative the structure, the more beautiful it becomes. The Taj Mahal of Agra or the Pyramids of Egypt are examples of the sublime.

2. *Images*—In a work of architecture, separate images of its constituents are more or less absent. Owing to its visual character, the entire form of the architectural work in itself acts as an image. It appears to our vision detached from its actual geographical position.

3. *Symbols*—Symbolisation is an important element of architecture. Both as an art symbol, as well as its constituents acting as symbols, a work of architecture abounds in symbolisation. An example of the former, the Taj Mahal is famous as the epitome of romance throughout the world. In the latter, where the symbol is the element of art, various patterns or engraved motifs, even the shape of the art work serve as symbols. Example in religious architecture—the cross of a church, the Swastika in a temple etc.

4. *Imagination*—Like all the arts, imagination is of surmount importance in architecture. The total art form depends on the imaginative genius of the architect. The manner in which the structure of the architectural work is organised, the choice of motifs, the size, the total idea or feeling associated is responsible for the overall impact of the form.

Poetics or Poesis

The term *Poesis* includes all forms of verbal art meant to be heard or read. It is a broader term than either literature or drama, since all types of poetry, literary forms, drama and even prose are included in it. It is a direct equivalent of the word *Kavya* in Hindi.

The primary illusion in poesis is virtual life. The word 'life' is used in two different senses with reference to art. One is in which 'life' is the organic character of the art work, having an inherent rhythm. The other sense is as the semblance of experienced events. It is in this sense that poesis creates the illusion of life. This illusion is established by the opening line or verse. According to S.K. Langer, '...all 'creative writing' is poesis, and so far as it works with words alone, creates the same illusion, virtual memory or history in the mode of an experienced past'.[56]

Even though poesis or poetics creates an illusion of life, it is not a mere representation of experienced events. It gives an insight of what can be possible which in reality may seem impossible. It is more comprehensive than actual events and human nature. We can even get a better understanding of reality through poesis.

The words *imitation* or *representation* used to explain the theories of Plato and Aristotle seem to be misleading. Plato in his *Phaedrus* has said of poetics,

'You will allow that every discourse ought to be constructed like a living organism, having its own body and head and feet; it must have middle and extremities, drawn in a manner agreeable to one another and to the whole'.[57]

This view of Plato about poetics or poesis has been echoed in Aristotle's poetic criticism also. In his book *Aristotle's Theory of Poetry and Fine Art,* S.H. Butcher has elaborated on Aristotle's view as follows :

> 'A work then of poetic art, as he conceives it, while it manifests the universal is yet a concrete and individual reality, a coherent whole, animated by a living principle—or by something which is at least the counterpart of life—and framed according to the laws of organic beauty. The artistic product is not indeed in a literal sense alive; for life or soul is in art ... the result of the proper form being impressed upon the proper matter'.[58]

In Indian Aesthetics, the very basis of formulating a theory on fine arts has been 'Nāṭya' or drama. 'Nāṭya' has been referred to as the highest form of poesis, i.e., 'Kāvya'. The earliest work that gives a comprehensive theory about the fine arts in Indian

Aesthetics is the *Nāṭya Śastra* by Bharat Muni. He has propounded the theory of 'Rasa' with 'Nāṭya' as the focal point.

Another canonical work on Indian Aesthetics relating to poesis is *Kāvyālankāra* by Bhāmaha. About poetry he says—'words and meanings together form poetry'[59]. He talks of 'vakrokti' as an essential element of poetry. The word 'vakrokti' is a composite Sanskrit word made by the union of 'vakra' and 'ukti', thereby meaning an indirect way of saying. In Western Aesthetics also it is acknowledged that instead of the direct ordinary language, a language consisting of word bound images and symbols is used, so that discursive symbol of language becomes presentational symbol in poesis. K.C. Pandey's evaluation of the word 'vakrokti' is 'the mode of presentation of ideas in words, which gives aesthetic pleasure to those who are possessed of aesthetic susceptibility'.[60] Another element which Bhāmaha considers essential for poesis is embellishment (Alankāra). Embellishment in poesis according to him consists in the 'striking manner of putting a striking idea in equally striking words'.[61]

The basic elements of art in poesis are as follows:

1. *Beauty*—The laws of beauty are abided by poesis as well. Purity of medium in this case would be sweetness of the sounding word. Harsh letters hamper the beauty of poesis. Balance and rhythm play a very important role in poesis, so does harmony. Santayana has talked of euphony in poetry, which can be equated to 'chhand' in Hindi, that takes care of all the three as Euphony arises from the similarity and regulated succession of sound, or from meter and rhyme. According to Santayana[62], euphony is the sole element responsible for beauty in a lower level of poetry. In great poetry, it provides the musical element. In higher level of poetry, euphony is supplemented by fanciful juxtaposition of phrases. This is what is implied by 'vakrokti' in the Indian poetic tradition. In Indian aesthetics, the prime source for beauty in poesis is the manifestation of 'Rasa', which is what great poetry is about.

2. *Images*—Images in poesis are in the form of words. Instead of direct prosaic language, a language consisting of word bound images is used in poesis. For example, Tennyson's—'Cast thy troubles on the lord: that anchor holds', uses the image of fact of life—'casting anchor and also combines the symbol—deep water for trouble.

3. Symbols—Just like images symbols are also used in poesis. The discursive symbols of language become presentational in poesis. The total import is not a mere addition of the individual meaning but a projection of the inherent idea or feeling.

e.g. 'Should dissappointment, parent of despair,
strive for her son to sieze my careless heart,
... chase him away, sweet hope with visage bright,
and frighten him, as the morning frightens night'.

The above verse from 'To hope' by Keats use the symbols 'brightness of morning' and 'darkness of night' for hope and despair respectively. The literal meaning would be a boy being chased away and frightened by brightness. The total import would be that, just like the brightness of morning dispells the darkness of night, hope removes all despair.

4. Imagination—The element of imagination in poesis is present in a very high degree compared to other fine arts (particularly plastic arts). The semblance of life experiences that is created in poesis is pure imagination with the appearance of the real. Events are projected as if they are actually taking place or have occurred. Even if the matter is based on reality and not fiction, the mode of presentation requires imagination.

MUTUAL RELATIONSHIP BETWEEN THE FINE ARTS

As seen in the previous section, there is an inherent relationship between the elements of various fine arts even though they may differ in their medium of expression. The difference lies in their combination and proportion. It is important to study the elementary relationship between the fine arts in the context of the present thesis, since it deals with the assimilation of one form of art with the other. The enumeration of the basic elements and the description of each fine art according to specific elements has already been discussed. In this section, the mutual relationship and unifying factors between the fine arts are being studied.

The perception of art is mostly through the so called higher senses of sight and sound, with the other senses playing indirect roles. Sometimes there is a 'fusion of sensations by which the experience of one sense impression conjures up that of another type'. The Encyclopedia Britannica calls this fusion of sensation *synaesthesia*. According to J. Chiari, synaesthesia is 'an interpretation of the senses, conveying an effect of oneness'.[63] Sounds often evoke visual images such as colours. In Indian canonical literature, a separate colour equivalent for each note has been determined, though the equivalents vary with different authors (as will be seen later). According to Matang :

Padmapatraprabhah śaḍja ṛshabhah śukavarṇakah /
kanakābhastu gāndhāro madhyamah kundsannibhah/73/
pancamastu bhavet kṛṣnah pīītavarṇastu dhaivatah/
niṣādah sarvavarṇo'yam vigyeyāh swarvarṇkāh/74//

— Bṛhaddeśî, p. 46

i.e, 'sa' is rosy, the colour of lotus petal, 're' takes the colour of parrot, green, 'ga' is golden, 'ma' is white, 'pa' is black, 'dha' is yellow and 'ni' has a mixed tone.

Painters speak of the 'tone' of certain colours. Richard Strauss wrote 'tone poems' or musical compositions with narrative or pictorial content, while Debussy called one of his piano pieces 'sounds and perfumes on the evening air'. Synaesthesia has been a favourite with symbolist poets. 'There are perfumes fresh as children's flesh', wrote Bandelaire, 'soft as oboes green as meadows ...'.[64]

While discussing about the theory of the aesthetic senses, Benedetto Croce in his *Aesthetic* mentions Dante's analogies such as 'sweet colour of the oriental sapphire' (fusion of gustatory and visual sense impressions), 'dense air', 'fresh rivulets' which 'parch the more the throat of the thirsty' (olfactory and tactile impressions). According to him, 'the belief that a picture yields only visual impressions is a curious illusion ... The bloom on a cheek, the warmth of a youthful body, the sweetness and freshness of a fruit, the edge of a sharp knife, are not these two impressions obtainable from a picture? Are they visual ? What would a picture mean to an imaginary man, lacking all or many of his sense, who should in an instant acquire the organ of sight alone? The picture we are looking at or believe we see only with our eyes would seem to his eyes to be little more than an artist's paint-smeared palette'.[65]

On the subject of unity of arts, Croce believed that by uniting various arts, it is not necessary that we obtain a more powerful effect. For example, some plays can be quite effective with a simple reading, whereas others may need full scenic display complete with songs, musical instruments, colours, statuary, architecture.

Each have a different purpose and 'the power of the means cannot be compared when the purposes are different'.[66] A much better perspective of the unity of various arts can be had by first differentiating them. As Langer says, 'if you trace the differences among the arts as far minutely as possible, there comes a point beyond which no more distinctions can befound among the several arts, there lies their unity'.[67] Further she says— '...we need not accept this unity by faith and reject as vicious all inquiries that call it in question, its demonstration is the result of such inquiries. Here we have certainly the deepest relationship among the arts, they all exemplify the general principles of art'.[68]

All arts give a semblance of living form in a virtual realm. The realm is different in different arts, such as virtual space in painting, virtual time in music, virtual life or a semblance of events lived and felt in the case of poesis and so on.

In most Rāgamālā paintings, there exists confluence of music, painting and poesis (poetry). The primary illusion of virtual space consists of the painting with the notes of Rāgas and the poetry becoming the elements of the painting. Such assimilation is possible only if there is some affinity between the arts. Sometimes it is objected that such a mixture of arts is not correct. To such an objection, a quotation by Reynolds may be cited, who writes of opera thus, 'It is conformable to experience, and therefore agreeable to reason as connected with and referred to experience, that we should ... be delighted with this union of music, poetry and graceful action joined to every circumstance of pomp and magnificance calculated to strike the senses of the spectator. Shall reason stand in the way and tell us that we ought not to like what we know we do like?'[69]

In *Feeling and Form,* Langer throws light on the unifying factor between the arts, '...the oft asserted fundamental unity of the arts lies not so much in parallels between their respective elements or analogies among their techniques, as in the singleness of their characteristic import, the meaning of *significance* with respect to any and each of their *significant form* (which really has significance) is the essence of every art; it is what we mean by calling anything *artistic*'.[70] Whereas Clive Bell used the term *significant form* (see p.8) only for visual arts, Langer extended it to include all arts.

COMPARISON OF FINE ARTS

As shown in the preceding section, the fine arts are mutually related in the expression of the 'significant form'. This form conveys an effect of 'livingness' within a virtual realm. The illusion of virtuality is different in each fine art as also the medium of expression. The level of similarity is higher among the romantic arts of music, painting and poesis, on the basis of the elements of images, imagination, symbols etc. However, according to the illusion of virtuality, the plastic arts of painting, sculpture and architecture show a common ground. The difference is in the abstraction. For instance, in painting it is a scene, in sculpture it is kinetic volume and in architecture it is virtual domain or place. The primary illusion in all three cases is virtual space. However, in the present thesis, the subject is concerned primarily with the fine arts of music, painting and to a lesser extent poesis. Therefore, the similarities between these three arts are being discussed in the present section. The differences between all the fine arts have been given in Table 4 of Appendix I.

Music and Painting

The similarities between music and painting hold special significance in the context of the present thesis. Depiction of music through paintings can only be accomplished when there exists an analogy of forms between the two arts. The process involves assimilation of one form into the other. This in turn implies that there remains one primary illusion and the other form becomes an element of that illusion. The primary illusion here is virtual space (the abstraction of a scene in two dimensional) of painting. Music has been transferred as an element (a component of virtual space) of the painting.

It has already been seen in an earlier portion of this chapter, the essence of all arts is 'significant' or 'expressive' form. This form gives a semblance of 'livingness'. In music, this is achieved primarily via the rhythm. Even if the rhythm is absent outwardly, there is a rhythm inherent within the structural organisation of the notes which can accomplish a 'livingness'. It denotes the tensions and relaxation and the other phenomena of life. In case of paintings, this livingness is produced by a three dimensional effect in a two dimensional space through the clever use of light, shade and lines. The element 'Lāvañya yojanaṁ' is also responsible for this property. In case of depiction of figures, the correct posture can also give a semblance of motion or 'livingness'.

The laws of beauty such as balance, rhythm, harmony and purity of medium apply to both music and painting as has already been discussed. The other basic elements such as symbols, images and imagination also find expression in both the arts. Similarly, aesthetic experience (Rasaniśpatti) is a goal for both the arts. This is more so because music as well as painting, particularly in the Indian tradition, are feeling oriented. 'Bhāva' or feeling, which is an important element of painting (one of six unique elements) finds equal if not more footage in music.

The musical modes depicted in the Rāgamālā paintings are called Rāgas and Rāginîs, which form the basis of Indian Classical music. The word 'Rāga' is derived from the root 'Rañj' of Sanskrit, which means 'that colours' (particularly in the sense of red colour, like in 'Anurāg'). Just like love colours the hearts of people giving them eternal bliss, so does Rāga colour the hearts of the listeners to give them absolute bliss. Thus the relationship of colour and music is deep rooted in the Indian tradition. Also, as has already been said earlier, a separate colour has been determined for each note in Indian Classical music—*Padmapatraprabhah* etc. Even in the West, equivalents have been determined between colours and notes. From the 18th century onwards various experiments have been conducted to prove a definite relationship between the two. In 1670 A.D., Newton propounded the theory that light is the source of colours. During his experiments, the similarity between the ratio of distance covered by the colours on a spectrum and that of double frequency of notes struck him. In 1688-1757 A.D., a mathematician Prof. Lewis. B. Cassil, was probably the first person to consider the concept of colourful music. Later, Bishop Issacs County of New York attached a projector to an ordinary organ such that it produced colours on a screen along with music. Towards the end of the 19th century, Bostonomy from Milan succeeded in completing an unsuccessful attempt of Remington in establishing a relationship between colours and the double frequency of notes. Other important names in this field are Lewis Frewey, Gram Waldt, Hector, Mukish, Sckriabein, Wilfred etc. Herbert Spencer established a relation between the primary colours of the prism—red, yellow and blue with the notes Sa, Ga and Ma respectively (representing the sound oo, oo, m) which also echoes the ancient Indian perspective. This is according to the ṣaḍja—madhyama bhāva. Hirendra Kumar Basu follows the ṣaḍja—Pancamabhāva replacing ma with pa. According to him, Re comes between Sa (red) and Ga (yellow), therefore it is orange. Between Pa (blue) and Re (orange) is Ni which is violet. Between Pa and Ni is Dha which is indigo blue. Between Ga (yellow) and Pa (blue) is Ma, which is green. Hence,

V — Ni
I — Dha
B — Pa
G — Ma
Y — Ga
O — Re
R — Sa

Music and Poesis

A major similarity between music and poesis lies in the fact that the prime source for both is sound. Since ancient times, music and poesis have mostly been interlinked. Whether in other parts of the world or in the Indian tradition, the chanting of hymns is perhaps the earliest example of such a linkage. During the vedic age in Indian tradition, the verses of Rgveda served as lyrics for the hymns (stotras) of Sāmveda[71]. In modern times, music and poesis have evolved as independent arts. It is no longer necessary for either poetry or drama to be musical. Likewise, music without words (instrumental or in its pure form) does not essentially requires discursive meaning to convey its importance. Still, their assimilation is easily accomplished and is desirable. This is so because they both have the basic characteristics of art. The expressive form which gives a semblance of livingness is an essential feature of both. Here the analogy of both the art forms is heightened by the fact that this semblance of livingness in both is achieved primarily through rhythmic meter (Chhand). Of course, there are other factors also, which have already been discussed earlier individually.

The basic elements of art are present in both the arts. Expression of 'bhāva' or feeling is an aim for both, which results in aesthetic experience or rasaniśpatti. The element of imagination is present in both in a similar proportion. Both are 'occurent arts'.

Painting and Poesis

Since ancient times, many scholars have drawn relationships

between painting and poesis. A famous saying in the west describes painting as silent poetry and poetry as verbal painting. Among Indian scholars, Vāmana relates poesis to painting in his kāvyālankārasutravritti, III vs (1), thus

Yathā vicchadyate rekhā caturam citrapanditaih/
Tathaiva vāgapi prāgyaih samastguṇagumphitā//

i.e. just as adept painters differentiate the line, so do poets inculcate various qualities through words. Elsewhere, Vāmana talks of 'aujjwalya' or brilliancy in painting which is comparable to 'kānti' in the words of a poem.[72] This property is responsible for 'livingness' of form in both and can be included in the element 'lāvanya yojanaṁ' of painting. Two other elements of painting find expression in poesis as well—*Bhāva* and *Sādrśya* (of which can be said are universal in romantic arts). In the Rāgamālā paintings, just like music, poesis has also been assimilated as an element (a component of the virtual space) of painting. Thus, it is imperative that a common analogy of form exists between poesis and painting as well.

The basic elements of art, viz.,—beauty (form), images, imagination and symbol (symbolic representation) are present in both. The laws of beauty of form—balance, harmony, rhythm and purity of medium are also exemplified in both. This point has already been discussed individually in both cases. In the Indian tradition drama, which has been included in poesis, has been described as a succession of paintings. In painting only a single scene is depicted whereas in drama, a series of scenes are shown.

References

1. Gill, Eric, 'Art and a Changing Civilisation', London: Lane, 1934.
2. *Encyclopedia Britannica*, pt. 2, pp. 484-485.
3. *Ibid.*
4. *'Yathā kalāṁ yathā śapham yathā riṇaṁ sannayāmasi'*—Ṛgveda 8/47/17.
5. *'śakto muko'pi yat kartum kalā sanjaṁ tu tat smṛtaṁ'*, Śukranitih, Mihirchandraji, 2012 vs 4/264.
6. *'kalayati swaroopaṁ āveśyati, vastum vā tatra—tatra pramātari kalanameva kalā*—Śivasutravimarśini, in 'kāvya aur kalā tathā anya nibandha', p. 42.

7. Pandey, K.C., 'Comparative Aesthetics,' Vol. II. Western Aesthetics, p. 512.
8. Saxena, S.K., 'Aesthetical Essays', p. 53.
9. Sharma, H.L., 'Indian Aesthetics and Aesthetic Perspectives', p. (xi).
10. 'kalpanā ko sākār rupa denā kalā ki sārthakatā hai', Gupta, Syamala, in 'Saundarya Tattva Mimansa', p. 38.
11. Meredith, J.C., 'Critique of Aesthetic Judgement'—translation of an article by Kant.
12. Croce, Bendetto, 'Aesthetic,' p. 13.
13. Langer, S.K., 'Feeling and Form,' p. 262.
14. Langer, S.K., 'Philosophy in a New Key,' p. 221.
15. Saxena, S.K., 'Aesthetical Essays,' p. 53.
16. *'tatra vibhāvānubhāva vyabhicārī sanyogādrasnişpattih'*—Nātyaśāstra of Bharata.
17. Pandey, K.C., 'Comparative Aesthetics,' vol. I, 2nd edition.
18. Sangît Ratnākar 1/21.
19. Stanislavsky, Konstantin, 'My Life in Art', 1924.
20. Collingwood, R.G., 'The Pinciples of Art'.
21. Croce, 'Aesthetic', pp. 114-115.
22. Knight, R.P.,—'An Analytical Inquiry into the Principles of Taste', p. 6.
23. Sparshott, F.E., 'The Structure of Aesthetics', p. 64.
24. *Ibid.*
25. 'citta ko ārdra karne wālā—Shukla, Ram Lakhan in 'Bhāratiya Sandarya śāstra ka tattivka vivecan evaṁ lalita kalāyen'.
26. Sharma, H.L., 'Aesthetic Education and the Grammar of Art,' p. 15.
27. Langer, S.K., 'Feeling and Form', p. 25.
28. Harvard University Press edition, p. 8 (from Langer, S.K. 'Feeling and Form', p. 33).
29. Sharma, H.L., 'Aesthetic Education and the Grammar of Art,' pp. 92-93.
30. Inge, Vol. 1, pp. 231-34.
31. Apte, V.S., 'The Practical Sanskrit—English Dictionary', Vol. 1, 1957.
32. *Encyclopedia Britannica,* pt. 12, p. 103.
33. *Ibid.*
34. *Ibid.*
35. 'bimba — vidhān kalā kā kriyā paksha —' etc.—Vimal, Dr. Kumar, 'Saundarya Śāstra ke Tattva,' p. 217.
36. Langer, S.K., 'Philosophy in a New Key', p. 5.
37. Langer, S.K., 'Feeling and Form', p. 26.
38. *Ibid.*
39. *Ibid.*

40. Ghosh, R.K., 'Aesthetic Theory and Art', pp. 16-17.
41. Langer, S.K., 'Feeling and Form', p. 25.
42. *Ibid.*
43. Bhatkhande memorial lecture sponsored by the Musicological Society, Baroda, held in Delhi, 1 Dec. '98.
44. Saxena, S.K., 'Aesthetical Essays', p. 130.
45. Langer, S.K., 'Philosophy in New Key', p. 209.
46. Passage from one note to another without a break.
47. 'The symbolism that conveys the idea of vital reality,' Langer, S.K., 'Feeling and Form', p. 82.
48. Langer, S.K., 'Feeling and Form', p. 127.
49. *Ibid.*, p. 128.
50. *Ibid.*, p. 75.
51. *'Rupabhedāḥ pramāṇāni bhāvalāvaṇya yojanaṁ/sādṛśyaṁ varnikābhanga iti citram ṣaḍaṅgakaṁ'.*
52. Ray, Nihar Ranjan, 'Bharatiya kala ke Ayama', p. 121.
53. Langer, S.K., 'Feeling and Form,' p. 89.
54. *Ibid.*, pp. 94-95.
55. *'Gṛhaṁ kśetramārāmah setubandhastaṃtākamādhorā vā vāstuh'// Arthaśāstra* of Cānakya.
56. Langer, S.K., 'Feeling and Form,' p. 279.
57. 264 C, Butcher, S.H., 'Aristotles' Theory of Poetry and Fine Art, p. 189.
58. *Ibid.*
59. 'Śabdārthau sahitau kāvyaṁ—Kāvyālnkāra of Bhāmaha.
60. Pandey, K.C., 'Comparative Aesthetics', Vol. 1, Indian Aesthetics, p. 492.
61. *Ibid.*, p. 493.
62. Saxena, S.K., 'Art and Philosophy,' p. 240.
63. Chiari, Joseph, 'Symbolism from Poe to Mallarme', p. 51.
64. Selected Poems from 'Flowers of Evil', translated by Wagner Geoffrey.
65. Croce, 'Aesthetic,' p. 18.
66. *Ibid.*
67. Langer, S.K., 'Problems of Art', pp. 78-79 (from, 'Aesthetic, Theory and Art', Ghosh, R.K.).
68. *Ibid.*
69. Reynolds, Joshua, The Idler no. 82 (1759) in Reynolds 1835/1786, Thirteenth Discourse II, 68 (from Sparshott 'The Structure of Aesthetics').
70. Langer, S.K., 'Feeling and Form', p. 25.
71. *'tasmādṛcyadhyuḍhaṁ sāmgîyate'.*
72. *'aujjwalayam kāntih'*/kāvyālaṅkārasutravritti, III, 1.25.

2
The Indian Tradition of Classical Music

INTRODUCTION

Till now, a general evaluation of music has been done as a fine art. Along with the other fine arts, an analytical view of music has been put forward relative to other arts. This has been accomplished by studying the basic as well as individual elements of music and their involvement in the creation of the musical 'presence' or 'expressive form'.

The present thesis deals with the depiction of music through paintings in the Indian tradition. Therefore, a brief summary of the historical development of the Indian tradition of classical music as well as painting is being given. This chapter deals with the Indian tradition of classical music.

NOMENCLATURE AND SYSTEMS OF MUSIC IN THE INDIAN TRADITION

Nomenclature

The Hindi word for music is 'Sangît' which finds its derivation from Sanskrit, in the sense of 'Samyak geetaṁ'. It is inclusive of not only vocal and instrumental music but also dance as complementary to each other as expresed in the śloka,

Geetaṁ Vādyaṁ Tathā nrittaṁ trayaṁ Sangîtamucyaté

—*Sangît Ratnākar*, 1/21

Hindustāni and Carnātic Music—The Two Systems of Indian Classical Music

Originally, a single system of classical music was prevalent throughout India, as is evident from ancient canons of musical literature. Same kind of notes having similar intervals consistent with same grāmas, murchanās and jātîs were universally acceptable.

From about 8th century A.D. onwards, a series of invasions which were mostly confined to the nothern region influenced, our music. Whereas in the north, Classical music assimilated other foreign nuances, the music of the southern region remained largely unaffected. This resulted in the formation of two different systems of classical music in India namely Hindustāni (or North Indian) classical music and Carnātic (or South Indian) classical music.

The Śuddha or pure notes of the Hindustāni system are those of the tonal scale, Bilāval. It is similar to the European Major scale, with a slight difference in the frequency of certain notes (such as—the frequency of A or Dha in the Hindustāni System is 405 instead of 400 in Western System). The pure notes of the Carnātic system are those of the tonal scale, Mukhāri or Kanakāngi. The pure or Śuddha state of notes in the Carnātic system is the lowest and all other are sharps. In the Hindustani system, with the exception of ma, the lower state is that of the flat note. The notes of both the systems are given in Table 1.

There have been various systems of classification of Rāgas in Hindustāni classical music apart from the Rāga-Rāginî system which has been followed by the Rāgamālā. In ancient period it was (1) Grāma-Murchhanā-Jāti classification, (2) Rāga classification of Sangît Ratnakar and (3) Śuddha, Chāyālag and samkeerna Rāga (Mataṅga) classification. In the medieval period, the classification was (1) Rāga-Rāginî and (2) Mela-Rāga. In the modern period, the classification of Rāgas is based on (1) Ṭhāṭ and (2) Rāgāṅga.

In Carnātic system, the Rāga or 'Pan' was classified in a similar manner uptil the ancient period (upto Mataṅga). Apart from the sampoorna (Heptātonic) Rāgas (Panas) there were also Auḍava (Pentatonic) and Ṣāḍava (Heratonic) Panas just as in Hindustāni Music Pans were also differentiated according to the time of singing-Pagal (day time), Iravuppan (night) and Poduppan (all times).

Table 1

Notes of Hindustāni, Carnātic and Western Systems of Music

Hindustāni	*Carnātic*	*Western*
Ṣaḍja (Tāra) (Śa)	Sadja (Tāra) (Śa)	C
Śuddha Niṣāda (Ni)	Kākali Ni	B
Komal* Niṣāda (Ni)	Ṣaṭśruti Dha	B^b
Śuddha Dhaivata (Dha)	Chatuhśruti Dha (Śuddha Ni)	A
Komal Dhaivata (Dha)	Śuddha Dha	A^b
Pañcama (Pa)	Pañcama (Pa)	G
Tivra** Madhyama (Ma)	Prati Ma	F
Śuddha Madhyama (Ma)	Śuddha Ma	F
Śuddha Gandhāra (Ga)	Aṅtara Ga	E
Komal Gandhāra (Ga)	Sādhāraṇa Ga (ṣaṭaśruti Ri)	E^b
Śuddha Rishabha (Re)	Chatuhśruti Ri (Śuddha Ga)	D
Komal Rishabha (Re)	Śuddha Ri	D^b
Ṣaḍja (Sa)	Ṣaḍja (Sa)	C

* Flat

** Sharp

In 14th-15th century A.D., the philosopher musician Vidyāraṇya Mādhavācārya *(Sangîtsāra)* discussed the genus—species (Janya—janaka) scheme for the first time. He classified fifteen basic and fifty subordinate Rāgas. In 1640 A.D., Venkatmakhi in his *Caturdanḍiprakāśikā,* established seventy two Melakartās from twelve notes. Of these, only nineteen were in practical use.

In the 20th century A.D., Pt. V.N. Bhātkhande incorporated this method of classification in the Hindustāni system. He devised ten Melas or Ṭhāṭs to determine the Rāgas of the Hindustāni system of music. The equivalents of these Ṭhāṭs in Carnatic system are given in Table 2.

In both the systems, many Rāgas have similar names but structurally they are different, such as Hindol (Hindolaṁ), Śri and Sohani. The converse is also true, i.e., there are Rāgas in both the systems where the names are different, but structurally they are same. For example, Bhupāli of Hindustāni Music is the same as Mohanarṁ of Carnātic Music.

Table 2

The Ṭhāṭs of Hindustāni Music Corresponding to Melakartas of Carnātic Music

S.No.	*Name of Ṭhāṭ in H.M.*	*Corresponding Melakartā in C.M*
1.	Yaman (Kalyāṇa)	Mecakalyāṇi
2.	Bilāval	Dhiraśankarābharaṇaṁ
3.	Khamāj	Harikāmbhoji
4.	Bhairava	Māyāmālavagaula
5.	Purvî	Kāmavardhani
6.	Mārvā	Gamakakṛya
7.	Kāfi	Kharaharapriyā
8.	Āsāvari	Naṭabhairavi
9.	Bhairavi	Hanumatodi
10.	Toḍi	Śubhapantuvarāli

HISTORICAL DEVELOPMENT OF INDIAN CLASSICAL MUSIC

A brief summary of the historical development of Indian classical music is being given on the basis of references in Sanskrit, Tamil and Hindi canonical literature. The overall historical development of Indian Classical music has been broadly divided into Vedic, Post Vedic (Classical), Medieval and Modern Period.

Music in Vedic Period

The period in which the four great pillars of ancient canonical literature, the Vedas viz-Rik, Sāma, Yajur and Atharva, came into existence is referred to as the Vedic Period. The advent of this period is believed to be from 6000 B.C. to 800 B.C.

In the Ṛgveda, the oldest (roughly around 1000 B.C.) of the four Vedas, the words Gîr, Gātu, Gāthā, Gāyatra, Gîti and Sāma have been used to denote music. When the mantras of Ṛgveda, the 'Richas', are set to music, they form the hymns of Sāmaveda and are called 'Stotra'. Thus, Sāmaveda is essentially musical in content as is also obvious from the title 'sāma'.

The Vedic modes were three fold. These were termed as Ārcika, Gāthika and Sāmika which constituted one, two and three notes respectively. During religious rites, the Richas were sung in Ārcika with the help of a single note, Brāhman vākyas and

Gāthas in Gathika with two notes and Sāma in Sāmika with three notes. The notes of Sāma were thus, three, namely Udatta, Anudatta and Swarita. In the Vedic Period, notes denoted the lower and higher pitch of sound as an extension of their counterpart in language. This is indicated by the fact that the swaras or notes of Ṛgveda as well as Sāmaveda are named as Udatta, Anudatta and Swarita[1]. Later, the seven notes evolved from these basic notes as—kruṣta, pratham, dvitîya, tritîya, caturtha, mandra and atisvārya. According to the Nāradîya Śikshā (NŚ), the notes of Sāma are related to laukika (present) as stated in the śloka,

yah sāmgānām prathamah sa venormadhyamah smṛtah/
yo dvitîyah sa gandhārah tritîyaṣtvrishabhah smṛtah// 1-5-1//
caturthah ṣaḍja ityāhuh pañcamo dhaivato bhavet/
ṣaṣtho niṣādo vigyeyah saptamah pañcamah smṛtah//1-5-2//

The gist of the above śloka in summarized in Table 3.

Table 3

The Sāma Notes of Vedic Period Corresponding to Laukik Notes

S.No.	*Sāma*	*Laukika*
1.	Prathama	ma (म) madhyam
2.	dvitîya	ga (ग) gandhār
3.	tritîya	re (रे) riṣabha
4.	caturtha	sa (सा) ṣaḍja
5.	mandra	dha (ध) dhaivata
6.	atisvārya	ni (नि) niṣāda
7.	kruṣta	pa (प) pañcama

It is believed that initially four and then five notes evolved from the three basic notes, to which 'ni' and 'pa' were added later. 'Ga' and 'ni' of Sāma were flat in relation to the modern notes. Thus, this octave is equivalent to the mode of modern Rāga Kāfi.

Many musical instruments were prevalent during the Vedic Period, such as—Dundubhi, Āḍambara (Percussion), Aghāti (Metallics), Flute, Tunav, Conch (śankha) (Wind), Kānḍavîṇā (stringed), Picol etc., comprising each category of instruments, viz.—Tat (stringed), Avanadya (percussion), Suśir (wind) and Ghan (metallic).

Music in Post Vedic (Classical) Period

(i) Epic Period (700 B.C.—150 A.D.)

After the Vedas, the two great epics—Rāmāyaṇa and Māhābhārata form important constituents of ancient Indian literature. Many direct and indirect references to music in these epics show that Indian music had developed to a great extent during this period.

(a) Rāmāyaṇa—This wonderful epic in Sanskrit was composed by the poet Vālmîki. The basic story line is about the life of Rāma, the son of king Dāśaratha of Ayodhyā, a kingdom in northern India. The period attached with this epic varies from 600 B.C. to 300 A.D. (about 400 B.C.).

The importance of music during that time is reflected by the fact that the epic is composed in lyrical form (the verses are in 'Anuśṭap chhand). The sons of Rāma, Lava and Kuśa were profficient in 'mārg'[2] music and it is believed that they originally sang this lyrical epic under the tutelage of Valmiki.

Music has been refered to as 'Sangît' or 'Gandharva'. The word 'Ātodya' has been used to describe instrumental music. Singing of 'Jātîs' was prevalent during that time. A mention of seven śuddha Jātîs has been made in Rāmāyaṇa. Like the present day Rāgas, these were the ancient melodic types and probably provided the matrix for the evolution of Rāgas. Important musical instruments of that time were Śankha (Conch), Veṇu (Flute), Mudduka (Brass trumpet). Wind instruments, Bherî, Dundubhi, Mṛdaṅga, Paṭaha, Ghaṭa, Muraj, Celika, Paṇava and Dindima—Percussion instruments and Viṇa (the name common for stringed instruments at the time).

(b) Mahābhārata—This colosal epic in Sanskrit consisting of one lakh verses was composed by Veda Vyās. The period attached to this epic is roughly between 500 B.C. to 450 A.D. (300 B.C.). Since the basic theme of Mahābhārata is the conflict between the Kauravas and Pāndavas, there are not as many references to music as in Rāmāyana. Still, various instances and references in this epic show that music occupied an important place in society. Uttarā, the princess of Virāṭa Nagara, learned music from Arjuna during the period of Agyātavāṣ (anonimity) of the Pāṇḍavas. Thus, music enjoyed Royal patronge at that time. There is a mention of various instruments in the Mahābhārata, such as—Mṛdaṅga,

Jharjhara, Bheri, Paṇava, Āṇaka, Gomukha Āḍambara, Śankha, Dhundubhi, Vîṇā, Veṇu, Kānsya etc.

(ii) Music in Buddhist and Jain Literature

The Jātaka tales constitute an important part of Buddhist literature. These tales are based on the past lives of Buddha and contain many references to music. The Jātakas were said to be prevalent during the 3rd century B.C. since some scenes from these tales are depicted in reliefs near the stupas of Bharahuta and Sāncî. During this period, both Sāma as well as laukik music was in practice. Sāmaveda was taught accoring to Vedic tradition and Gāndharva was included in the arts. Various universities were established during that time which imparted eductaion in disciplines such as philosophy, medicine, literature and arts.

Some universities like Nālandā and Vārānasi had independent faculties for music which were headed by a prominent musician.

There is a popular fallacy that music was taboo for Buddhists. This does not hold true. Buddha was not against all types of music. He was only against the 'Samajja' or sensual music in which people took drinks and behaved indulgently.

There are several references to musical instruments in the Jātakas. One such Jātaka relates the story of Guttila, a previous incarnation of Bodhisattva. Guttila was the court musician of Kāśi, who was adept at singing as well as playing the Vîṇā. Another musician, Musila of Ujjayani, came to learn music from him. One day, the king arranged a performance for both of them and rewarded Guttila more than Musila. Musila did not like this and a competition was held between the two. During the competition, Guttila kept on breaking the strings of his Vîṇā one after another while singing. Even after six strings were broken, the Vîṇā kept repeating the music with a single string. Guttila won the competition.

Thus, the seven-stringed or saptatantri Vîṇā was popular in that era. An excellent plucking technique had been developed such that by pressing certain points on a single string, all the musical notes could be produced.

Some other instruments that were prevalent at that time were, Stringed-Parivādini, Vattlali, Mahatî, Nakulî, Kacchapî, Vipanici and Tumbuvinā, Percussion—Āḍambara, Paṇava, Bherî, Mṛdanga, Dimdima and Dundhubi, Wind-Śankha, Vamśa, Kāhala and Śṛnga (horn), Metallic-Jhallari, Kānsya, Kumbhathana or Jallali (Jaltarang).

Ample reference to music is found in Jain scriptures also. The *Sthānāṇga sutra (Ṭhānānga sutta),* which dates to about 2nd century B.C., discusses the avoidable demerits as well as good qualities for music. The three grāmas or fundamental tone systems, viz.—Ṣaḍja, Gāndhāra and Madhyama, have been mentioned. The originating points of seven notes in human body and the relation between the notes and sounds of animals have also been mentioned.

Apart from *Sthānanga sutra, Rājapraśnîya sutra (Rāyāpasenîya sutta), Anuyogadvāra sutra, Nandî Sutra* and *Vṛhat Kalpasutra* contain references to music. Various musical instruments have been mentioned in the Jain works such as—*Vamśa* (Flute), Śankha (Conch), Kāhala, Maddala, Jhallari, Hudukka, Paṇava, Muaṅga (Mṛdaṅga), Bherî, Dundubhi, Diddima (Ḍimdima), Kānsya, Bhramarî, Sughosa, Vîṇā, Vipancî, Vallaki, Kacchapi etc.

(iii) Music in Ancient Tamil Literature (1st-3rd Century A.D.)

Ancient Tamil Literature has several references pertaining to music. Information from Tamil books written during this period reflects the universal character of music at that time (i.e., the division of Hindustāni and Carṇātic music had not yet taken place). Important among these books (from a musical point of view) are, *Silappaḍikāraṁ, Purānānuṛu, Pattupāṭṭu, Paripāḍal* and *Tivākaraṁ.*

In *Purānānuṛu* and *Pattupāṭṭu* (100-200A.D.), the drum has been mentioned with greate, reverence. There were three types of drums;

(*a*) The battle drum (yuddha bheri);
(*b*) The judgement drum (nyāya bheri); and
(*c*) The sacrificial drum (played during rituals).

The importance of the drum was such that, during a war if the drum was captured the army was considered to be defeated.

Another book of the same period, Paripāḍal, mentions seven modes called 'Palāi'. The ancient Tamil drama, '*Silappaḍikāraṁ*', written around 2nd century A.D., sheds light on the type of music that was prevalent during that time not only in the South, but throughout India. The term used for music in Tamil was 'Isai', which consisted of singing, dancing and instrumental music. Four varieties of Pans or Rāgas arose from four yāla or modal shifts (equivalent to murchanā). The smallest audible unit (śruti) was called 'Alaku' which were twenty two in number as in Nāṭya Śāstra (described subsequently). Different types of lutes (Vîṇā) were termed 'yāz' which were differentiated according to the number of strings, such as—Airiyaz—7-21, Makaryāz-17, Sakotyāz-14 etc. Another Tamil book, *Tivākaraṁ* (2nd-3rd Century A.D.) mentions about the Sampoorna, Ṣādava and Auḍava varieties of Rāgas in which the former has been called 'Pan' and the latter two have been called 'tiraṃ'. Thus, ancient music had already reached an advanced stage of development by this time.

(iv) Music in Nāṭyaśāstra (2nd Century B.C.—5th Century A.D.)

This Sanskrit work on Dramaturgy is believed to be the earliest comprehensive work on Indian Aesthetics. The author of this pioneering work is 'Bharata'. Some hold the view that it is a compilation of various authors of the name 'Bharata',[3] the first one being 'Ādi Bharata'. Music was an essential part of ancient Indian drama. Thus, out of a total of thirty-six chapters (comprising 5,600 verses), six chapters beginning from chapter 28 have been devoted fully to music.

The twenty-eighth chapter begins with a description of rules relating to instrumental music. The fourfold classification of instruments (Ātodya) has been discussed, viz.—Tata (stringed), Avanaddha (percussion or membranophnoic), Suṣira (wind blown) and Ghana (cymbals). This system of classification was later adopted by the west (19th century A.D.). The 'Kutapa' or orchestration has also been mentioned, as a feature of drama. Two important types of Kutapa—Tata and Avanadya Kutapa comprising stringed and percussion instruments respectively have been mentioned. The ensemblage of stringed instruments in Tat Kutapa is to the accompaniment of vocal music and flute whereas the orchestra of percussion instruments in Avanadya Kutapa are played by themselves. For music, the term 'Gāndharva' has been used, for which Bharata says,

'Yattu tantrîkṛtaṁ proktaṁ nānātodyasamāśrayaṁ/
Gāndharvamiti tajjneyaṁ svaratālapadātmakaṁa //9//

i.e., that which is dependent on different kinds of instruments, stringed instruments and consists of notes, rhythm and verbal content is 'Gāndharva'.

According to Nāṭyaśāstra, notes can be produced either through the wooden lute (Dāravîvîṇā) or the human lute (Śārîrîvîṇā). Thus

'Dvayadhiṣṭhānāh svarā vaiṇāh śārîrāśca prakîrtitāh/
Eteṣāṁ sampravaksyāmi vidhānaṁ lakṣaṇāvitaṁ//13//

Thus the rules of vocal music have also been enumerated along with instrumental music. The elements of music produced from the wooden lute consist of seven musical notes (svaras), two basic scales (Grāmas), fourteen derived scales (murchanās), 84 tānas, i.e., murchanās reduced to six or five notes, three registers (sthānas), vrittis, śuṣka, sādhāraṇa or intermediary notes, varṇas, alaṅkāras, dhātus, śrutis and Jātîs. Elements of vocal music (Śārîrvîṇā) consist of notes, Grāmas, alaṅkāras, varṇas, the three registers (sthānas), Jātîs and sādhāraṇa or intermediary notes.

(a) The Pure Notes

The seven śuddha notes are given as follows :

Ṣaḍjaśca rṣabhaścaiva gāndhāro mdhyamastathā/
pancamo dhaivataścaiva saptamo'tha nisādavān//23

i.e., ṣaḍja (sa), ṛṣabha (re), gāndhār (ga), madhyama (ma), pañcama (pa), dhaivata (dha) and niṣāda (ni).

Futher, the author dicusses the four types of notes sonant (Vādi), consonant (Samvādi), assonant (Anuvādi) and dissonant (Vivādi). Vādi is the prominent note of the Jāti and is the same as amśa. The others have been explained wth reference to Vādi as,

'Tatra vadanādvādi, saṁvadanāt samivādi,
Vivadanādvivādi, anuvadanādanuvāditi/30

i.e., that which communicates with the vāḍi is samvādi, that which debates with the vādi is vivadi and that which follows the vadi is anuvādi.

An interval of 9 or 13 śrutis between the notes has been indicated as being conducive to consonance. A difference of śrutis leads to dissonance. Two fundamental tonal systems, 'Grāmas' have been mentioned, viz. Ṣaḍja and Madhyama Grāma. These were the foundational scales that determined the śruti intervals between the notes of the octave. The total number of śrutis has been given as twenty two. Their distribution among the notes of Ṣadja Grāma is as follows :

Catuhśrutirbhavet ṣaḍjah ṛṣabhastriśrutih smṛtah/
Dviśruti ścaiva gāndhāro madhyamaśca catuhśrutih//34
Pancamastadvadeva syāt triśutirdhaivato matah/
dviśrutiśca niṣādah syāt ṣaḍjagrāma vidhirbhavet//35

i.e. — Sa — 4
Re — 3
Ga — 2
Ma — 4
Pa — 4
Dha — 3
Ni — 2

By lowering one sruti of the Pa note the śruti distribution in ma—scale is obtained, thus

Sa — 4
Re — 3
Ga — 2
Ma — 4
Pa — 3
Dha — 4
Ni — 2

(b) Demonstration of the Twenty Two Śrutis

The magnitude of one śruti, which the author calls 'Pramāna' has been demonstrated scientifically in the NŚ by a method called *'sāraṇā catuṣṭayi'*. There are four steps in this process.

1. Two vîṇās of identical proportions, strings, bridges etc., tuned to a given pure note murchanā in Ṣaḍjagrāma are to be taken. Let one vîṇā be called (a) which is to remain untouched and the other (b) in which the strings are to be loosened, for convenience.[4] The note pancama of (b) is to be lowered by an interval as much as the breadth of a hair or 'keśa' that has been called 'kaiśiki'. In this manner, (b) will be tuned to Madhyamagrāma. The remaining notes are also to be lowered by the same interval so that (b) is again tuned to Ṣaḍjagrāma.
2. In the second *sāraṇā,* the notes of (b) are to be lowered once again (by a larger interval 'mahati') such that

gāndhāra and niśāda of (b) resound with the same pitch as that of rṣabha and dhaivata of (a).

3. The strings of (b) are to be slackened first such that rṣabha and dhaivata of (b) are now in consonance with ṣaḍja and pañcama of (a) respectively. The interval has been called 'upamahati'.
4. The fourth time when the notes of (b) are lowered by loosening the strings, the notes pañcama, madhyama and sadja of (b) will resound with the same pitches as those of madhyama, gāndhāra and niśāda of (a) respectively.

In this manner, the distribution of twenty two śrutis becomes clear. (see Table 4 given in Appendix I)

(c) The Modified Notes

Other than the seven pure notes two modified notes called 'svarasādhārana' have also been mentioned in NŚ. They have been compared to the transitional period between the Spring and Winter seasons, thus

yatha chāyāsu bhawati Sîtam prasvedo bhavati cātapasthasya/
Na ca nāgato vasanto na ca niśśesah śiśirakālah//
Iti kālasādhāraṇatā/64

i.e., just like while standing in the shade, one feels cold but standing in the sun one perspires. Neither the spring has come fully, or the winter season has gone. This is 'sādhāraṇa' of the seasons. In the same way, śvara sādhāraṇa' lie between the interval of two notes. They are called 'kākali' and 'antara'. Thus,

'Svarasādhāranaṁ kākalyantarasvarau. Tatra dviśrutyutkṛṣto niṣādah kākalî samjnobhavati. Tadvat gāndhāro' ntrarasaṁ jnobhavati/66

When nisāda is raised by two śrutis, it becomes kākali and when gāndhāra is raised by two śrutis, it becomes antara gāndhara.

(d) Murchanās

After the demonstration of śrutis, the author of NŚ describes fourteen 'murchanās' in two Grāmas. 'Murchanā' or derived scales have been defined as

'Kramāyuktāh svarāh sapta murcchanetyabhisamjnita/51

i.e., the seven notes in a particular sequence are called 'murchanā'. Though it has not been specified, but the manner in which he names the murchanās, the sequence seems to be in descending order. The names of the murchanās are given in Table-5 in Appendix I. Based on these murchanās, 84 murchanā tānas have been derived by deleting one or two notes from each.

(e) Jātîs

These were musical modes with fixed combinations of notes. Apart from the seven pure Jātîs mentioned in the Rāmāyaṇa, the NŚ gives eleven 'vikrita' Jātîs. That is, eighteen Jātîs are mentioned in the NŚ. Apart from these, eleven hybrid or Samvāyaja Jātîs are also mentioned. Their tenfold characteristics have also been discussed elaborately.

The Jātîs belonging to the sa-scale are Ṣāḍjî, Ārṣabhî, Dhaivatî, Naisādi, Ṣaḍjodîcyavatî, Saḍjakaiśikî and Saḍjamadhyamā. The Jātîs of ma-scale are Gāndhāri, Madhayamā, Pañcami, Gāndhārodîcyavā, Gāndhārpancami, Madhyamodîcyavā, Raktagāndhāri, Nandayantî, Kārmāravî, Āndhri and Kaiśiki.

Of these, the Suddha Jātîs of sa-scale are Ṣādjî, Ārṣabhî, Dhaivatî and Naisādi. Those of ma-scale are Gāndhārî, Madhyamā and Pañcami. The modified notes are used in Ṣaḍjamadhyamā of sa-scale and Madhyama and Pañcami of ma-scale (see Table 6 in Appendix I).

(f) The Tenfold Characteristics of Jātîs

According to the Nāṭya Śāstra,

Daśakaṁ jātilakṣaṇaṁ
Grahāmśau tāramaṅdrau ca nyāso'panyāsa eva ca/
Alpatvaṁ ca bahutvaṁ ca Ṣāḍavauduvite tathā//102

i.e.—the ten characteristics of a Jāti are Graha, Aṁśa, Tāra, Maṅdra, Nyāsa, Apanyāsa, Alpatva, Bahutva, Ṣāḍava and Auḍuvita.

1. *Graha*—The note with which a Jāti begins, is termed 'graha', In pure Jātîs, the aṁsā is also the graha.

2. *Aṁśa*—'Aṁśa' is the prominent note (same as sonant) of the Jāti in which resides the dominant sentiment. It is responsible

for the charm of melodic expression. It is used repeatedly as graha, apanyāsa, saṁnyāsa and nyāsa. It determines the range of tara—mandra.

3. *Tāra*—The upper limit for the ascent of notes in a Jāti has been given either uptil the fourth note from aṁśa or even the fifth or seventh note.

4. *Maṅdra*—The lower limit for the descent of notes in a Jāti has been given either uptil aṁśa or nyāsa or apanyāsa.

5. *Nyāsa*—the note used at the end of a Jāti is 'nyāsa'. In pure Jātîs, aṁśa is also nyāsa.

6. *Apanyāsa*—The note used at the end of the first half portion of a Jāti is called 'apanyāsa'.

7. *Alpatva*—When notes (other than āmśa) are used sparingly, it is called 'alpatva'. This is done in two ways either by skipping of non or by nora-repetition.

8. *Bahutva*—When notes are used abundantly, it is called 'Bahutva'. This is done in two ways—by using the note fully or by repeating it often.

9. *Ṣāḍavita*—Hexatonic usage (by omitting one note) in a Jāti is 'Ṣāḍavita'.

10. *Auḍavita*—Pentatonic usuage (by omitting two notes) in a Jātî is 'Auḍavita'.

Presentation of the Jātîs according to different 'rasas' or sentiments on the basis of the prominent note has also been disclosed in the NŚ. After that the author goes on to discribe the varṇas—alaṅkāras used in music. He has mentioned four types of 'Gîtîs'—Māgadhi, Ardhamāgadhi, Sambhāvitā and Pṛthulā, which were sung according to the 'vrittis'—Citrā, Vārtik and Dakṣinā.

In the thirty first chapter, there is a detailed description of 'tālas' or rhythmic beats. Popular tālas of that period were cancatpuṭa, cāpapuṭa, ṣaṭ pitaputraka or pancapāṇi, samparkaṣṭāka and udghatta. The method of showing the tālas by hand-gestures has also been given. The thirty second chapter deals mostly with the description of a particular type of song called 'Dhruvā'. This type of song was supposed to be sung before, after as well as during the course of a play. Five kinds of Dhruvā have been mentioned, viz.

1. *Prāveśikî,* which was the entrance song.

2. *Naiṣkrāmikî,* which was the exit song, to be sung at the end of a scene or the play.

3. *Ākṣepikî*—Between Prāveśiki and Naiskrāmikî, when there was still time for a scene to start or for a change of mood, the 'Ākṣepikî' was employed along with dance in fast tempo.

4. *Prāsādikî*—This type of Dhruvā was used to reinforce the dominant mood of the play.

5. *Antarā*—This type of Dhruvā was sung when there was a gap or was used to cover up some mishap during a performance. It was also used in situations of grief, anger, loss of memory, etc.

The merits and demerits of singers and instrumentatalists have also been discussed. A detailed description of various percussion instruments, stringed instruments etc., has also been given. Thus, the Nāṭya Śāstra is not only the earliest available comprehensive treatise on ancient Indian drama, it also consists of an exhaustive account of the fundamental theory of ancient Indian music.

(v) Music as in 'Bṛhaddeśi' of Mataṅga (7-8th A.D.)

Next to the 'NŚ', this Sanskrit book on music is of particular significance to gain knowledge of the historical development of ancient music. The word 'Rāga' in the strict sense has been mentioned for the first time in this book. In his own words, Mataṅga says,

> *'Rāga mārgasya yadrupaṁ yan noktam Bharatādibhih/*
> *Nirupyate tadasmābhir Iakṣya—lakṣaṇa—saṁyutaṁ//262*

i.e.—The form of the course of 'Rāga' music that has not been discussed by the likes of Bharata is being discussed by me in both its practical and theoretical aspects.

He has also given veiws of earlier authors, prominent among whom are Bharata, Yāstika, Kaśyapa, Śārdula, Durgaśakti, Dattila and Kohala. 'Bṛhaddeśi' consists of eight chapters out of which the chapters on instrumental music and dance are not available. Mahārānā Kumbha in his 'Sangeet Rāja' sheds light on the chapter of instrumental music, which was available to him. Mataṅga played the Citrā vîṇā and invented the Kinnarî vîṇā. He is supposed to have placed fourteen to eighteen movable frets for the first time on this seven stringed vîṇā. He also played the flute and is supposed to have constructed one of metal in place of the wooden flute.

During Mataṅgal's period, 'Gāndharva' had started giving way to the 'Desî'[5] Rāga music. The 'Grāma (Mārgi) Rāgas' and their varieties Bhāṣā and Vibhāṣā (Desî) existed along with the Jātîs of Gāndharva. Later, when other rāgāṅga and the like evolved by a relaxation of rules, Bhāṣā and Vibhāṣā along with Grāma Rāgas were included in Mārg and the others in Deśî music.

Dr. Thakur Jaidev Singh in *Indian Music* has distinguished three stages of development of our music during this transitional phase.

1. Gāndharva or Jāti music.
2. Mārga music (Grāma rāgas—their varieties and sub-varieties)
3. Deśî music (Rāgānga, Kriyānga etc., during the period of Śārngadeva).

The description of Jātîs in Bṛhaddeśî is similar of that to NŚ. After that Mataṅga defines Rāga as,

Yo'sau dhvaniviśeṣastu svaravarṇavibhuṣitaḥ/
Ranjako janacittānāṁ sa ca rāga udāhṛtaḥ// 264

i.e.—that special melodic configuration consisting of notes and 'varṇas' or embellishments which colours or delights the minds of people is called 'Rāga'. Further, he gives the etymology of the word 'Rāga' as born from the act of colouring or delighting.

The rendering of fifty six Rāgas has been given according to seven Gîtis, viz.—

Śuddhā (5), Bhinnā(5), Gauḍi(3), Rāga(8), Sādhārani(7), Bhāṣa(16) and Vibhāṣā(12)

1. *Śuddhā*—Complete (with all seven notes) and rendered in all three registers in straight and attractive notes with śrutis of equal magnitude.

2. *Bhinnā*—Bhinnā is of short duration, mobile, curvaceous and spreads out upwards in attractive notes of high-low registers.

3. *Gaudi*—This Gîti consists of continuous rendering of beautiful and attractive notes in the three registers along with a variety of Gamaka[6] called 'Ohāti'. Ohāti is obtained by the shaking of notes in the lower register.

4. *Rāga (vesarā)*—'Vesarā' is in which the notes move with speed. The reason for calling it 'Rāga' has been given through a

quotation of Kaśyapa according to which 'where the element of colourful or delightful beauty (Rāga) is seen in its totality in all the four varṇas that is Rāga. It consists of Gamakas—delightful arrangement of notes.

5. *Sādhāraṇi*—This is a combination of all other Gîtis.

6. *Bhāṣā*—This Gîti consists of smooth, well composed colourful with 'kākus'[7], shaken, soft, luminous with 'mālavikāku', attractive and graceful melodic phrases. It is rendered in such a manner that delights people.

7. *Vibhāṣā*—This Gîti consists of gamakas that are attractive, numerous, luminous, shaken, orginating from chest region, even, high and very high, smooth, in which madhyama shines brightly in between, that are delightful to the ear and are attractive. The composition of Vibhāṣā Gîti should be spontaneous and according to the liking of people.

The Bhāṣās have been divided into four types—*mula, sankîrṇa, deśaja* and *chāyāmātrānuga*. The viewpoint of Yāṣṭika has been given about the origin' of these Bhāṣās—Vibhāṣās as,

> *Grāmarāgodhbavā bhāṣā bhāsābhyaśca vibhāṣikā/*
> *vibhāṣābhyaśca sanjātastathā cāntarabhāsikā//10*

i.e. Bhāsās evolved from Grāmarāgās, Vibhāṣās from the Bhāṣās and Antarabhāṣ ās from Vibhāṣās.

These Bhāsās-vibhāsas were later amalgamated with the Rāga-Rāginî system and supplied the nucleus for the 'Rāginîs'. This view is endorsed by the fact that in a 14th century Jain lexicon '*Sangitopaniṣadsāroddhār*, the Rāginîs have been mentioned under the heading of 'Bhāṣa'.

After the description of Bhāṣās, the Deśîrāgas have been discussed. Three types of Deśî Rāgas have been mentioned; viz.—Rāgānga, Bhāṣānga and Kriyānga. The Rāgāngas were a reflection of Grāmarāgas in the same way as the Bhāṣāngas were a reflection of Bhāṣās and did not necessarily follow the Mārga rules rigidly. The Kriyānagas were related to the expression of particular sentiments.

The etymology of the note in Bṛhaddeśî has been given as,

Rājr diptāviti dhātoh svaśabdapurvakasyaca svayam yo rājate yasmāt tasmādeṣa svarah smṛtah//

i.e., the word 'svara' or note is formed by adding the prefix 'sva' meaning self in front of the Sanskrit root 'rājṛ' meaning 'luminous'. Thus, a note is that which is self luminous. Like Bharata, Mataṅga has also given the fourfold notes, viz.—Vādi, Saṁvādi, Anuvādi and Vivādi. Thus

Vadanād vādi swāmivat saṁvadanāt saṁvādi amātyavat/
anuvadanādanuvādi parijanavat vivadanād vivādi śatruvat//

i.e., like the master, the Vādi (sonant) orders, like the minister, the Saṁvādi (consonant) confers, like the servants, the Anuvādi (assonant) follows orders and like an enemy, the Vivādi (dissonant) causes dispute.

Matanga has defined murchanā very clearly as the ascent and descent of the seven notes in a particular sequence. He has differentiated two types of murchanās—

1. Seven note murchanā
2. Tweleve note murchanā

The murchanā of seven notes is four fold—

1. Purvā (complete, with all seven notes)
2. Ṣāḍavā (hexatonic)
3. Auḍuvita (pentatonic)
4. Sādhāraṇā (with sādhāraṇa svaras—kākali 'ni' and antara 'ga').

There are fourteen Purṇā murchanās of the two Grāmas. The Ṣaḍava and Auḍuvita have been called 'tāna' instead of murchanā, since the pre-requisite of having seven notes is not fulfilled for calling them murchanā. According to Mataṅga, as opposed to murchanā, the notes in a tāna are arranged only in ascending order. These are eighty four in both Grāmas (49 ṣāḍava and 35 auḍava). Out of the fourteen complete murchanās, a total of fifty six murchanās of seven notes can be obtained by including the sādhāraṇa notes. The twelve note murchanā, according to Mataṅga, is required for the sake of establishment of tāra and maṅdra in Jāti, Bhāṣā and the like.

A type of song of the Desî category of music called 'Prabandha' has been described in Bṛhaddeśî for the first time. He has discussed forty eight Prabandhas. A more meticulous description of Prabandha can be obtained from Sangît Ratnākara of Śarngadeva, it will be explained under the heading of Sangît Ratnākara.

(vi) Sangît Makaranda of Nārada (7th-9th Century A.D.)

The 'Sangît Makaranda' (S.M.) of Nārada is of particular significance regarding the Rāga-Rāginî system of classification. Though the word 'Rāginî' has not been used in S.M., a direct reference to the feminine nature (Stri or Yoshita Bhārya) has been made. Whereas in 'Bṛhaddeśî, even though the names of Grāma Rāgas are masculine and those of Bhāṣās—Vibhāṣās are feminine, Matanga has not made any deliberate attempt towards such a classification. There has been some controversy regarding the exact time period of S.M. owing to the mention of this system and also because of the author's name 'Nārada'. Various works on music have been attributed to Nārada such as *Nāradiya Śiksha, Pancama Sāra Samhitā, chatvārimschatta Rāga Nirupaṇaṁ* etc., apart from S.M. The time period of these works ranges from 2nd-3rd century A.D. to 15th century A.D. Thus, 'Nārada' is definitely not a single person. In 'A critical study of Sangeet Makaranda by Dr. M.V. Vijay Lakshmi, various finer points regarding the controversies concerning the exact period of this work have been discussed elaborately. After much discussion, the time period ascribed to S.M. is not earlier than 7th century and not later than 9th century.

The S.M. consists of two portions—Sangeetādhyāya and Nrityādhyāya. Each portion has four chapters or 'Pādas'. It is not a very elaborate book (consisting of merely 560 ślokas) but is unique in its treatment of Rāga classification. Nārada has classified Rāgas in at least four different ways. Apart from the Gender classification, S.M. is the ealiest work to discuss the time concept of Rāgas. He has classified the Rāgas according to the number of notes and also according to the method of using notes in a Rāga (Kaṁpana).

(1) Gender Classification

Nārada has classified Rāgas as Male (Puṅlinga), Female (Strî) and Neuter (Napuṅsaka) according to various sentiments. Thus

Raudra' dbhute tathā vîre puṅrāgeh parigiyate/

śṛngār hāsya karuṇam strî rāgaiśca pragîyate
bhayānake ca vîbhatse śānte gāyannapuṁsake//63

i.e., the furious, marvellous and heroic sentiments are attributed to the male Rāgas, the erotic, comic and pathetic sentiments are ascribed to the female Rāgas and the neuter Rāgas give expression to the horrible, fearful and calm sentiments (generalised). He has enumerated twenty Rāgas in the masculine category, twenty four in the femine category and thirteen in the neuter category. The table is given in Appendix I. Two other variations of this classification have also been given, viz.—8 main and 23 feminine (yosita)—3 each and 6 main—36 Uparāgas (which probably gave rise to 6 male Rāga and 36 female Rāginî system).

The classification according to the number of notes is—

1. Sampoorna—(having all seven notes) in number. These are eleven.
2. Ṣāḍava (having six notes). These are also eleven in number.
3. Auḍava (having five notes) these are eight in number.

According to method of production of note (Kaṁpana) he has given three categories—

1. Muktānga Kampita (notes are shaken purposely)
2. Ardha vikaṁpita (only halfshaken) and
3. Kampa Vihina (notes are steady).

In the classification according to the time of singing, Nārada has first of all categorised the Rāgas broadly as Suryānsha and Candramānsha. The former are supposed to be sung at day time while the latter (except Gaudi-noon Rāga) are evening Rāgas. Then, there are the morning (Prātah Kāla) Rāgas and noon (Madhyānha) Rāgas. The hours of the day have been divided according to 'Praharas'. There are eight praharas in twenty-four hours, each of three hours duration. The Suryānsha Rāgas are nineteen 19 in number, noon Rāgas are fourteen and Candramānsha Rāgas are seventeen (see Table 8(d) in App. I). The time of singing for morning and evening Rāgas has been determined on the basis of the following pattern, thus

Praharaikodayādarvāk praharaikodayopari/
deśākṣî bhairavā śuddhā nādaṁ yatpraharodhbhavaṁ//20

i.e., Deśakṣî and Śuddha Bhairava should be sung at a prahara (three hours) from sun rise.

In the same way Varātikā and Śuddha Drāvatika should be sung at a prahara from sunset. Malhāri, Māhuri and Āndoli should be sung a prahara after sun rise in the same way as Rāmakriti, Cāyānāṭa and Ranji should be sung during three hours after sunset. Gauda should be sung at noon while Śuddha and Sālaṅga Nātika should be sung after three praharas of sunset.

In his treatment of basic concepts like Nāda, Nārada is unique in mentioning five varieties—Nakhaj, Vāyuj, Charmaj, Lohaj and Śārîraj. He has mentioned Rāgālapti and Rupakālapti but is silent about Gîtis and Grāma Rāgas. In other areas, he has mostly followed Mataṅga.

(vii) Music in Bharata Bhāṣyaṁ of Nānya Deva

This Sanskrit commentary on 'Nātya Śāstra' was originally called '*Saraswati hṛdayālaṅkārā* by the author himself, who has side-by-side used the name 'Bharata Bhāṣyaṁ' or 'Bharata Vārtikā' as well. Nānya Deva was a Rāṣṭrakuṭa prince who ruled over Mithilā from 1097 A.D. to 1133 A.D. The manuscript of 'Bharat Bhāṣyaṁ,' which is kept in the Bhandarkar Oriental Research Institute, Pune, consists of 15 chapters out of a total of 17 chapters (16 and 17 are missing). It comprises approximately 8-9,000 ślokas, which means it is even larger than NŚ itself.

Though Bharata Bhāṣyaṁ basically elaborates on N.Ś., there are references to other authors also, such as Dattila, Kaśyapa, Nārada and Mataṅga. Bharata Bhāṣyaṁ also discusses certain topics that have not been mentioned in N.Ś. For instance, the Gāndhāra Grāma, which does not find a place in NS', has been discussed in detail, along with Ṣadja and Madhyama Grāmas. The three Grāmās of Nānya Deva according to their śruti distribution are,

1. Ṣaḍja Grāma—4 Sa, 3 Re, 2 Ga, 4 Ma, 4 Pa, 3 Dha, 2 Ni
2. Madhyama Grāma—4 Ma, 3 Pa, 4 Dha, 2 Ni, 4 Sa, 3 Re, 2 Ga
3. Gāndhāra Grāma—4 Ga, 3 Ma, 3 Pa, 3 Dha, 4 Ni, 3 Sa, 2 Re

He has given a detailed description of Jātirāgas and Grāmarāgas along with elaboration of notes. He mentions five

Gîtis—Śuddhā, Bhinnā, Gaudi, Vesarā, and Sādhāranā. He has also allocated different times periods for the Gîtis. Seven Grāma Rāgas, six Mula Rāgas, six Mukhyā Bhāṣās and twenty Desākhyā Bhāṣās have been mentioned. Uparāgas are thirty. Another Svarākhyā are forty[8]. He has given Rāgas according to the Gāndhāra Grāma also. He has mentioned Purva and Prasiddha Kṛiyangas along with Bhāṣās, Vibhāṣās and Antarabhāṣās.

Music in Medieval Period

(i) Music in 'Sangît Ratnākara' of Śārṅgadeva (1210-1247 A.D.)

'Sārṅgadeva's Sangît Ratnākara is a monumental pillar in the realm of the history of Indian classical music. He has attempted the mammoth task of reorganising the fragmented principles of music and linking them to his contemporary practical music (i.e., connecting *lakṣaṇa* to *lakṣya)*. During his period, there were so many contradictory and varied view points that it was essential to discard the obsolete and rearrange the existing. The commentaries of Kallinath and Singh Bhupal have also contributed towards this end. 'Nihśaṅka' Śarṅgadeva has re-established the principles of music in a comprehensive manner and is next only to NŚ's Bharata. Sangît Ratnākara serves as a connecting link between the ancient and the modern for both the streams of Indian classical music—Hindustāni and Carnātic. The book consists of seven chapters for which it is also referred to as 'Saptādhyāyi'. A brief description of the chapters is given below:

(A) Chapter I—Svaragatādhyāya

This chapter deals with the various aspects of the note—svara. It is divided into eight-sections (Prakaranas) as:

1. *Padārthasangrahaprakarṇa*—This section serves as an introduction to the work. The authors' lineage, sources of reference, definition of music and a summary of contents have been discussed in this section. Starting with an invocation, he goes on to describe his ancestry. He belonged to the family of sage Vṛṣagaṇa of Kashmir. One of his descendants called Bhāskara, migrated to the South and was a great exponent of Ayurveda. His son, Soḍhala followed his father's footsteps and received the patronage of King Bhillama and subsequently King Singhaṇa of the Yādava dynasty. Śārṅgdeva was Soḍhala's son.

Śarṅgadeva has referred to earlier authors from whose works he has gained knowledge, such as Sadāśiva, Śiva, Brahma, Bharata, Kaśyapa, Mataṅga, Yāṣṭika, Durgaśakti, Śārdula, Kohala, Visākhila, Dattila, Nārada, Tumburu, Nānyadeva, Bhoja, Someśa, Jagadeka, Abhinavagupta etc. Thereafter, he gives the characteristics of music[9] and its branches Mārga and Deśî. Among the triology of vocal, instrumental music and dance, he has given importance to vocal music[10]. Then he describes the significance of music. In the end, he gives a synopsis of the contents.

2. *Pinḍotpatti-prakarana*—Music depends on Nāda (Sound). There are two kinds of Nāda—Āhata and Anāhata, where the former is created (struck) and the other is uncreated (unstruck). Both are manifest in the human body, therefore the embodiment within the human body has been discussed in this section. Śārṅgadeva has given a detailed description of the finer points of the human body including the manifestation, growth of feotus and birth of a child according to Ayurveda. He has described the chakras (psychophysical centres) according to Haṭhayoga. In the end he states that Nāda is a means for enjoyment as well as salvation.

3. *Nāda-sthāna-śruti-svara-Jāti-kula-devatā-ṛṣi-chhanda-rasa-prakarṇa*—In this section, Śārṅgadeva gives the etymology of nāda, śruti and svara. He gives his interpretation of the *sāraṇā catuṣṭayi* of Bharata. He has distributed twenty two śrutis into fives classes (Jātîs) (Table 10, Appendix I) and givens their nomenclature. Three sthānas or registers—Maṅdra, Madhya and Tāra of the notes have been mentioned. He has mentioned twelve modified or 'vikrita' notes (Table 9, Appendix I). Apart from that he has also mentioned the caste, colour, sage, deity, metre and rasa of the notes (Table 12, Appendix I). The fourfold notes—Vādi (Sonant), Samavādi (Consonant), Anuvādi (Assonant) and Vivādi (dissonant) have also been described. The Definition of note has been given as follows:

Śrutyanantarabhāvi yah snigdho 'nuranānātmakah
Svato ranjayati śrotṛcittaṁ sa svara ucyate//24

i.e., that creamy (soft/viscous) and resonant sound which immediately follows the sruti elights the listeners mind by itself is called 'svara' or note. Śārṅgadeva has given the seven notes Ṣaḍja, Ṛṣabha, Gāndhāra, Madhyama, Pāncama, Dhaivata and Niṣāda. He has also given their common usage as Sa, Re, Ga,

Ma, Pa, Dha and Ni (which he has used in the elaboration of Jātîs and Rāgas).

4. *Grāma-murchanā-krama-tāna-prakaraṇa*—Earlier, the tonal aspect was treated individually, by taking up nāda, śruti and svara. In this section, their organisation within Grāma-murchanā etc., is being dealt with. The fundamental group of tones which forms the basis for murchanā etc., has been called 'Grāma', as conveyed from the śloka,

Grāmah svara samuhah syānmurchanā" deh samāṣṛayah/[11]

Further, he has discussed Ṣaḍja, Madhyama and Gāndhāra Grāmas, with the first two being prevalent on Earth and the latter in Heaven. The distribution of śrutis among the notes in the three Grāmas is same as that given by Nārada. He has also given the decities and time period of singing the melodic types associated with the Grāmas. The 'murchana' has been defined as follows:

Kramātsvarāṇaṁ Saptānāmārohaścāvarohaṇaṁ/
murchanetyucyate grāmadvaye tāh saptasapta ca//9//

i.e., the successive ascent and descent of the seven notes constitutes 'murchanā'. There are seven murchanās each in the two Grāmas (of this world). Their names and order of notes are given in Table 11 of Appendix I. The murchanās have been classified as Śuddhā, Kākalikalitā, Sāntarā and Ubhayagatā. In all, there are fifty six murchanās. When one or two notes are omitted from Śuddhā murchanās, śuddha tānas (hexatonic and pentatonic) are formed. There are forty nine hexatonic and thirty five pentatonic Śuddha tānas in both Grāmas. The total number is therefore, eighty four. When the notes of the complete or incomplete murchanās are no longer in successive order, permutational or kuta tānas are formed. The number of complete kuṭa tānas out of fifty six murchanās is two lakh eighty two thousand and two hundred forty. The number of incomplete kuṭa tānas are as follows :

Hexatonic	—	720
Pentatonic	—	120
Tetrtonic	—	24
Tritonic	—	6
Bitonic	—	2
Monotonic	—	1

He has given the *khañḍameru* or permutation indicator to calculate the number of permutions and also find out Uddiṣta (indicated note series) or Naṣta (missing note series).

5. *Sādhāṛaṇa prakaraṇa*—Śarṅgadeva has talked of four varieties of svara sādhāraṇa. Apart from the two mentioned by Bharata (kākali 'ni' and antara 'ga'), he has mentioned śaḍja and madhyama sādhāraṇa and how they are employed in obtaining the twelve modified notes. He has also mentioned Jāti sādhāraṇa.

6. *Varṇa alaṅkāra prakaraṇa*—Śarṅgadeva has given the four types of Varṅas or tone patterns—Sthāyi, Ārohi, Avarohî and Sañcarî as his predecessors. In the treatment of Alaṅkāras (embelishments), he has been very explicit. According to him (Alaṅkāras specific arrangements of Varṇas (tone patterns). He has described as many as sixty three Alaṅkāras which were popular during his time. Some of them are in practice even today, (e.g. Prasannamadhya—sa, sa, sa, Niṣkarṣa—sa sa, re re, Ākṣepa—sariga, riga ma, ga ma pa etc).

7. *Jātî-prakaraṇa*—Śārṅgadeva has described the seven Śuddha and eleven Saṁsargaja vikrita Jātîs of Bharata. The modified or vikrita varieties of the Śuddhā Jātîs are twenty three each except for Ṣāḍji, which has fifteen. Instead of the ten characteristics of Jātis that Bharata enumerated, Śārṅgadeva has discussed thirteen characteristics. He has referred to Samnyāsa and Vinyāsa seperately and has also included Antara mārga.[12] Thereafter, he describes the Jātîs individually, giving the elaboration of notes as well.

8. *Gîti-prakaraṇa*—The author begins this section with a description of Kapāla and Kambalagānas. The Kapāla songs originated from the Śuddhā Jātîs and Kambala songs form the Pañcami Jātî. After that, he describes the Gîtis. *Gîti* has been defined as an 'act of singing' enriched with tonal and verbal patterns that are set to a definite tempo. In this section, Śārṅgadeva has discussed only the Padāśritā (based on verbal structure) and Tālāśita Gitis (based on rhythm). These are fourfold — Māgadhi, Ardhamāgadhi, Sambhāvitā and Pṛthulā. The Svarāśrita Gîtis (based on tonal structure) are described in the chapter). With this section, the 'Svaragatādhyāya' of Sangît Ratnākara comes to an end.

(B) Chapter II—Rāgavivekādhyāya

In this chapter, Śārṅgadeva has expounded the complete concept of Rāga'. He has given a tenfold classification of Rāgas, with the total number, of Rāgas in each category amounting to two hundred and sixty four. Though Mataṅga has also mentioned most of these categories, he has left out Upāngas and is not very systematic about the other categories. This chapter consists of two sections. They are,

1. *Grāmarāga uparāga-rāga—bhāṣā-vibhāṣā—antarabhāṣa viveka prakaraṇa.* This section begins with the description of five types of Grāmarāgas[13] on the basis of five Gîtis. Out of the seven Gîtis of Mataṅga, the Bhāṣa and Vibhāṣa Gîtis are derivatives of Grāma Rāgas. Thus, Śārṅgadeva has not included them in his five Gîtis which are—Śuddhā, Bhinnā, Gauḍî, Vesarā and Sādhāraṇî. Their features are the same as those given by Mataṅga. The Rāgas associated with these 'Svarāśrita' Gîtis are also known by the same name (Śuddha etc.) There are seven Śuddha, five Bhinnā, three Gauḍā, eight Vesarā and seven Sādhāraṅa Grāma Rāgas (see Table 13 in Appendix I). Subsequently he mentions the Uparāgas, Rāgas, Bhāṣās, Vibhāṣās and Antarabhāṣas (see Table 14 in Appendix I).

2. *Rāgaṅgādi nirṇaya prakaraṇa*—In this section, Śārṅgadeva discusses four varieties of Deśi Rāgas, viz. Rāgāṅga, Bhāṣāṅga, Kriyāṅga and Upāṅga.

(*a*) Rāgāṅgas—Deśi Rāgas which have the influence of some Grāmarāga, e.g. Bhairava from Bhinnaṣaḍja, Toḍi from Ṣāḍava etc.,
(*b*) Bhāṣāṅgas—Deṣî Rāgas associated with Bhāṣās etc.
(*c*) Kriyāṅgas—These were more feeling oriented.
(*d*) Upāṅgas—These consisted of aṅgas (or parts) of all the three types.

Śārṅgadeva has enumerated the Deśî Rāgas as Prākprasiddha (well known in ancient times) and Adhunāprasiddha (modern well known Rāgas). The former are thirty four while the latter are fifty two in number. Finally he gives their characteristics and also the notations. For example, in the Adhunāprasiddha Rāgas, the description of 'Mālavakaiśika' has been given as,

—atha mālavakaiśikah //70//
kaiśikîjātijah ṣaḍjagrahāṅsānto' Ipadhaivatah/
sakākalîkah śaḍjādimurchaṇārohivarṇavān //71//

prasannamadhyalaṅkāro vîre roudre' dbhute rase/
vipralambhe prayoktavyah śiśire prahare' ntime //72//
dinasya keśavaprîtyay,
sā sa pā mā mā ma risa nisasari .... ririri pa pa sa nisa ityālāpah (elaboration)
gagapa magapapani .... ni ri sa nisa iti karaṅam
sa sa pa pa ga ma pa
can drā bha ra ñam—etc.
ityākśiptikā (composition)[14]

The gist of the śloka is that 'Mālavakaiśika' is derived from Kaiśikî Jātî having ṣaḍja as its initial, fundamental and final note. The use of Dhaivata is rare. It has Śaḍja murchanā in the ascending Varṇa having kākali note. It is embellished with *prasanna madhya* Alañkāra and expresses the sentiments of valour, wrath and bewilderment and love in seperation. Its time of singing is the last quarter of the day in winter for the appeasment of Keśava (Kṛṣṇa).

After that, Mālavaśrî has been described as a Rāgāṅga of Mālavakaiśika. The other Rāgas have also been described in a similar manner.

(C) Chapter III— Prakîṇakādhyāya (miscellaneous)

In the previous chapter, Śārṅgadeva had discussed the various melodic types. How the basic structure of these melodic types is incorporated into compositions and the actual presentation depends on the composer *(Vāggeyakāra)*[15] or the performer, quality of the medium (voice/instrument), inflections *(kāku)*, embellishments such as shaking of the notes (Gamakas) and Ālapti. All these factors have been taken up in this chapter and their various categories have been discussed elaborately.

(D) Chapter IV—Prabandhādhyāya

This chapter deals with 'Prabandha' and all its varieties. Śārṅgadeva begins with the definition of *Gîta*[16] and its two types, viz. Gāndharva and Gāna. The former belonged to the mārga music consisting of Jatîs, Grāmarāgas, Uparāgas, Rāgas, Bhāṣās etc., whereas the latter belonged to the Deśi music comprising Rāgaṅgas etc., and these compostional forms. The classification of Gāna is two fold—Nibaddha and Anibaddha. Śārṅgadeva has defined them as,

'baddham dhātubhiraṅgayśca nibaddhamabhidhîyate /
ālaptirbandhahînatvādanibaddhamitîrita//5

i.e., that which is bound with 'dhātus' and 'aṅgas' is called *Nibaddha,* where as that which is free of any such bonding is *Anibaddha.* Ālapti is included in the second category. Nibaddha is threefold—Prạbandha, Vastu and Rupaka. Śārṅgadeva treats them as synonymous to each other. Some later authors (such as Mahārāṇā Kumbha and Nānya Deva) have distingushed them according to the number of dhātus and aṅgas. 'Dhātus' are different sections or structural parts which are fourfold in Prabhandha. They are,

(i) *Udgrāha*—This is the first section from where the Prabandha begins.
(ii) *Melāpaka*—The next section joins the third and first sections, thus it is called 'melāpaka' or the joinder.
(iii) *Dhruva*—The third section is called 'dhruva', since it remains fixed and is never omitted.
(iv) *Ābhoga*—The last section is called 'ābhoga', as it concludes.

A fifth dhātu called *antara* has also been mentioned, which is so called because it occurs in between *dhruva* and *ābhoga.* This dhātu is found only in the Sālaga suḍa variety. At least two dhātus should be present in a prabandha. On the basis of elimination of melāpaka or both melāpaka and ābhoga, there are three types of prabandhas.

(a) *dwidhātu*—In which melāpaka and ābhoga are omitted (consisting of two dhatus)
(b) *tridhātu*—In which melāpaka is omitted (consisting of three dhātus)
(c) *caturdhātu*—Having all four dhātus.

'Aṅgas' are the integral elements which are six in prabandha. They have been likened to the parts of a human body. The six aṅgas of prabandhas are:

(i) *Svaras*—When the notes 'sa, re, ga etc' are pronounced by their names, together with their respective musical intonation, they constitute the element svara. A modern adaptation of this element is the 'sargama gita', or swarmālikā.

(ii) *Taal/tāla* —The topic of tāla has been taken up in the next chapter. It is described as the (rhythmic) base upon which music has been established.[17] This element is significant in prabandha, since it literally 'binds' the prabandha.

(iii) *Tena*—This element signifies auspiciousness. 'Tena' is a derivative of the word 'tat', which refers to the supreme being 'Brahma' in passages such as 'Om tat sat', 'Tat tvam asi' etc. Thus, by the inclusion of this element, the prabandha is said to be characterised by Brahma himself. In modern times, the composition of Tarānā and 'nom-tom' elaboration (ālāpa) of 'Dhrupada' can be called a modified version of tena.

(iv) *Biruda—'Birudam guṇanāma'*, i.e., the description of qualities of great personalities, kings or gods and goddesses.

(v) *Pada*—Other than biruda, the verbal text of the prabandha through which meaning is conveyed, constitutes pada.

(vi) *Pāṭa—pāṭovādyākṣarotkarah'*, i.e., the reproduction of sound obtained from musical instruments through syllables. This element can be traced in some modern styles of music also, such as 'Caturaṅga' and 'Tārānā'.

At least two aṅgas should be present in a prabandha. According to the number of aṅgas, five Jātîs of prabandhas have been mentioned. They are

(a) *Medini*—Having six aṅgas
(b) *Ānandini*—Having five aṅgas
(c) *Dîpaṇi*—Having four aṅgas
(d) *Bhāvanî*—Having three aṅgas
(e) *Tāravalî*—Having two aṅgas

Alternately, they are also called śruti, nîti, senā, kavitā and campu respectively. The prabandhas have also been classified on the basis of specified and unspecified tāla. metre etc. The former are called 'Niryukta' and the latter are called 'Aniryakta'. For the actual description of various prabandhas, Śārṅgadeva has given a threefold classification as follows :

1. *Suḍa*—In Kallinath's commentary, 'suḍa' has been described as a regional term indicating a group of compositions. It is of two types,

(*a*) Śuddha suḍa—elā, karaṇa, dheṅkî, vartani, jhombaḍa, lambha rāsa and ekatālî.
(*b*) Chāyālaga or Sālaga suda—dhruva, mañṭha, pratimañṭha, nihsāruka, aḍḍatāla, rāsa and ekātalî.

2. *Ālikrama*—The word 'āli' means a line or row and 'krama' means sequence. Thus, Ālikrama indicates a series of prabandhas sung in sequence. By themselves, Āli prabandhas are twenty four, but when combined with Suḍa, they are thirty two. When a variety of Suḍa is present in between the Āli series, then also it is called Ālikrama.
3. *Viprakîrṇa*—These are independent compositions to be rendered at specific occasions. They are thirty six in number.

(E) Chapter V—Tālādhyāya

This chapter deals with the concept of 'tāla' in detail. 'Tāla' has been defined as

'tālastalapratiṣthāyāmiti dhātordhayin smṛtah/
gitaṁ vādyaṁ tathā nṛttaṁ yatastāle pratiṣṭhitaṁ//2

i.e., 'tāla' has been derived from 'tal' which is the base upon which an object is fixed. Similarly, tāla is the base or foundation upon which vocal, instrumental music and dance are established.

The various elements of tāla such as kriya (niśabda and saśabda), laya, yati, etc., have been discussed. The tālas have been classified as Mārga and Deśî.

(F) Chapter VI—Vādyādhyāya

The four categories of instruments viz.—stringed (*tat*), wind *(suṣir)*, percussion *(avanadya)* and metallic *(ghana)* have been discussed in a similar manner as Bharata.

(G) Chapter VII—Nartanādhyāya

This chapter deals with the various elements of dance.

(ii) Sangît Samayasāra of Pārśvadeva (13th Century A.D.)

Pārśvadeva was a prominent musical authority of the medieval period belonging to the Digambara sect of Jainism. He has not mentioned Śārṅgadeva (nor has Śārṅgadeva referred to him), which might be becuase they were contemporaries. He has been quoted by a commentator of Śārṅgadeva, Singh Bhupāla (C.1330 A.D.). Earlier authorities mentioned by Pārśvadeva include Bharata, Mataṅga, Dattila, Bhoja, Kaṣyapa, Yāṣtika, Kohala, Someśvara, Jadadekamalla, Mātṛgupta and Pramārdi. The book consists of ten chapters, out of which nine are available.

A unique feature of Sangît Samayasāra is that Pārśvadeva (or *Sangitākara,* as he calls himself) has mentioned sixty six śrutis, twenty two in each register. The names are also unlike any mentioned by earlier authors, but the distribution among notes is the same, i.e. 4324432 of sa, re, ga and so on respectively. The etymology of the note has been given in a manner similar to that of Mataṅga. He has refuted Kohal's veiwpoint of considering the note as continuous and omnipresent, since it cannot cross time and space. He has distinguished the note from other sounds by its unique characteristic of 'giving rise to rāga'.[18]

The points of origin of the seven notes within the human body have also been discussed as follows :

(*a*) The note ṣaḍja is called so, since it is obtained from six areas—the nose, throat, heart, palate, tongue and teeth.

(*b*) Arising from the navel and creating the sound of a bull through the passage of air from the throat and head, the second note is called ṛṣabha.

(*c*) Arising from the navel and obtained from the throat and head, it is pleasing to the Gandharvas therefore, it (the third note) is called Gandhāra.

(*d*) Since it is obtained in the middle portion through the passage of air arising from the navel to the heart, the fourth note is madhyama.

(*e*) As it is obtained from air passing through five areas the navel, lips, throat, head and heart, it (the fifth note) is called pañcama.

(*f*) Dhaivata is called so, as it is obtained from air arising from the navel which establishes itself upon the throat, palate, head and heart.

(*g*) Air arising from the navel which touches the throat, palate and head gives rise to niṣāda, where all the notes end.

In the treatment of murchanās he has followed Mataṅga. He has discussed both Saptasvara and Dvādaśasvara murchanās.

The names in both cases are the same.

He gives the distribution of Grāma Rāgas as follows:

Seven śuddha, five Bhinna, three Gauḍā, eight Vesara, seven Sādhārañа and eight Uparāgas.

In the 2nd chapter, he begins with a description of the characteristics of Deśî according to Mataṅga. He goes on to give the etymology of Nāda, the types of Gamakas, Gîta and its varieties—Nibaddha and Anibaddha. Then he describes the varieties of Ālapti. He gives sixteen varieties of Ālapti. They are—Rāgālapti, Roopakālapti, Pranjala, Viṣama, Anakṣara, Satāla, Atāla and the Śuddha and Sālaga varieties of each. He has referred to Ālapti as an 'Anibaddha form' of Gîta which is used in the beginning of Prabandhas and all Gîtas. He has mentioned four Varṇas and thirteen Alaṅkāras.

In the third chapter, he defines various technical terms such as ṭhāya, jiva svara (another term for vādi or amṣa), sthāna (registers), various kākus etc.

In the fourth chapter, he gives the characteristics of Rāgaṅgas, Bhāṣāṅgas, Kriyāṅgas and Upāṅgas and their distribution is as follows:

Rāgaṅgas	—	20
Bhāṣaṅgas	—	47
Upāṅgas	—	31
Kriyāṅgas	—	3

He has described only the popular Rāgas out of these 101 rāgas. e.g. Bhairava—

Bhinnaṣaḍja samudbhuto manyāso dhāṅśabhuṣitah //
samasvaro ripatyaktah prārthane bhairavah smṛtah //18//

i.e. Arising from Bhinnaṣaḍja, with ma as nyāsa and dha as aṁśa, omitting re and pa, the notes of Bhairava are equiposed and is suitable for prayer.

The fifth chapter deals with the description of prabandhas. The five jatis of the prabandhas have been named as champu, kavitā, senā, niti and śruti. In addition to Niryukta and Airyukta prabandhas of Śārṅgadeva, Pārśvadeva has mentioned Ubhayātmaka (combination of both) prabandhas also. The number of Śuddha suḍa prabandhas given by Pārśvadeva is eleven as compared to the eight given by Śārṅgadeva.

In the sixth chapter, the various musical instruments have been discussed. The seventh chapter is concerned with the elements of dance. The various abhinayas have been described elaborately. The chapter deals with the subject of tāla. The ninth chapter, comprises the different categories of *Vāggeyakāra,* the merits and demerits of singers and related topics.

(iii) Saṅgîtopaniṣatsāroddhāra of Sudhākalaśa (14th Century A.D.)

This book written in 1350 A.D. is of special significance in the development of Rāgamāla. It contains the earliest known iconographic details (Dhyānas). Thus, it is only natural that in the earliest available Rāgamālā painting (given in Plate 7), the Rāgas and Bhāṣās conform to the Rāgas and Bhāṣās given in this book (see Table 15). The Bhāṣās have been clearly identified as feminine in these Dhyānas. It consists of six chapters, which are as follows :

(a) Gitaprakaśana adhyāya (Chapter I)

In this chapter, Sudhākalaśa gives the importance of Gîta and describes Deśî saṅgît according to Śārṅgadeva. He discusses three types of notes—*sachetana, achetana* and *ubhayātmaka.* Nibaddha and Anibaddha have also been discussed. The three categories of Nibaddha—Prabandha, Roopaka and Vastu has also been given. During his time, the Prabandha seems to have become obscure, so he does not give its details. He has mentioned six aṅgas of Roopaka in which Rāga has also been included. Pāṭa and Pada have been combined.

(b) Tālaprakāśana (Chapter II)

In this chapter, the author describes the origin of music according to Jainism, since he himself hails from the community. According to Jain tradition, music is believed to have originated from the Śaṅkhanidhi, which is one of the nine mythical nidhis of cakravartin. He has also given the Śaiva and Vaiṣṇavaite viewpoints which believe music to have originated from Śiva and Hari respectively. Thereupon, the units and elements of tāla have been discussed in detail. Seventy three tālas have been divided into twelve groups according to the number of mātrās. The pāṭa (bola) of these tālas have also been given.

(c) Rāgādiprakāṣana (Chapter III)

The origin of the seven notes pertaining to different parts of the body has been discussed in the beginning of this chapter. The origin of 'sa' has been atributed to the throat, 're' to the heart, 'ga' to the nose, 'ma' to the navel, 'pa' to the heart, cerebrum and throat, 'dha' to the forehead and 'ni' to a combination of all these parts. He has mentioned twenty one murchanās and forty nine tānas, but the names differ from those of earlier authors. He has given twenty two śrutis, but the names are different. Some to them such as Nādanta, Niṣkala, Guḍā are closer to those mentioned in Sangît Samayasāra. Thereafter, he give the classification of Rāgas. The six main Rāgas and their six Bhāṣās each are given in Table 15 of Appendix I. In Deśî Rāga classification he gives Rāgāṅgas, Bhāṣāṅgas, Kriyāṅgas and Upāṅgas.

The iconographical details of the Rāgas and their Bhāṣās have been given for the first time. For example, Śri and its Bhāṣās have been described as follows :

Śri

śrirāgo'tha gauravarṇah so'ṣṭahastacaturmukhah//
pāṣābjapustakaṅkuśabîjapurbhṛtkārah/
vîṇā karadvaye'sya syādekaśca varadah karah//
vikhyāto'yaṁ haṅsayāno brahmamurtirivāparah/

—sl. 76 and 77

i.e., fair complexioned and having eight hands and four faces, Śri is seated on the lotus throne. She holds the vîṇā and holy books in two of her hands. The swan is her carrier.

The Bhāṣās of Śri

Gauḍibhāṣā pîta vastrā gaurāṅgî gajavāhanā//
kolāhalā raktavastrā gaurā tu śukavāhanā/
dhumrābhā krṣṇavasanāndhālî śukaravāhanā//
dravaḍî raktacîra syāddhemābhāmatsya vāhanā/
mālavakaiśikî gaurā krauṅcgāraktacîvarā//
raktābhā devagāndhārî pîtacîrāśvagāminî/

— sl. 80-82

i.e., Gauḍî is fair complexioned, adorns yellow clothes and rides an elephant. Kolāhalā wears red clothes and the parrot is her carrier. Āndhāli is greyish and rides a hog. Dravadi wears red clothes and fish is her carrier. Mālavakaiśiki is fair adorning red clothes and her vehicle is the crane. Devagāndhāri has a rosy constenance adorning yellow clothes and rides a horse.

Similarly, the visual description of other Rāgas and their Bhāṣās have also been given. Then he describes the Alaṅkāras. He gives the number of Alaṅkāras according to Śivamata as twelve, then mentions eighteen Alaṅkāras conforming to Gaurimata (prasanna, Akṣipta etc).

The fourth chapter deals with the four categories of musical instruments. The fifth and sixth chapters are devoted to the elements of dance.

(iv) Mānakutuhal of Rājā Mān Singh Tomar (1486-1517 A.D.)

Uptil now only Sanskrit treatises have been discussed (except the Tamil works). 'Mānakutuhala' or the curiosity of man, was originally written in Hindi by Rāja Mān Singh Tomar of Gwalior (1486-1517A.D.) and later in 1666 A.D. translated into Persian by Faqîrullah. The original is no longer available. Thus, the *'Tarjuma-i-Mānakutuhala and Risālai-i-Rāga darpana'*, a combination of two treatises comprising the translation in the earlier portion (till second chapter) and Faqirullāh's own contribution in the latter, is the only available access to Mānakutuhala.

Rājā Mān Singh was a great patron as well as composer of music. Many proficient musicians (Nāyakas) were patronized by him, like Nāyaka Bakhshu, Nāyaka Pāṇḍavi, Nāyaka Bhinnu, Nāyaka Dhondee and Charjoo. It is said that after confering with these musicians, the book Mānakutuhal was compiled. The 'Dhrupada' style of Hindustāni music was also initiated in its present form by the Rājā's own compositions as well as Nāyaka Bakhshu's compositions. The details of this style will be given in the later part of this chapter.

The book consists of details regarding the Rāgas, Rāginîs and Putras following *Hamumanmata* (Table 28 in Appendix I). Three categories Śuddha, Saṅkira(na) and Sālaga have been given to include the Rāgas, Rāginîs and Putras and any new inventions respectively. Another three categories according to the number of notes have been given, viz.—*Sampurana* (all seven notes), *Khādo* or Śāḍava (six notes) and *Oḍo* or Auḍava (five notes).

The six Śuddha Rāgas have been allocated the six seasons, viz.—Bhairon (Bhairava) in Śiśira, Mālakauns in Hemanta, Śri in Śarada, Megha in Pāwasa, Dîpaka in Grîṣma and Hinḍola in Basanta ṛtu along with their Rāginîs and Putras.

Faqirullāh has also discussed the contributions of Amîr Khusrau, who invented various new melodic structures by combining Persian *maqāms* to Hindustāni Rāgas. For example, by mixing Shahnāz to Khaṭa Rāga, he introduced Zilaf and by combining Nay-rez to Aiman, he innovated Yamanî. Twelve such innovations of Amîr Khusrau have been mentioned in *Risālai-Rāg'adarpana*. He has also mentioned seventeen Rāgas contributed by Sultān Hussain Shāh Sharqi of Jaunpur. Many present styles have been the boon of these two eminent musicians. The details will be given later.

(v) Rāga Taranginî of Panḍit Locana (1670-1705 A.D.)

This Sanskrit work devoted to music has been ascribed the date between 1670-1705 A.D. by Prof. C.S. Pant after much research work.[19] The book consists of five chapters. In the first chapter, he has given the iconography of masculine Rāgas. He has used the word 'murti' or icon to describe the dhyānas. He has given six masculine Rāgas following the *Hanumanmata.* They are—Bhairava, Kauśika, Hindol, Dîpaka, Śri and Megha. An example of his description is as follows :

Bhairava—
Chappai

Śirahaṅgaṅga aṅgahi bhuaṅga bhuṣana śaśibhālah,
viṣamanayana cita uditacayena āsana gajakhālah/
nara kapāla dhara dhavalarupa kara śula sulacchana//
jaga sakala rāga rāginibhavana ādi rāga jehi kahata sava/
saba samayegeyaguna ati nipuna bhairava sunisukhadeta bhuva//
Padmañca
Lalāṭe śîtāṅśuhkila jaṭila .... bhasitaih//
aica
trinetrastaccaikam ..... bhairavaiti//[20]

The import of the above verses is that Rāga Bhairava has been described in the form of Lord Śiva. The river ganges is flowing from his head which adorns the moon. His ornament is the snake. He wears a necklace of heads and carries the triśula. It is the first Rāga that is sung at all times.

Similarly Mālavakauśika has also been described. The description is very close to that depicted in the painting given in Plate B of Chapter 4.

Each masculine Rāga has five Rāginîs (see Table 17 in Appendix I). He describes their iconography in the second chapter. In the third chapter he discusses the origin of nāda and popular

Deśi Rāgas. In the fifth chapter he has discussed svara, śruti, vîṇā, Rāga saṁsthānas, time of singing Rāgas and Nāyikā bhedas. He has discussed the *saṁsthānas*[21] of Rāgas in the context of the vîṇā. These are twelve in number, i.e.

'tāstu saṅsthitayah prācyo rāgaṇaṁ dvādaśasmṛtāh'

He enumerates seventy five Rāgas derived from these twelve saṁsthānas. The table is given in Appendix I. His pure scale is equivalent to modern Kāfi of Hindustāni system.[22]

(vi) Svaramelakalānidhi of Rāmāmātya (1550 A.D.)

After Vidyāraṅya Mādhavācārya of Vijayanagar, Rāmāmātya, who also hailed from Vijayanagar, was the second person to enumerate 'melas'.[23] His pure scale was also Mukhāri. As against fifteen melas of Vidyāraṅya, Rāmāmātya enumerated twenty melas. Later, in 1620 A.D., Venkatamakhi devised seventy two melakartas out of which nineteen were in actual use.

An important contribution of Rāmāmātya was that he was the first person to discard the repetative modified notes of Śārṅgadeva. He reduced the number of modified notes to seven and further according to the principle of *pratinidhitva*[24] (representation), he again deleted two more notes. Thus, his modified notes are similar to the modified notes used in Modern period in the Deccan. Table 19 in Appendix I shows Rāmāmātya's notes.

(vii) Rāgamālā of Puṅdarîka Viṭṭhala (1557 A.D.)

Puṅdarîka Viṭṭhala, who hailed from Satanur village in Karnātaka, has authored three more treatises on music as well as dance, other than *Rāgamāla.* They are—*Sadrāgacandrodaya, Rāgamañjarî* and *Nartana-nirñaya.* Though he belonged to the southern part of India and adopted the Mukhari (or Kanakāngî) as his śuddha scale, he has discussed both southern and northern systems of Rāgas and classified them under nineteen melas.

He wrote *Sadrāgacandrodaya* under the patronage of Burhān Khān of Khāndeśa. After the fall of Burhānapur, the capital of Khāndeśa, he took service with Mādho Singh and Mān Singh Kacchwas of Āmera, who were feudal chiefs of Akbar (1556-1605 A.D.). Under their patronage, he wrote *Rāgamañjari. Rāgamālā* and *Nartananirṇaya* were written probably on inspiration from Akbar himself. He also had some knowledge of Persian Rāgas, called 'Parad'.

In his Rāgamāla, Puṅḍarîka Viṭṭhala, has given his own enumeration of masculine Rāgas, feminine Rāginîs and their Putra (sons) Rāgas, though the number remains thirty six for the Rāgas and Rāginîs (6 for Rāgas, 30 for Rāginîs and 30 for Putras). The table is given in Appendix I.

(viii) Rāgavibodha of Somnath (1609 A.D.)

This Sanskrit treatise was written during the reign of Jahāngir (1605-1627 A.D.) by Somnath, who hailed from Andhra Pradesh. The book contains five chapters along with his own commentary in Sanskrit (viveka). His concept of modified notes is quite close to Rāmāmātya, since intially he accepts only seven modified notes (instead of the twelve) given by Śārṅgadeva. He uses the term 'mṛdu' instead of 'cyuta' before the modified 'sa', 'ma' and 'pa' notes as conveyed from the śloka,

'iti saptoktāh śuddhā vikritānsaptaiva vacmi sah nāmnā/23
.... mṛduparasamapāh samapatṛtîyaśruti sthityā//24

Then he goes on to mention the tîvra, tîvratara and tîvratama modifications for 're', 'dha', 'ga' and 'ma'. Out of these he discards the tivra and tîvratara terms for 'ga' and 'ma'[25] (only tîvratama 'ga' and 'ma' remain), for 're' and 'dha', he keeps the term 'tîvra'.[26] Thus, three modified notes are added to the earlier seven, making the total number of modified notes ten. The table is given in Appendix I.

In the 2nd chapter, he describes various vîṇās. The third chapter deals with the melas. He gives the possible number of melas as nine hundred and sixty. For practical purposes, he gives only twenty-three melas.

In the fourth chapter, the concept of Rāgas is discussed according to previous authors such as Mataṅga and Śārṅgadeva. He also mentions the *Rāgārṇava* mata (Table 26 in Appendix I) of thirty six Rāgas and Rāginîs. Then he categorises *uttama, mādhyama* and *adhama* Rāgas. After that the gives the graha, amśa, sampoorṇa characteristics of Rāgas in the context of the melas.

In the fifth chapter, he gives an important statement regarding the structure of Rāgas. According to Somnath,

'susvaravarṇaviśeṣaṁ rupaṁ rāgasya bodhakaṁ dvedhā/
nādātma ca devamayaṁ tatkramato' nekamekaṁtu//11

i.e., the structure of a Rāga is twofold 'nādātma' and 'devamaya'. The former is the elaboration of notes or tonal structure and the latter is the iconography or pictorial structure. He has given both types of structural descriptions in his treatment of Rāgas. First he discusses the 'Nādatma rupa' of each Rāga. For example,

Toḍi tu

ga o ri ga o ri sa o sa ri pa ma o ga o ri ga o ri sa o ... etc.
... 2 drut // drut Padmaṁ / iti
prātagativyāścatvāro rāgāh / /
toḍi tu garigeti / ...
.... sa o ga ri sa ni dha dha ni sa o ri ni dha pa ma ga o ri sa//[27]

After that, the 'devamaya rupa' is as follows :

Toḍi

Kalitavipañcî vipinelālitahariṇāruṅāmbarā hariṇî/
dhavalāṇgarāgaracanā mṛduvacanā bhuṣitā toḍi//180

i.e., holding the vîñā close to her body, she enchants the deer. Fair complexioned and adorned in white clothes (the colour of the sun), the sweetness of voice is her embellishment.

Similarly other Rāgas have been described.

(ix) Sangît Darpaṇa of Dāmodara Miśra (1625 A.D.)

This 17th century Sanskrit treatise on music is basically known for its iconographical details of various Rāgas. The concept of notes, grāma, murchanā, tānas etc., has been given identical to the earlier authors such as Bharata, Mataṅga and Śārṅgadeva. For this reason, there seems to be a wide gap between the *lakṣya* and *lakṣaṇa,* since the Rāgas that have been described were prevalent during his own period.

Sangît Darpaṇa is of special significance regarding its 'dhyāna' or iconographic formulas. He seems to have standardized these pictorial versions of the Rāgas and Rāginîs by inculcating the common or more inticing features from various books. He has mentioned all the matas of Rāgas and Rāginîs (Śiva, Rāgarnava etc.), but has given the detailed iconography following

Hanumanmata. Since Dāmodara Miśra has given the standard iconography of Rāgas and Rāginîs, the demonstrative miniatures given in the present thesis follow his dhyānas. The dhyānas depicted in the plates A, B and C of Chapter 4 which follow Sangît Darpaṇa, have been described in that chapter.

Music in Modern Period

(i) Rādhā Govinda Saṅgît Sāra of Mahārājā Sawāi Pratāp Singh Deo of Jaipur (1779-1804 A.D.)

This non Sanskrit book written in *Dhundāḍî* dialect is of special significance regarding the advent of the modern Hindustāni system of music. Many popular Rāgas that are prevalent today and have not been mentioned in any previous book find place in this pioneering work. In the Poona Gāyan Samaj edition, the pure scale has been established as 'Bilāval'. The book is quite volumnous comprising seven chapters. The seventh chapter deals with the topic of Rāgas. The author has given characteristic features of Rāgas and Gîtis on the basis of previous musical authorities. Thereafter, he gives a description of Rāga-Rāginîs following *Hanumanrnata*. Some difference occurs in the names of Putra Rāgas, which are given in Table 28b of Appendix I.

The descriptions and the 'dhyāna' formlae are similar to those of Sangîta Darpaṇa. An additional feature is the test of authenticity for each Rāga or Rāginî.

(ii) Usulun Naghmāt-e Āsifi of Ghulām Rezā Bin Mohammad Panāh (18-19 Century A.D.)

This Persian book is historically significant regarding the Rāga-Rāginî classification. The author has condemned all the four matas (Bharata, Kallinātha, Hanuman and some Someśvar mata) of Rāga-Rāginî classification as baseless. During his time, there remained no structural link between the Rāgas and various Rāginîs grouped together. Even if there had been some relationship originally, they had evolved into totally different melodic structures. The ancient pure scale of Kāfi had been replaced by Bilāwal.

In Usulun Naghmāte-Āsifi the author has first elaborated the four matas (Tables 23 to 27 in Appendix I) according to another Persian work Tohfat-ul-Hind' by Mirzā Khān (17th Century A.D.). Then, pointing out their defficiencies, he gives his own mata (Table

23 of Appendix I). He has attempted to relate the Rāginîs to their Rāgas on the basis of structural or tonal similarities.

(iii) The Works of Bhātkhande (1860-1936 A.D.)

Paṇḍit Viṣṇu Nārāyaṇa Bhātkhaṇḍe is aptly regarded as the architect of the present day Hindustāni music. He accomplished the enormous task of re-establishing the theoretical aspect of Hindustāni classical music and co-ordinating it with the prevailing practice of music. Not only that, he also paved the way for future growth and development of music by initiating institutional studies in Hindustāni music. His single handed achievements were of such a great dimension that they triggered off a renaissance of Hindustāni music.

Some of his major contributions have been listed below :

(*i*) His most significant contribution to Hindustāni music was the classification of Rāgas into ten *ṭhāṭas*[28] (Table 2). Though it had its origin in the southern *Mela* system, it was a practice in the Rampur *Gharānā*[29] to prepare the tonal base of a pupil by rehearsing these ten different arrangements of notes. Since he too belonged to this tradition, he got the novel idea to classify all the Rāgas according to these basic modes.

(*ii*) Another contribution of Bhātkhaṇḍe is his interpretation of the traditional time theory of Rāgas. He has unveiled a very systematic procedure of assigning specific time periods to specific types of Rāgas.

(*iii*) Paṇḍit Bhātkhande evolved a comprehensive notation system as an aid for learning as well as keeping a future record of musical compositions. During those days, all knowledge was imparted orally, thus only the musicians were the source of compositions. These musicians treated their 'Gharānedār' compositions more as a treasure and were highly reluctant to part with them. With great difficulty, he collected a substantial number of compositions in his notation for the first time. About 1,200 compositions have been given in the six parts of his 'Kramik Pustak Mālikā' series.

(*iv*) It is to Bhātkhaṇḍe's credit that various ancient Sanskrit texts related to music could be edited and published, which might otherwise have been lost to the students and connoisseurs of music.

(*v*) Pt. Bhātkhanḍe realised the need for proper institutions to popularise music among the masses. During his period, students had to depend on the eccentricities and whims of select individuals to impart training and wasted many productive years just to appease them. This had led to a lack of enthusiasm among students to pursue their interest in music. Understanding the implications of such a situation, Pt. Bhātkhanḍe established the Mādhava Sangît Vidyālaya (1918 A.D.) in Gwalior and Marris College of Music, Lucknow (1923 A.D.). Thus, a healthy academic environment was provided for interested students, who were later given the opportunity for specialisation under able musicians.

(*vi*) Books written by Pt. Bhātkhanḍe include

(*a*)	Śrimallakṣyasaṅgîtaṁ	—	Sanskrit
(*b*)	Abhinav Rāga Manjarî	—	Sanskrit
(*c*)	Abhinav Tāla Manjarî	—	Sanskrit
(*d*)	Hindustanî Sangîta Paddhātî in 4 parts	—	Marāṭhî (translation in Hindi as Bhātkhanḍe Sangita Shāstra)
(*e*)	Kramika Pustaka Mālikā in 6 parts	—	Marāthî & translation in Hindi
(*f*)	Swara Mālikā	—	Book of notations using Gujarātî characters
(*g*)	Geeta Malika	—	Journal consisting of musical compositions

(*h*) A comparitive study of Music systems of the 15th, 16th, 17th and (18th centuries (English)

THE STYLES OF HINDUSTĀNI CLASSICAL MUSIC

Dhruvapada

One of the purer styles of classical music is the *Dhruvapada* or *Dhrupada* style. The word *Dhrupada* is the Hindi version of the Sanskrit word *Dhruvapada*. Etymologically, *Dhruvapada* is a combination of two words—*dhruva* and *pada*. The former refers to that which has a definite structure or is fixed, whereas the latter refers to the verbal content. Thus, literally 'Dhruvapada' means 'a composition of words or padas within a definite structure'.

A unique feature of Dhruvapada or Dhrupada is that equal importance is given to the three basic elements of music, viz. svara (notes), tāla (rhythm) and pada (text). A singer of Dhrupada requires great mastery over the rhythm. The purity of note and text is equally emphasized. In forms such as Khyāl, the element of svara often overshadows the other two elements.

There are different viewpoints regarding the origin of Dhrupada. Some link it to Rāja Mānsingh Tomar of Gwalior,[30] whereas a significant number beleive it to be a gradual development of the Prabandha described by Śārṅgadeva. Books such as Usualun Naghmāte—Asifi and Anoop Sangîta Ratnākar of the medieval period throw light on such a development. In the definition of Dhrupada given by Bhāvabhatta in the swarādhyāya of Anoop Sangît Ratnākara, the four parts of Dhrupada have been named as the Dhatus of prabandhas—Udgrāh, Dhruva, Ābhoga and Antara as conveyed through the śloka.

Gîravāṇamadhya deśîyabhāṣā...
... udgrāha dhruvakābhogāntaraṁ dhruvapadaṁ smṛtaṁ/
—Anoop Sangît Ratnākara of Bhāvabhatta, p. 47

In the present day Dhrupada, the Udgrāha and Dhruva have been combined as 'Sthāyi', Antarā and Ābhoga are as it is. In between there is Sancāri. These days Apart from that, the elements (aṅgas) of svara, tāla and pada are present in Dhrupada, as already stated. The aṅgas Viruda, Tenaka and Pāṭa may also be present. The Norn-Tom Ālāpa or elaboration of Rāga in the beginning of Dhrupada represents the aṅga Tenaka.

The Dhrupada is usually accompanied by the Pakhāwaja. Earlier it was believed to be accompanied by the Vîṇā as well. Now-a-days, this style has become a rarity and faces the danger of extinction. The schools of Dhrupada are referred to as Bānis, viz.—Khanḍāra, Nauhāra, Dāgura and Gobarahāri.

Khyāl

This style of Hindustāni music is the most prominent and popular as compared to other styles of vocal music. The artist has full freedom to use his imagination within the framework of the Rāga.

The Arabic word 'Khyāl' itself indicates imagination or contemplation. This term is said to have been coined by Amir Khusrau in the thirteenth century. Many people associate his name along with Sultan Hussain Sharqui of Jaunpur (15th Century) for the advent of this style. It is true that Amir Khusrau brought about the 'Qawwāl' and Sharqui the 'Kalawant' variations of this style and were responsible for popularising Khyāl. The names of Sadārang and Adārang (18th century) are also linked to the rise of Khyāl, since many of their compositions are still in practice. But none of them actually 'invented' the style. It was basically a gradual evolution of the ancient musical forms already in existence. According to Thakur Jaidev Singh, 'Sādhārani Geeti with the predominant use of Bhinnā'[31] became Khyāl. The elaboration of Rāga in this style seems to have inculcated elements from *Rupakalapti*—(1) Pratigrahanikā (as elaboration in between Sthāyi and Antarā and subsequently linking it with *mukhdā),* (2a) Sthāya Bhanjani (Bol Banāva) and (2b) Rupaka Bhanjani (Boltāna and tānas).

The development of Rupakālapti took shape as 'Khyāl' in Hindustāni music and 'Pallavi' in Carnatic music. Both these styles are first rendered in slow tempo and subsequently in fast tempo.

The Khyāl style flowered under different schools (Gharānās) such as Gwalior, Agra, Jaipur, Delhi, Kirānā and Patiala which played a significant role in the continuous evolution of this style to this day.

Ṭhumri

This style along with Ṭappa is often included in a 'semi classical' category of music, owing to a slight relaxation of the rules regarding Rāga. It is basically a feeling oriented style which may be accompanied by dance (usually kathak). The word '*Ṭhumri*' itself is indicative of dance as '*ṭhum*' or '*ṭhumak*'. Its origin as an independent style is attributed to the Nawāb Wājid Ali Shah of Oudh in the nineteenth century. Before that, there have been references to 'Ṭhumri' as a Rāginî of Rāga Śri according to Bharata Mat in books like Tohfat-ul-Hind and Usulun Naghmāte-Asifi.

There are two types of Ṭhumris, one in which the Rhythm is predominant and the other in which the note is predominant. The former variety is rarely heard these days. There are two schools of the latter variety, viz. Purab anga (prevalent in Lucknow and Benaras) and Punjāb anga (prevalent in Punjab).

The Ṭhumri style is accompanied by the Tablā in tālas such as Dipacandi, Punjābi, teentāla, Dādrā and Kaharwā. Similar styles by the name of Dādrā and Kaharwā are also prevalent, but they are rendered only in Dādrā and Kaharwā tālas respectively. Their tempo is slightly faster than Ṭhumri. The Ṭhumri is initially rendered at a slower pace which is later increased to the accompaniment of Kaharwā tāla.

Dhamār

This is a sister style of Dhrupada of a lighter variety. A typical feature of this style is the description of Lord Kṛṣṇa playing Holī[32] with Gopis. Thus, another name for this style is Hori. This style is characterised by its accompanying Dhamār tāla.

Ṭappā

The Ṭappā style is believed to have been evolved by Ghulām Nabi Shori or Shori Miān in the nineteenth century and became popular alongside the Ṭhumri. It is also believed to have been influenced by the folk music of Punjab Hills. There is a mention of 'Dappā' in Rāga Darpana also, which indicates Ṭappā was prevalent earlier perhaps in a slightly different form. The ancient Vesarā Gîti is sometimes linked to this style, since this Gîti comprises mainly of swift notes. In the composition of Ṭappā also, notes are rendered very swiftly. The Rāgas and tālas used for Ṭhumri are relevant for Ṭappā as well.

Tarānā

This style is similar to the fast tempo[33] (Drut) Khyāl with the exception that the text of the composition consists of seemingly meaningless words such as tanā, dir, yalali, dernā etc. The Tarānā is said to be a contribution of Amir Khusrau, who developed it on the basis of existing styles in Indian as well as Arabic musical systems such as Nirgeet and Naubā[34] respectively. An equivalent of Tarānā is also prevalent in the South by the name 'Tillānā,' which is usually accompanied by dance.

THE TRADITIONAL SCHOOLS (GHARĀNĀS)

The practical aspect of Indian classical music prevalent in modern times is largely the product of traditional schools. Be it the Bānis of Dhrupad style or the aṅgas of Ṭhumri or the Gharānās of Khyāl or Bāz in case of instrumental music, by highlighting different aspects of different styles, the various schools have contributed immensely to the multifaceted development of Indian classical music. In the South, the term used for traditional schools is 'Sampradāy. The origin of such traditional schools can be traced right to the Brāhminical oral tradition of the Vedic Age, in which the teacher or *Guru* taught the pupil or Śiṣya the Vedic chants and scriptures orally.

The traditional schools of the Khyāl style known as Gharānās evolved with the rise of Khyāl around the seventeenth and eighteenth century. Although these Gharānās followed the basic structure of the Khyāl style, their approach towards its form was different. The difference in proportion of the tonal and rhythmic elements often became the distinguishing features of these Gharānās. For e.g., the Kirānā Gharānā is more liberal towards the tonal aspect, whereas the Āgrā Gharānā is known for its exceptional rhythmic patterns. Some other distinguishing factors of different Gharānās are:

(*i*) The composition or *Bandish,*
(*ii*) Voice Production,
(*iii*) The elaboration or *Baḍhat/Ālāpa,*
(*iv*) Rhythmic patterns using words or notes,
(*v*) Tānas and Boltānas,
(*vi*) The choice of Rāgas.

On the basis of these factors, the characteristic features of some important Gharānās are being described below:

Gwalior Gharānā

One of the three oldest and established schools (the other two being Āgrā and Delhi), this Gharānā is renowned for its unique *Gāyaki*[35] which is complete in itself. This Gharānā was founded by Natthan Pîra Bakhśa, who shifted to Gwalior from Lucknow along with his nephews Haddu-Hassu and Nattu Khān, whom he had adopted. The Haddu-Hassu brothers inculcated nuances from the Gāyaki of Bade Muhammad Khān (Kawwāl bacche) and strengthened the foundation of the Gwalior Gharānā. Their followers include a gamuṭ of musical greats such as Pandit Dikśit, Nisār Hussain Khān, Shankar Pandit, Krisna Rao Shankar Pandit,

Eknāth Pandit, Rāmkṛṣṇa Buā Vaze, Bāl kṛṣṇa Buā Ical karanjikar, Pt. Visnu Digambar Paluskar and the list goes on.

The Characteristic Features:

(*i*) The compositions are very innovative. Sometimes the influence of Ṭappā style can also be seen. A typical characteristic of this Gharānā is the complete rendition of the Sthāyi as well as Antarā before beginning the elaboration of Rāga.

(*ii*) The method of voice production is given full importance in this Gharānā. A full throated voice is desired having a range of all three registers. The voice has to be bold in order to incorporate the Gāyaki of Gamakas.

(*iii*) The elaboration of Rāga is done slowly in a definite sequence according to the structure of the Rāga in a simple and effective manner.

(*iv*) There is equal emphasis on all the aspects such as Ālāpa, Boltāna, tāna and rhythmic patterns.

(*v*) Most of the popular Rāgas are sung in this Gharānā.

Āgrā Gharānā

Alakhdāsa and Mulakdāsa are said to be the founders of this Gharānā. The son of Alakhdāsa, Hāji Sujān Khān was proficient in Dhrupada style. Mulak Dāsa had two sons-Sarasranga and Śyāmranga. One of the sons of Śyāmranga was Khudā Bakhśa (Ghagghe Khudā Bakhśa), who went to Gwalior for training under Natthan Pîra Bakhśa. Khudā Bakhśa's son Ghulām Abbās Khān is said to have added the Rhythmic patternry to a basically Gwalior like Gāyaki, thereby giving an independent form to Agrā Gharānā. Prominent musicians of this Gharānā include names like Ustad Vilāyat Hussain Khān (Prān Piyā), Ustad Yunus Hussain Khān and the all time great Ustad Faiyyāz Khān (Prem Piyā) whose legacy was carried by Pt. Dilip Chandra Bedi, Pt. S.N. Ratanjankar, Ustad Atā Hussain Khān and the like.

The Characteristic Features:

(*i*) The composition is sung in a comparatively slower tempo than Gwalior Gharānā. A prominent influence of Dhrupada can be noticed, e.g., in the initial Norn-Tom Ālāpa.

(*ii*) The voice production is uninhibited having a certain depth in keeping with the overall Gāyaki.
(*iii*) The Ālāpa cannot be considered as an asset of this Gharānā, except for the contributions of individuals like Ustad Faiyyāz Khān. The method is close to that of Gwalior Gharānā added with a depth of its own.
(*iv*) Bol Bānt or rhythmic innovations using select phrases has touched new heights in this Gharānā. There is ample use of Sargam or interweaving of notes with rhythm.
(*v*) Rare Rāgas also find place in this Gharānā.

Delhi Gharānā

One of the earliest Gharānās, it was founded by Miān Achpal. His disciple, Kutubbaksh received the title of 'Tānras Khān' from the last Emperor of Delhi, Bahādur Shāh Zafar (1837 A.D.). Ustad Chānd Khān was a great exponent of this Gharānā. His followers include Tānsamrāt Ustad Naseer Ahmed Khān, Ustad Hilal Ahmed Khān, Prof. Krishnā Bisht (former Dean of Faculty of Music and Fine Arts), Dr. Bhārati Chakravarty and Ustad Iqbāl Ahmed Khān who is the present 'Khalifā' of this Gharānā.

The Characteristic Features:

(*i*) The compositions are known for their creativity and beautiful structure (Pālaki, Paṭari or Khānāpuri and the like).
(*ii*) Full emphasis is laid on voice production.
(*iii*) Before taking up the Vilambit Khyāl to introduce the Rāga, Norn-Tom alāpa is rendered. The elaboration of the Rāga is done both note by note and phrase wise. A distinguishing feature of the Baḍhat (vistār or elaboration) of Delhi Gharānā is this, that while developing a note, even higher notes are judiciously used. The style is highly ornate.
(*iv*) Layakārî is an important aspect of this Gāyakî.
(*v*) Delhi Gharānā is known for its variety of tānas with their striking names, e.g., fande ki tān, talwār kāṭ tān, jhule ki tān etc.

Jaipur Gharānā

This Gharānā was established Ustad Karāmat Ali and Ustad Mubārak Ali (Lucknow wāle). The Gāyakî of this Gharānā is predominently Ustad Allādiyā Khān's contribution. Leading exponents of this Gharānā are Kesarbai Kerkar. Mallikārjun Mansoor, Moghubai Kurdikar and presently her daughter Kishori Amonkar.

The Characteristic Features :

(*i*) The compositions are short but rendered in a very slow tempo, which is a difficult task. The drut or fast tempo composition is not obligatory.

(*ii*) They have their own method of voice production (Ghumāvadār). A full throated rich voice is desired.

(*iii*) During the baḍhat itself, small tānas are used liberally giving rise to an embellished style of singing.

(*iv*) A special characteristic of this Gharānā is that the notes and rhythm are thoroughly interlinked throughout the performance. Seperate rhythmic artistry is not given much importance.

(*v*) This Gharānā is known for singing lesser known Rāgas such as Khokhar, Pat Bihāg, Triveni etc.

Patiala Gharānā

The foundations for this Gharānā were laid by Ali Baksh and Fateh Ali, also known as Aliāh-Fattu. They received training from Tānras Khān of Delhi Gharānā. The present Gāyakî of Patiala Gharānā has been predominantly influenced by the individual style of Ustad Bade Ghulam Ali Khān Saheb. The Gāyakî of this Gharānā is a cross between the embellished style of Jaipur Gharānā and note predominant Kirānā Gharānā. Some special features of this Gharānā are :

(*i*) The compositions are a fine example of an emotive confluence of music and poetry.

(*ii*) Blemishless voice production ranging all three octaves.

(*iii*) A balanced blend of layakārî and elaboration of the notes.

(*iv*) There is ample use of Gamaka and the tānas are characterised by their exceptionally fast pace and intricacy. Some element of Ṭappā, Qawwāli land use of Punjābi words is also there.

(*v*) Ṭhumri (Punjab anga), Tarānās and Bhajans are also rendered after the completion of Khyāl.

Kirānā Gharānā

The name of Binakār Bande Ali Khān is associated with the origin of this Gharānā, but its Gāyaki was fully established by Abdul Karim Khān and Abdul Wahid Khān. Some prominent musicians of this Gharānā are Savāi Gandharva, Suresh Māne, Hirābai Badodkar, Gangubāi Hangal, Vasava Rāja Rājguru, Mānik Verma and of course, Pt. Bhimsen Joshi, who has popularised classical music among the present generation to a great extent.

The Characteristic Features :

(*i*) There is a practice of singing Ṭhumri after the completion of the Khyāl (Vilambit and Drut).

(*ii*) The voice production is unique in its smoothness. A typical character is the gental flow of notes embellished with meenḍs.

(*iii*) The Ālāpa or Baḍhat is the main ingredient of this Gāyaki. The elaboration is accomplished by emphasising important notes of the Rāga and weaving intricate patterns around those notes.

(*iv*) Popular Rāgas of this Gharānā include Toḍi, Puriyā, Darbāri, Malkauns etc.

Apart from the Gharānās mentioned, there are other important Gharānās also such as Indore (Bhendi Bazār), Rampur—Sahsawān, Vishnupur, Mewati etc. Basically, Gharānās or Sampradāys are the pivot of the traditional character consistent with Indian classical music.

References

1. *uccairudātta, nîcairanudātta, samāhārahswarita.*
   —*Aṣṭdhyāyi of Pāṇini* (7th century B.C.)
2. Pure classical stream of music.
3. One who combines deep knowledge of Bhāva, Rāga and Tāla.
4. Not named so in Nāṭyaśāstra (NŚ).
5. Popular folk inspired stream of music.
6. The word 'Gamaka' has been used in the sense of vocal embellishments such as shaking of notes etc.
7. A change of pitch, volume, ancent, a reflection of a note into another or that of a phrase of Rāga into another.
8. śl. 21 and 22 of Rāgadhyāya, Bharata Bhāṣyaṁ, p. 226.

9. *gitaṁ vādyaṁ tathā nrittaṁ trayaṁ saṅgîtaṁ ucyate,* Sangît Ratnakara 1/21, p. 10.
10. *nṛtaṁ vādyānugaṁ* etc. 24, p. 11.
11. Sangît Ratnākara, Shringy and Sharma, p. 160.
12. Non repetetive and overlapping, the use of rare notes in between Nyāsa and other notes in order to provide variety (usually in modified Jātis).
13. In a commentary (Kalānidhi) by Kallinath, they are so called because they are derived from Jātîs, which are associated with the Grāmas.
14. śl. 70-72, Sangît Ratnākara, Vol. II, Shringy and Sharma, p. 63.
15. The composer of verbal as well as melodic form.
16. A delightful arrangement of notes—'*Rañjakaḥ svarasaṅdarabho*' Sangît Ratnākara, p. 209.
17. *tālastalpratiṣṭhāyāmiti...yatastālaṁ pratiṣṭhitaṁ,* Sangît Ratnākara, 5/ 2.
18. *Rāgajanako dhvaniḥ svara iti lakṣaṇam,* Sangît Samayasāra of Parśvadeva (translation by Ācārya Bṛhaspati), p. 13.
19. Pant, C.S., Lochana's Rāga Tarangini (Article in the Journal of Madras Music Academy, Vol. XXXVI, pp. 69, 71-72).
20. Rāga Tarangini, pp. 3-4.
21. Generic grouping of the notes of Rāgas in a manner similar to modern ṭhāṭs.
22. Rāga Tarangini, translation by Baldeva Miśra, p. 121.
23. Generic groups of notes of Rāgas prevalent in South (equivalent in North—ṭhāṭ).
24. Notes with interval of only one śrūti were treated as same.
25. *gasya masya ca ṣaṭśrutikatve tîvratama ityekaiva saṅgyā,* Rāga Vibodha of Somnath, ed. Subramanya Sāstri, p. 25.
26. sl. 3 and 4, *Ibid.*, p. 80.
27. Rāga Vibodha of Somnath, ed. Subramanya Śastri, pp. 145-146.
28. Generic gruop of seven notes in ascending order.
29. Traditional school in Hindustāni Music basically of Khyāl style (details given later).
30. Rāga Darpaṇa of Faquirullāh, translation by Shahab Sarmadee, Indira Gandhi National Centre for the Arts, p. 97.
31. Singh, Thakur Jaideva, the evolution of Khyāl, pp. 127-132.
32. A festival of colours.
33. Sometimes there is a slow tempo 'Khyālnumā' Tarānā also, but it is very rare.
34. Ahmed, N.P., Hindustāni Music—A study of its development in seventeenth and eighteenth centuries, pp. 126-127.
35. Particular method of singing.

3

The Indian Tradition of Miniature Painting

INTRODUCTION

In the Rāgamāla miniature series, the primary illusion is of virtual space. Thus, the main form is the painting, in which music is the ingredient. Just like music, the art of painting also has a long tradition of Indian history. As *Gharānās* are the schools in Indian musical tradition, so are *kalms* the schools in Indian tradition of painting. This chapter deals with a brief study of the historical development and schools of the Indian tradition of painting.

NOMENCLATURE

In various ancient Sanskrit texts the terms, Ālekhya or 'citraṁ' are used to refer to painting. 'Ālekhya' is derived from the root Ālikh, denoting to write, delineate or draw lines[1]. The word 'citraṁ' conveys the meaning of selection in 'ciyate' *i.e.—ciyate iti citraṁ*[2]. According to Dr. R.L. Shukla, this selection is of the six elements of painting—Rupa bheda etc. (explained earlier). In Ṛg Veda, the word 'citraṁ' has been used in the sense of a wonderful combination of various hues in praise of the sun[3].

Rai Kṛṣṇa Dās defines painting as 'the depiction of a sensuous form and presentation of related aspects on a level surface (which may be curvaceous also—such as the outer surface of an earthern pitcher etc.), using one or more colours either dissolved in water, oil or any other medium or dry. The basic surface usually comprises wall/plaque, stone, wood, cured or raw mud ware or sheath, ivory, leather, cloth, palm leaf or paper.[4]

The popular base for miniature paintings has been ivory, palm leaf and more recently paper (14th century A.D. onwards). Before going into the details of miniature paintings, it will be appropriate to discuss the general historical background of paintings.

HISTORICAL DEVELOPMENT OF PAINTING IN INDIA

A study of the historical development of painting in India can be accomplished by two approaches,

(*i*) through a study of references in ancient texts and
(*ii*) through a study of archeological evidences.

A Study of References to Painting in Ancient Texts

A cursory glance at various ancient texts reveals a plethora of mythological sayings associated with the origin of painting. Even though they may seem exaggerated, they do convey some underlying facts about the nature and situation of painting during their particular periods of time. Three such popular accounts are:

(*i*) The Sage Nārāyana created the painting of Urvasi taking the juice of a mango and endowed it with life to teach the *apsaras* a lesson. He later taught the art to Viśvakarmāṅ.[5]

(*ii*) Princess Uṣā requested her companion Citralekhā to establish the identity of her future husband as perceived in a dream. Accordingly, Citralekhā creates a series of portraits ranging from those of Gods, spirits, demons to those of mortals until the princess recognises the person she desired as Aniruddha, the grandson of Kṛṣṇa.[6]

(*iii*) The account of king Bhayajit drawing the picture of a Brahmin's son and Brahma instilling life in the picture. Here also, Viśvakarmāṅ is deemed as the knowledgeable about citralakṣaṇas, from whom Nagnajit learns the same.[7]

A general observation from the above notions is that the name of Viśvakarmāṅ is usually associated with the art of painting. From the account of Citralekha, it may be observed, that painting was popular among women. Also, from all three accounts, it can be safely deduced that portraiture was the most common form of painting in ancient India.

As stated earlier during a discussion of the elements of painting in Chapter 1, the theoretical evaluation of sculpture and painting has been included in books relating to Architecture. Thus, a portion of works such as *Viṣṇudharmottaraṁ, Samrāṅgaṇa sutradhāra, Vāstuśāstraṁ, Mānasollās, Śilparatnaṁ* and *Aparājit prachha* contains many references to the art of painting also.

(a) References to Painting in the 'Viṣṇudharmottaraṁ' (6-7th Century A.D.)

Even though there are indirect references to the art of painting in earlier works such as Ṛg Veda (as already mentioned), a detailed treatment regarding the same is not available until the *Viṣṇudharmottaraṁ,* particularly its third part, under the title of *Citrasutraṁ.* (Ch—35-43).

In the 2nd chapter of *Viṣṇudharmottaraṁ* part III, the mutual relationship between the arts of painting, dance and music has been highlighted. A knowledge of each has been deemed essential for a proper understanding of any art as in indicated from the following śloka,

Vinā tu nṛtya śāstreṇa citrasutraṁ sudurvidaṁ/
jagato na kriyā ...
... ātodyena vinā nṛtaṁ vidyate
na kathamcana//

—V.D., PIII chapter 2, Sl. 6-9

In the 25th Chapter, the Rasadrṣtis have been mentioned. The 26th chapter discusses the *mudrās* or positions of hands. In the 27th chapter the method of preparing colours has been discussed. In the 35th chapter, the account of sage Nārāyaṇa relating to the origin of painting has been given. In the 41st chapter, four types of paintings have been given, viz.—Satya, Vainika, Nāgara and Miśra. Satya is the true reflection of the external world (Lok Sādṣyaṁ). Vainika is the proportionate square type painting, while Nāgara or the urban painting may sometimes be circular. Miśra is the mixed type of painting.

The *Viṣṇudharmottaraṁ* (V.D.) mentions eight attributes of a painting. They are sthāna (position), pramāna (measurement or proportion), bhulamba (perpendicular from the base), madhuratva (sweetness), vibhaktatā (divisibility), sādṛṣya (likeness), ksaya (diminution) and vṛddhi (development). Apart from these the line, shading, embellishments and colour composition have been given due importance.

Thus,

Rekhāṁ praśansantyācāryā vartanāṁ ca vicakṣaṇāh/
striyo bhuṣaṇamicchanti varṇāḍhyamitare janāh//
—V.D., Ch. 43, S1. 9 *citrasutraṁ*

i.e.—the master artists praise the skill of drawing lines in a painting, connoissuers appreciate the work of light and shade, women marvel at embellishments and the common person praises the colour combination.

(b) Samarāṅgaṇasutradhāra of Bhojadeva (11th Century A.D.)

After V.D., the *Samarāṅgaṇasutradhāra* of Bhojadeva cites various references pertaining to painting. One such reference in the seventy first chapter shows the popularity of this art over other arts as conveyed from the śloka,

citraṁ hi sarva śilpānāṃ mukhaṁ
lokasya ca priyaṁ/

Eight *aṅgas* or features of painting have been given as—Vartikā, Bhumibandhana, Lekhya (or Lepya), Rekhā Karma, Karṣakarma (or varṇakarma), Vartanākarma, Lekhana (or Lekhakarma) and Rupakarma.[8]

Later, in chapters 81, 82 and 83, the five kinds of men and women, Rasa and Dṛshti (expressions) and positions of hands (mudras) have been given similar to V.D.

(c) Aparājitapracchā of Bhuvanadeva (11-12th Century A.D.)

The Chapters 224-231 are related to painting. These include a description of Eulogy of citra, units of measurements, materials of images (Aṣṭadhātu and other metals), citrapatra, kanṭakas, colours—paṭṭṭapatravartanā—lepa karma—preparations of the ground of painting, objects of painting (kirti mukha—Vyālas of 16 kinds), characterisitics of men and women, thirty six kinds of implements (Āyudhas) and sixteen kinds of ornaments.

(d) Mānasollās (Abhilaṣitārthachintāmaṇi) of Someśvaradeva (1129 A.D.)

In the 2nd part of the book, there are details regarding painting. After describing the characteristics of a good painting, preparation of ground for painting, brushes of three types, colours—pure and mixed, positions of five kinds—Ṛju, ardha-rju, sāchi, ardhākshi, bhittikā, he discusses Viddha, Aviddha, Dhuli and Rasa citras.

Viddha is the particular type of portrait that affects the heart of the beholder and makes a lasting impression on the mind. Aviddha is the sketch type of portrait based on the artists temporary fancy. A Rasacitra directly affects the emotions of a beholder while a Dhulicitra is the painting made of colour dusts and is suitable for landscapes.

The qualifications of a painter have been given as follows :

pragalbhaibhārvakaistajgyaih
sukṣmarekhā viṣāradaih
.... nānā rasa samudbhavam//

i.e., a successful painter is one who can create a painting full of rasas and rasadṛshties, the sentiments and emotions to the satisfaction of royal pleasure, who is an expert at fineness of line and skillful in creating designs of patras, adept at colours and employment of light and shade.

Apart from these canonical works, the commentary of Yashodhar Pandit on Vātsyāyan's *Kāmasutra* gives a description of six aṅgas of painting, as already mentioned in the first chapter. References to painting abound in the literary works of eminent Sanskrit poets like Kālidāsa, Bāṇa and Bhavabhuti. In almost all the works of Kālidāsa as well as Bāṇabhatta, there is a mention of citraśālās or art galleries. References to citrācāryas or master artists are found in *Mālivikāgnimitra* of Kālidāsa and *Uttara-Rāma carita* of Bhavabhuti, which indicate their importance in royal courts. References to portrait paintings, particularly those by imagination in the absense of models are ample in the works of Kālidāsa, who calls them 'Bhāvagamya citras'. For e.g., the painting of Yakṣiṇi in Megheduta and that of Śakuntalā and her companions in *Abhigyāna Śakuntalaṁ.* Bāṇabhatta has used the term 'Samkalpalekha' for the same.

Kālidāsa has portrayed God as the supreme artist. A reference to this effect occurs in A.Ś when king Dusyanta makes the following comment to Viduṣaka relating to Śakuntalā's exceptional beauty as given in the śloka,

citre niveśya parikalpitasatvayogā
—A. Śākuntalaṁ II. 6

i.e., she must have been created by instilling life into a picture. Again, the capacity of a painting, to complement natural defficiencies is indicated through an observation made by Vidhusaka while praising Śakuntalāś divine beauty in the context of her picture. Thus

Yadyat sādhu na citre syāt kriyate tattad anyathā
Tathāpi tasyā lāvanyam rekhyā kincidanvitaṁ//
—*A. Śākuntalaṁ* V. 15

i.e., the ability of a painting to complete nature has fallen short in this case, because her beauty is beyond the supreme power of art.

The nature of colours used for painting at that time is also revealed by certain references in Kālidāsa's as well as Bāṇa's works. For example a verse in *Meghadutaṁ* of Kālidāsa describes the clouds as 'Slyly sneaking away in the form (guise) of smoke through the window apertures of the lofty mansions of Alakā being ashamed of their conduct in having caused damage to the beautiful pictures painted there by allowing water particles to settle on them'.[9] This indicates that the colours were easily spoilt by water and as revealed in Bāṇa's Kādambari, by perspiration of the fingers. Bāṇa has described the various natural hews of flowers, fruits and birds explicitly. For example the description of the purple Jambu fruit with its bluish-red tinge resembling the eye of a cuckoo, the pomegranate seed likened to a pearl smeared with blood and the Amalakî fruit, green as the lotus leaf are remarkable, thus,

Āmattakokila locanacchvirnnîlapāṭalah ---- nalinîdalaharinti ....
..... prācînāmalakîphalānî
—*Kādambari* p. 36.

In comparision to the works of Kālidāsa and Bāṇa, where references to painting usually involve portraiture, Bhavabhuti's *Uttara-Rāma Carita* abounds in description of landscapes. All these references imply the proximity of painting to the lives of Indian people.

A Study of Archeological Records of Painting in India

Archeologically, there are several records of painting in India since prehistoric times. Many cave paintings have been discovered (as haematite brush forms) in Mirzapur, Singhanpur, Kaimur range and Vindhya hills. Mostly hunting scenes have been depicted in these pre-historic paintings. By the first century B.C. they had started assuming the shape of well defined frescoes such as those found in the Jogimara caves of Ramgarh hill in Sirguja (Central Provinces—now M.P.), known as 'mural paintings'. Such paintings reached the zenith of their development in the Ajanta paintings by the beginning of the Christian era.

Other than mural paintings, traditional Indian paintings are in the form of miniatures or in small format. Paintings of the concerned topic, Rāgamālā, occur in the form of miniatures. Barring the Ajantā school, most of the traditional schools of Indian painting are concerned with miniature painting. A description of traditional schools of Indian painting is being given in the following section.

THE SCHOOLS OF PAINTING IN INDIAN TRADITION

The post Christian era abounds in various traditional styles of exquisite Indian paintings. A.K. Coomarswamy has broadly distributed Indian painting into religious divisions for the sake of convenience, as

1. Buddhist
2. Jain
3. Hindu (Rajput and Deccan)
4. Eclectic (Mughal)

The various Schools of Indian painting fall into these basic categories. Detailed classification Indian paintings by A.K. Coomarswamy is given in Tabe 30(a). The author has also given a slightly modified version of this classification [see Table 30(b)]. A description of the various Schools of Indian painting is being given following the modified version. Thus, Buddhist painting which has been assigned the classical period, comprises Ajantā (First Century B.C. to 8 Century A.D.) as well as Pāla Schools (8-12th Century A.D.).

Ajantā School

The earliest examples of Buddhist painting are found in the renowned cave temples (Vihāras) at Ajantā situated at the head of one of the ghats leading down from the Ajantā Range to the valley of the Tapti River. According to Percy Brown, 'the greater part of the frescoes at Ajantā, supplemented by the remains at Bagh, and the friezes at Sigiriya may be regarded as records of the consummation of Buddhist painting, in India. These examples were executed at an interval of time which corresponds, for all practical purposes, to the outstanding creative age of the Gupta kings'.[10] The characteristic features of Ajantā school have been described by Percy Brown as 'a simple, bold style of painting emphasised by a spirited and vigorous outline. The scenes are well composed, some of the individual figures are very skilfully drawn, and the expressive treatment of the hands is noticeable'.[11] The frescoes usually follow a narrative style depicting scenes from the life of Lord Buddha. The basic aim of the Buddhist painter was 'to visualise the ideals of his creed' and 'to illustrate by pictorial parables all the beautiful sentiments of the Buddhist religion', thus imbibing within the spectator a feeling of the absolute. An example of a painting from Ajantā school can be seen in Plate 2 of Appendix II.

Pāla School

The Pāla school flourished in Bengal and Bihar under the Pāla Dynasty (8th-12th century A.D.) from where it spread to many Himalayan regions from Ladakh to Bhutan, Burma and Nepal. Tārā Nāth (1608 A.D.) sheds light on the early history of Buddhist art under the Pālas. According to him 'In the time of kings Devapāla (815-854 A.D.) and Srimant Dharma Pāla (770-815 A.D.), there was an artist named Dhiman. Along with his son, Bitpalo, he produced works in cast metal as well as scuplture and painting. The son gave rise to the Eastern Bengal style and the father to the Magadhi (Bihar) style.'[12]

A clear influence of the Ajanatā School can be seen in paintings of this style. An example of Pāla school is given in Plate 3 of Appendix II, which is an illustration from a palm leaf Buddhist manuscript in Bengali. According to Karl Khandalavala, 'the art of wall painting appears to have degenerated from the 10th century onwards owning to increase in patronage given to the sculptor guilds and the decrease in patronage given to painter guilds. The elaborately carved temples left little scope for fresco painting. In this scenario, an interesting development took place almost simultaneously in two widely distant parts of the country. This development consisted of :

(*a*) The production in Gujarat of illustrated manuscripts on palm leaf of Jain canonical works.

(*b*) The production in Bengal and Bihar of illustrated Buddhist manuscripts on palm leaf during the reign of the 'Pāla kings'.[13] Such illustrated manuscripts heralded the advent of miniature paintings.

Western India or 'Gujarati School'

The Jain paintings of Gujarat have been referred to by various names. The late N.C. Mehta grouped them under 'Gujarati Paintings', Rai Kṛṣṇa Das gave them the name 'Apabhraṁśa' owing to the colloquialised language of the manuscripts, while Dr. Moti Chandra called them 'Western India miniature paintings'.

The origin of these paintings has been linked to the 7th century A.D. murals of Sittanvasal (Madras) and 9th century A.D. murals of Ellora. The earliest known Jain miniatures are from the ll-12th century manuscript of *Niśitha Curni* (Plate 4 of Appendix II) on palm leaf. The palm leaf base was substituted with paper by about 14th century A.D. The earliest illustrated manuscript on paper is a *Klpasutra* of late 14th century (Plate 5 of Appendix II). An exquisite example of the Western India school can be seen in the illustrations of the *Kalpasutra* and *Kālakācārya kathā* manuscript of about 1400 A.D. (Plate 5 fig. 3 of Appendix II). One of the important characterisitic features of the Western India school is the depiction of three-fourth profile with a protruding eye in empty space.

In the pre-Mughal period, the Gujarati or Western India school flourished not only in Gujarat, but also in Rajputana, Malwa and Uttar Pradesh. According to K. Khandalavala, 'manuscripts in the Gujarat style influenced the art of painting even in the far Southern kingdom of Vijay Nagar which flourished from circa 1350 to 1565 A.D.'[14] It is now an established fact that the Rājput school has its origin from this Western India school. Various examples of the early phase of development of the Rājput school clearly indicate towards this fact. One such example is the *Kalpasutra* from Mandu of 1439 A.D. An illustration of this manuscript has been given in Plate 6 of Appendix II.

Rājput School

According to the classification of A.K. Coomaraswamy, the Hindu paintings comprise the Rājput and Deccan schools. The Rājput school includes not only the Rajputana region, but also areas covered by the Punjab hills such as Jammu, Kangra and Garhwal. The style prevalent in Rajputana region is usually referred to as 'Rājasthānî' and that in the Punjab hills is called 'Pahāri'. As mentioned above, the Rājput school has been a derivation from the Western India school. In the early paintings of this style, the angularity of the Western India school remains, but the protruding 'further eye' has been replaced by a 'large fish eye'. This feature can be observed in Plates 8 to 12 of Appendix II.

Rai kṛṣṇa Das has attributed the origin of Rājasthānî style from an influence of Kashmir style in Mewār on the Gujarat 'Apabhraṁṣa' school by 15th century A.D.[15] This statement by R.K. Das gets further weightage from a study conducted by Parvez Dewan, from which evidence has been obtained suggesting the prevalence of a Kashmir school before the Mughal era.[16] A.K. Coomarswamy has assigned the period spanning from 13th to 19th century A.D. to the Rājput (with reference to Rājasthānî style) school.[17] The earliest available illustrated palm leaf manuscripts in Rājasthānî style is the *sāvag paḍikamaṇa sutta cunni' (śrāvaka pratikramanya sutra curnî)* during the reign of Guhil Tej Singh in 1260 A.D. Another early example of an illustrated manuscript also belonging to Udaipur is the '*supāsanāh caritam*' (supārśvanāth *caritraṁ)* of 1422-23 A.D. The influence of Western India school is easily discernible in these examples. Thus, the Rājasthānî style was already in the formative stages before the Mughal era. Later, it was influenced by the Mughal school. There are four sub-schools of the Rājasthānî style :

1. Mewār (Chāwand, Udaipur etc.)
2. Mārwār (Jodhpur, Bikaner, Kishangarh, Pāli etc.)
3. Ḍhunḍhāḍa (Āmer, Jaipur, Śekhāwāti etc.)
4. Hāḍauti (Bundi, Kota etc.).

Rājput painters depicted scenes from day to day life, religious festivals, episodes from the legend of Kṛṣṇa, the seasons and of course their favourite theme 'Rāgamālā', which will be discussed in the later part of this chapter. The off shoot of Rājput school in the Punjab Himalayas known as 'Pahāri' style took root only after the 17th century A.D. A clear influence of Mughal school is observed in the paintings of Pahāri style, specially in the treatment of clothes. It is believed that in the absence of patronage during

Aurangzeb's reign (1685-1707 A.D.), artists from the Mughal court of Delhi migrated to the Punjab Himalayas and initiated the Pahāri style. The two major centres of this styles are Basohli and Kangra. According to Karl Khandalavala, 'what Ananda K. Coomarswamy called Jammu School, is now referred to as Basohli painting'.[18] The earliest dated example of this school belongs to the period of Kirpal Pal (1678-1695 A.D.). The birth place of the second centre was at Guler, which was founded by Raja Hari Chand of Kangra in 1405 A.D. Under Dalip Singh (1695-1730 A.D.), a near Basohli style of painting prevailed in Guler which was transformed into a highly sophisticated style by artists proficient in Mughal style. The names Manak (or Manaku) and Nainsukh and their sons are usually linked to this style. The Kangra/Guler style reached full bloom under Raja Sansar Chand (1775-1823 A.D.) of Kangra. The characterisitc features of this style are best summed up by J.C. French as 'Beautiful as is the line of the art of Guler and Kangra, its colour is equally fine. Clear, pure and bright, it is yet of a gossamer of lightness and delicacy. The artists of Guler and Kangra had the colours of the dawn and the rainbow on their palettes.'[19]

Deccan School

With the decline of the Bahmani Kingdom, an independent Islamic Kingdom of the Deccan in 14th Century A.D., provincial governors became independent rulers. The Ādil Shāhi Dynasty was founded in 1490 A.D. by Yusuf Adil Shāh, governor of Bijapur. Similarly, Malik Ahmad, governor of Junnar founded the Nizām Shāhi Dynasty of Ahmadnagar in the same year. Quli Qutb Shāh of Telingana founded the Qutb Shāhi lineage of Golconda in 1512 A.D. The provinces of Bijapur, Ahmadnagar and Golconda were major centres of painting in the Deccan. Bijapur is well known for its patronage to Rāgamālā miniature paintings. One of the greatest rulers of Bijapur was Ibrahim Ādil Shāh II (1580-1627 A.D.). The tradition of Rāgamālā paintings in the Deccan reached the zenith of its development under his patronage. According to Krishna Chaitanya, 'the last three decades of the sixteenth century saw the origin and stabilisation of Deccani Rāgamālā painting, that Ahmednagar and Bijapur both contributed to its evolution and that Ibrahim Ādil Shāh's love of music must have given it considerable impetus'.[20] A happy blend of Persian as well as Hindu elements can be seen in the paintings of Deccan school. According to Mark Zebrowski, 'even after the great Persianate schools of painting developed at the Deccani capitals in the late sixteenth century, provincial painting for Hindu rajas continued, particularly in the northern Deccan where influences from Rajasthan and Malwa were strong'.[21] The bold colours of Rājput painting have been combined exquisitely with blues, pinks and mauves. While in some paintings, Persian styled grilled windows and cypruses are depicted (e.g. Plate 14 of Appendix II), some paintings (e.g. Plate 15 of Appendix II) are characterised with a typical Hinduised treatment of clothes (transparent veils etc.) and foliage.

Mughal School

The Mughal school was a product of the Mughal dynasty founded by Babur (1526 A.D.). After his death, his son Humayun had to face fifteen years of exile, during which he took refuge in the court of Shah Tehmasp of Persia. While preparing an army, he also came in contact with Persian painting (such as those by Bihzad and his followers). He took such a fancy to it that he brought two Persian artists, Mir Syed Ali and Khwaja Abu Sammad along with him to India. They were specifically employed to illustrate a Persian manuscript 'Hamzāhnāmā'. Within a year of his arrival in India, he died and Akbar ascended the throne in 1556 A.D. Work on 'Hamzāhnāmā' began during his reign. An illustration from this work is given in Plate 16 of Appendix II which shows the prophet Elias saving prince Nur ad-Dar from the river (1564 A.D.). By this time, the earlier Rājput school had also evolved. Akbar recruited many indigenous painters from different parts of India such as Gujarat, Rajasthan and Kashmir. As many as forty such artists were present in his court. The Mughal school, which was initially an aristocratic style confined to the Mughal court as a provincial off shoot of Persian painting, achieved a more universal and secular character under Akbar's reign. With indigenous painters being involved and illustrated Persian translations of the epics, the Mughal school came to be recognised as an individual style of Indian painting. Various branches or 'Kalms' of this school came into being such as Delhi, Lucknow, Jaipur, Deccan, Patna and Kashmir. Mostly hunting scene, battles, historical episodes, portraits, court scenes, flora and fauna were the themes of this school. Local themes and Rāgamālās were not very popular in this school, though not entirely absent.

Modern School

The foundations of Modern School of painting in India were laid by Abanindra Nath Tagore in 1903 A.D. Motivated by a spirit to revive the traditional Indian art from degeneration, he along with a group of young Bengali artists started experimenting with different styles. The themes were taken from classical literature and were usually in small format.

MATERIALS, TECHNIQUES AND CHARACTERISTICS OF INDIAN MINIATURE PAINTING

The term 'miniature' is derived from a Latin word, minium, meaning 'red-lead' which was used to enhance initial letters. In the 17th century A.D., it became wrongly connected with minutus, signifying little, small, minute etc., and the expression began to be used to describe anything 'depicted on a small format',[22] including manuscript illustrations or even portraits of small size.

As already mentioned in an earlier portion of this chapter, the origin of miniature paintings in India was in the form of illustrations on palm leaf manuscripts. From 11th century A.D. to 19th century A.D., the tradition of painting miniatures blossomed in the various schools of Indian painting. The Rājput and Mughal schools are particularly renowned for their miniatures. In the Deccan also, some exquisite examples of miniatures are found. After the advent of paper, palm leaf was substituted by this more suitable medium. By the Mughal Period, different varieties of paper were produced in India. Some of these were Daulatabadi, Nizāmshāhi, Siālkoti, Hariri, Mughali, Hindi and Kardey. To prepare the base of a miniature painting, the artist pasted together two or more sheets of paper. The surface was then burnished by first dipping in a solution of alum, which was allowed to partly dry and subsequently rubbed with a piece of agate, until it achieved an enamel-like smoothness. The colours were often prepared by the artist himself. They were either extracts from plants (organic), mineral, chemical or metallic (Gold, silver etc.). Brushes were made from hair of animals or fibers and barks of trees. The finest brushes were made from hair obtained from tales of young squirrels.

A general observation of Indian miniature paintings shows certain typical characteristics. The most prominent of these is in the perspective of the subject. There appears to be no clear differentiation between foreground and background in the Indian miniature paintings. The subject seems to come to the fore in totality. The images are largest in the center and start tapering to smaller size towards the top as well as bottom of the painting. This characteristic is clearly evident in Rāgamālā paintings of Jaipur and Jodhpur sub-schools. Other characteristics, such as the style of showing the whiskers or moustaches of the Nāyaka, *dupaṭṭā* of the Nāyikā, the profiles (half, more than half or full) are School specific. These have already been discussed earlier.

DESCRIPTION OF RĀGAMĀLĀ MOTIFS IN VARIOUS SCHOOLS OF MINIATURE PAINTING IN INDIA

Depiction of music in Indian traditional miniature schools of painting has been in the form of Rāgamālā motifs. Even though there have been attempts in the West to depict music through the medium of paintings, they are mostly in abstract form. When depicted pictorially also, they are not expressing music as such. For e.g. Kandinsky has shown the scene of a concert, which cannot be called an interpretation of music. Whereas, Rāgamālā motifs actually transform the musical melodies into iconographical deities. It is not known whether the notes were also depicted in the ancient tradition, but since there are equivalents between colours and notes in ancient texts, the possibility cannot be ruled out entirely. An attempt has been made in the present thesis, to depict certain phrases of notes pictorially, which will be dealt with in the next chapter. Presently, some examples of Rāgamālā paintings in the various schools of miniature painting in India are being taken up. The theme of Rāgamālā was basically the domain of Hindu painting, comprising Rājput (Rājasthānî and Pahāri) and Deccan schools. Therefore, the Rāgamālā paintings available in these schools are being discussed.

Rāgamālā Paintings in Rājput Schools

(i) Rājasthānî Rāgamālā Paintings

The earliest available Rāgamālā paintings belong to a manuscript of *Kalpasutra* dated 1475 A.D. in the Western India style (Plate 7 Appendix II). Though Klaus Ebeling has included all the areas covering Western India under the Rājasthānî style, he has referred to this particular set as an 'iconographic dead end'.[23] This could be because the iconographies depicted in this Rāgamālā set have not been followed in later paintings though Bhairava has still been depicted in the form of Śiva (Trishul, Nandi cow and the snake around neck). However, another example of Rāginî Bhairavi (Plate 8 Appendix II) belonging to the same region has been established as the oldest available Rāgamālā painting in Rājasthānî style. This is probably because the iconography has been continued in later paintings also, e.g., the Rāginî Bhairavi of Bundi (Plate 13 Appendix II).

The next landmarks in the development of Rāgamālā paintings of Rājasthānî style are the Rāgamālā paintings of Chunār (1591 A.D.). By this time, the iconographic details had been standardised, as is seen from the typical depiction of Bhairva in the form of Śiva with *muṇḍamālā,* tilak on forehead etc. (Plate 9 of Appendix II).

The Chāwanḍ Rāgamālā paintings (1605 A.D.) belonging to the Mewār sub school form the next stage of development of Rāgamālā paintings of the Rājasthānî style. Upto this period, the paintings clearly show a Hindu character in the chakdār jāmā and fish eye. A typical feature of these paintings is an undulating sky line and faces with a broad nose and double chin. An example of this set of Rāgamālā paintings painted by Nisaradi/Nasiruddin is given in Plate 10 of Appendix II.

After that comes a Rāgamālā set from Pali belonging to the Mārwār sub-school painted by Virji in 1623 A.D. These paintings seem to have some Mughal influence (of Jahangir's reign) in the head gear and jama having four or six pointed ends.

In the Ḍhunḍhāḍ sub-school, there are exquisite examples of Rāgamālā paintings from Āmer kalm (about 1700 A.D.) and Jaipur kalm (1777-1802 A.D.). The paintings from Hāḍauti sub school comprising Bundi and Kota kalms show a very sound technical character. The Chunār Rāgamālā is included in this sub school as it was made during the reign of Bhoj Singh, son of King Surjan Singh of Bundi. The next Rāgamālā set from Bundi is obtained in 1625 A.D. (Plate 13 of Appendix II) and the earliest one from Kota is dated 1660 A.D.

(ii) Pahāri Rāgamālā Paintings

Paintings on the theme of Rāgamālā are available only after 1700 A.D. in the Pahāri styles. A number of Basohli Rāgamālā paintings have been given in Coomarswamy's *Rajput Painting* as paintings from Jammu. Karl Khandalavala has published a Basohli painting showing Rāginî Devagiri dated 1700-1730 A.D. in his *Pahāri Miniature painting.* M.S. Randhawa has published a painting in Basohli Kalm showing Rāga Naṭa in his *Basohli Painting.* This painting is part of a series from the Bharat kalā, Bhawan, Varanasi collection dated 1700-1720 A.D. and is believed to have been made during the reign of Dhiraj Pal.

Rāgamālā paintings are also available in the Kāngrā Kalm of Pahāri style from 18th to 19th century A.D. Earlier it was thought that the theme of Rāgamālā was very rare in Kāngrā Kalm. However, after the publication of various examples of Kāngrā Rāgamālā paintings, such an assumption becomes baseless. Apart from the Rāga Megha of Coomarswamy given in the 'Catalogue of the Indian collections in the Museum of Fine Arts, Boston (1926), a Kāngrā drawing of Rāginî Kānada was published by Hirananda Shastri in the 'Journal of the Bihar and Orissa Research Society, Vol. 17, p. 101. Subsequently, Karl Khandalavala published a Kāngrā painting of Rāginî Kakubha in *Indian Sculpture and painting,* P1. 14. Two more Rāgamālā paintings in Kāngrā Kalm have been given in Khandalavala's book *Pahari miniature Painting* dated 1780-1800 A.D. from the collection of Indian National Museum, New Delhi. They are believed to have been made during the period of Sansar Chand. Two examples of Kāngrā Rāgamālā paintings from the Nahar collection have been reproduced by O.C. Gangoly in his *Rāgas and Rāginîs,* Vol. 2, Plate 24, Fig. C and Plate 35, showing Rāginîs Gunakari and Deśākhi respectively. Rāginîs Mālati and Kedāra, from a series of late 18th century are found in the Indian National Museum, New Delhi and Bhārat kalā Bhavan, Banaras respectively. National Museum of New Delhi came into the possession of some sixty three Rāgamālā paintings in 1960 A.D. belonging to the Kāngrā style. According to M.S. Randhawa, these paintings have been dated century 1810 A.D.[24]

Rāgamālā Paintings in Deccan School

Examples of Rāgamālā paintings belonging to the Deccan school are available from the late sixteenth century A.D. onwards. The provinces of Ahmadnagar and Bijapur abound with exquisite specimens of Rāgamālā miniature paintings under the patronage of Nizām Shāhi and Ādil Shāhi Dynasties respectively. According to Douglas Barrett and Basil Gray, in their book *Paintings of India,*

Treasures of Asia series, the school of Bijapur was patronised by Ali Ādil Shāh I (1558-1580 A.D.) and his successor Ibrahim II (1580-1627 A.D.) and that the latter 'might have commissioned the Rāgamālā series in the 1590s'.[25] This set, which was earlier in the Bikaner Palace, is now dispersed between the National Museum, Baroda Museum and Khajanchi Collection. Plate 14 of Appendix II shows Rāga Śri from the Khajanchi collection published by Barrett and Gray.

A stray Rāgamālā painting from an unknown set is present in the National Museum belonging to the Ahmadnagar kalm of Deccan school. This painting depicts Rāga Hindol (Plate 15 Appendix II) in an ambience of spring (the season of this Rāga) shown by the medium of accompanying maidens squirting coloured water to celeberate Holi festival. It has been variously dated by difterent authors, but all have ascribed it to the late sixteenth century A.D. An absolutely same iconography and technique has been used in another painting of Rāga Hindola belonging to the second half of seventeenth century A.D. in the Bashir Mohammed collection, London. The only difference is in the presentation of the 'Nayaka' or hero/deity personifying the Rāga which shows a strong Mughal influence. This painting has been reproduced by Mark Zebrowski in his 'Deccani Painting' fig. 42 under the general designation of Northern Deccan.

THE MUSICAL IMPORTANCE OF PICTORIAL RĀGAMĀLĀ MOTIFS

Rāgamālā (literally 'garland of Rāgas') motifs, which are a portrayal of the iconographic forms of traditional Rāgas and Rāginîs, have great significance for Indian classical music. The depiction of particular motifs relating to a particular Rāga or Rāginî conveys a lot regarding the nature of the melodic form. The ethos of the Rāga or Rāginî is brought out in its pictorial expression. Not only that, the pictorial motifs sometimes hint towards the origin of the particular Rāga or Rāginî. It is well known that the roots of classical music in India are found in the Folk strains of yore. Certain motifs, like that of Toḍi and Āsāvari, which are quite consistent, might indicate the original ambience surrounding the Rāginîs. As suggested from various literary references, it was a standard practice among rice farmers to lure away deer herds from paddy fields by the means of music. Usually the women folk carried out this task. This practice seems to be the motivating source for the visual interpretation of Todi almost universally. Similarly, in the case of Āsāvari, there is always a depiction of snake charmers. Klaus Ebeling has linked it to the origin of Āsāvari as 'the tune of snake charmers from the mountain tribe of the Saveris,'.[26] The basis for iconographic portrayal of Rāga-Rāginîs can be traced to the age old tradition of mythological idolisation. Since time immemorial, Gods and Goddesses have been worshipped in the form of idols. Most of them have been associated with some musical instrument or the other, e.g., Śiva with Damru, Saraswati with Vîṇā and Kṛṣṇa with flute. The motive behind such an association could have been to give music a divine or honourable place in society. A similar motive is possible for the pictorial depiction of Rāgas and Rāginîs in the form of deities. Also, the structure of Rāga-Rāginîs that had already been established would be difficult to change once given a pictorial form. Apart from that, the pictorial representation of musical modes perhaps served as a simpler means of memorising the innumerable names of Rāgas, Rāginîs, Putras and Putra vadhus of the Rāga-Rāginî system of classification. Historically also, the type of instruments prevalent during the period of the miniatures, the extent of development of music and its place in society are reflected from pictorial motifs of Rāgamālā.

It should also be noted that apart from pictorial motifs, abstract paintings are also available in which Rāgas have been depicted. An excellent example, is the painting showing Megh Mallar in Jaipur City Palace Museum (Plate 17). However, the author has chosen to depict musical phrases pictorially in accordance with the dhyānas given in ancient texts.

References

1. Apte, V.S., The practical Sanskṛit-English dictionary, Part I, p. 359.
2. Shukla, R.L., Bhartiya saundarya śāstra ka tattvika vivecan evaṁ lalit kalāyen, p. 216.
3. *Citram devānaṁ* etc., Ṛg Veda 1/115/1.
4. 'Kiśi ek tal ... hoti hai, Das Rai kṛṣṇa, Bhārat ki citrakalā', p. 1.
5. Vide Viṣṇudharmottaraṁ, Pt. III, chap. 35.
6. Vide Viṣṇu Purāṇa, p. 465.
7. Bhattacharya, Tarapada, The Canons of Indian Art, p. 337.
8. *Ibid.*, p. 352.

9. Shukla, D.N., Vāstu Śāstra, p. 445.
10. Brown, Percy, Indian Painting, p. 38.
11. *Ibid.*, p. 33.
12. Healey, W.L.—Tara Nath's chapter on Buddhist Art, Indian Antiquary, 1875, Marg, Vol. IX, No. 2 (1956), p. 105.
13. Khandalavala, Karl, Pahāri miniature painting, p. 7.
14. *Ibid.*
15. Rājasthānî śaili ka udbhava ... etc.', Das, Rai Kṛṣna, Bharat Ki citrakala, p. 61.
16. Article by Altaf Hussain, *Times of India*, Nov. 3, '97.
17. Coomarswamy, A.K., Rājput Painting, p. 1.
18. Khandalavala, Karl, in forward of 'Rājput Painting' by Coomarswamy, A.K., p. 12.
19. French, J.C., Review of W.G. Archer's 'Indian Painting in the Punjab Hills', in Art and letters, Vol. XXVI, No. 1, (1952), p. 63.
20. Chaitanya, Krishna, A History of Inian Painting, p. 75.
21. Zebrowski, Mark, Deccani Painting, p. 46.
22. Mukherjee, B.N., Earliest Indian miniatures, p. 17.
23. Ebeling, Klaus, Rāgamālā Painting, p. 34.
24. Randhawa, M.S., Kāngrā Rāgamālā Painting, p. 20.
25. Barrett, Douglas and Gray, Basil, Paintings of India, p. 121.
26. Article 'Rāgamālā, India's visible music', Ebeling, Klaus in Span, 1973.

4
Pictorial Depiction of Music

INTRODUCTION

In the previous chapter, examples of Rāgamālā miniature paintings according to traditional schools of painting in India were taken up. These paintings were a visual interpretation of Rāgas and Rāginîs of classical music as prevalent during the medieval era. With the passage of time, the structure of Rāgas and Rāginîs has undergone a sea of change as is evident from a study of ancient, medieval and modern musical works. The iconography or *murti/devamaya*[1] rupa depicted according to dhyāna formulas given in various Sanskrit, Hindi or dialect verses also gave way to more popular romantic themes catering to the tastes of patrons. As a result, the basic ethos of a Rāga could not be portrayed. Also, there seemed to be no link to practical music. There have been some efforts to relate notes to colours as given in ancient texts or otherwise, in recent years. Apart from the names mentioned in the first chapter, the contributions of S.V. Vadnerkar and Tilak Gitai are significant landmarks in this direction. Their contributions are being discussed in the following section. However, there has not been any effort to depict actual phrases of notes through the medium of paintings in the Indian (or even western) tradition. The present research work endeavours to actually express phrases of notes characteristic of certain Rāgas through traditional miniature paintings in a modern mould. Three examples of such paintings are being given in this chapter along with graphs to aid the understanding of phrases depicted. The paintings have been made by the researcher using wash technique in water colour. The iconographies of the Rāgas shown are in standard form and particular reference has been taken from

'Sangît Darpana' of Damodar Miśra (1625 A.D.). The three Rāgas are—Bhairava, Mālkauns and Toḍi (Rāginî). The explanation of depicted phrases will be given after a general description of the said Rāgas.

SURVEY OF EARLIER EFFORTS ON THE SUBJECT

Since ancient times, relationships have been established between musical notes and colours, particularly in Indian tradition. Various Sanskrit works like Bharata's Nāṭya Śāstra, Mataṅga's Bṛhaddeśî, Sangît Ratnākara of Śārngadeva and Sangît Makaranda of Nārada contain equivalents between colours, emotions (Rasas) and notes. Mataṅga's relationship between colours and notes has already been given earlier *(padmapatra* etc.). Śārngadeva's equivalents are also more or less similar except that for rshabh he has given the colour pale yellow instead of parrot green.

More recently, the names of S.V. Vadnerkar, Hirendra Kumar Basu and Tilak Gitai are significant in the association of notes with colours. H.K. Basu has mostly followed the work of Herbert Spencer except that he has taken the consonance of Sa and Pa instead of Sa and Ma. The colours of the Spectrum have been taken in reverse order to represent the notes, as already stated in the first chapter. Tilak Gitai has presented a series of Rāgamālā miniatures in his catalogue/book entitled 'Rāgamālā—The missing link' in which he has used colour equivalents for notes and also formulated a means of showing elements of a painting according to the number of notes used as well as omitted the use of a colour corresponding to the omitted note. The association of colours with musical notes that he has used is

Sa	—	Blue
Re	—	Violet
Ga	—	Grey
Ma	—	Yellow
Pa	—	Red
Dha	—	Orange
Ni	—	Green

Shri S.V. Vadnerkar has shown notes through the medium of graphs e.g., in his article '*Bhavanon par citrit Rāga*' in the journal Sangît Kalā Vihār Jan. '79 issue, he has depicted the notes of Bihāg graphically (see Graph 4.1). He has also given a scheme of colours corresponding to notes and their differences in shades also according to modifications of notes, such as light green for komal Dha etc. His scheme of colours in relation to notes has been given in Table 29. Instead of coloured squares as given by the researcher, he has used separate symbols denoting different colours. He has also shown a method of depicting the mātrā of each note (full, half or quarter).

Even though substantial work has been done in this field, the actual depiction of musical notes had so far been considered an impossibility. The author's aim has been to depict phrases of select Rāgas in ascent and descent in order to bring forth the true melodic structure of the Rāga-Rāginî pictorially. For this purpose, three demonstrative paintings made by the author have been presented in this chapter along with graphs to aid the description of phrases depicted. Before explaining the phrases a general description of the chosen Rāgas-Rāginî is being given.

GENERAL DESCRIPTION OF THE DEMONSTRATED RĀGAS-RĀGINÎ

In the present thesis, the main objective of the researcher has been to pictorially depict musical phrases through the medium of miniature paintings. Such a depiction of musical phrases has been demonstrated practically by the author through paintings given in Plates A, B and C. In these paintings, the characteristic phrases of Rāgas Bhairava, Mālkauns Rāginî Toḍi have been depicted which have been explained with the help of graphs in this section. Before that, a general description as well as iconographic details are being given of each Rāga-Rāginî.

General Description of Rāga Bhairava

One of the prominent Rāgas since ancient times, it is counted among the six main Rāgas of the Rāga-Rāginî system. In the present Ṭhāṭa and Rāgānga systems also, it is the generic Rāga. In ancient times it originated from the Bhinna-Ṣaḍja Grāma Rāga and had a pentatonic (Auḍava) structure (See 2nd Chap., p. 56). The present day Bhairava is heptatonic (Sampoorna) with the sonant being dhaivata and consonant rishabha, which are also the flat notes, the rest being pure. Some remnants of the pentatonic variety in which the notes 're' and 'pa' were omitted are still seen in the modern Rāga Bhairava. During the ascent (Āroha) of the

Rāga, the note 're' and to a lesser extent 'pa' are weak and are generally omitted. The lack of 're' and 'pa' is more than made up in the descent (Avaroha). A typical characteristic of this Rāga is the unique undulation of the notes 're' and 'dha'. Some characteristic phrases of this Rāga are

Sa ga ma, re, sa, ga ma dha pa,
dha pa ma pa ga ma dha pa,
dha ma pa ga ma dha ni dha pa,
ma pa dha ni sa ni dha pa ma ga ma re sa.

The hallmark of Bhairava in purvānga is the association of notes 'ma re' through meenḍ with the characteristic undulation of 're'. In uttarānga, 'ga ma dha pa' is the phrase characteristic of this Rāga. The time prescribed for singing/playing this Rāga is early morning. The nature of Bhairava is sombre, therefore it is suitable for slower tempo and despite being an uttarānga vādi Rāga, it is elaborated in the lower and medium registers for the same reason. The iconography fo Bhairava in various musical works has been uniformly described as Lord Śiva as is evident from descriptions in the second chapter. In Sangît Darpaṇa of Dāmodara Miśra, the 'dhyāna' of Bhairava is given as

Gaṅgādharaḥ śaśikalātilakastrinetraḥ
sarpairvibhuṣitatanurgajakṛttvāsāḥ/
bhāsvatriśulakara eṣa nṛmuṇḍadhārî
śubhrāṁbarojayati bhairava ādirāgaḥ//
— Sangît Darpaṇa of Pt. Damodara, p. 81

i.e., one who has encaged the ganges in his locks, his head is adorned with the moon and has three eyes. He wears a snake around his neck as a necklace and carries the elephant skin. He holds a triśula in his hand, wears white clothes and a garland of heads. This is the first Rāga Bhairava.

The demonstrative painting of Bhairava given in plate A shows this iconography.

Description of Phrases of Notes Depicted in the Painting of Bhairava (Plate A)

The phrases of notes as depicted in the demonstrated painting of Bhairava (Plate A) made by the researcher are being described in this sub-section. Each phrase in being taken up according to a specific graph.

(1) Graph 2—dḥa ṇi sa re sa, ma ga ma dha pa

The notes depicted in the lower right and left portion of the painting have been shown in this graph. The same phrase, 'dḥa ṇi sa re sa, ma ga ma dha pa', has been shown in below right and below left portion according to the colour scheme of S.V. Vadnerkar (Table 29). Beginning from the green of the grass (dḥa), excluding the figure, straight upto the edge of the plains where the boundary of trees starts, the phrase ends at violet (pa) towards the right. Towards the left, again beginning from the tuft of grass, moving straight upwards and then curving towards the right for the blue of 'ga' and orange of 'ma', again tilting to the left for the green of dha, the phrase finishes at the first patch of violet (pa).

(2) Graph 3— dha ma pa dha ni ṡa

The phrase 'dha ma pa dha ni ṡa' has been depicted on the left and right sides of the figure in the painting of Bhairava. Towards the left side, starting from where the previous phrase ended, going upwards towards the belt of trees being treated as 'dha', to the mountains (ni) right upto the pink tinge (ṡa) of the sky, the phrase ends. Towards the right of the figure of Śiva, starting from the green patch near the elephant skin, is 'dha' below which are the orange flowers showing 'ma' going upto the elephant skin is pa, which goes towards the green belt (dha), reaching to the mountains (ni) and finally to the sky (ṡa).

(3) Graph 4—ṡa ġa ṁa ṙe sa

The phrase—'ṡa ġa ṁa ṙe ṡa' depicted in the top right portion of the painting of Bhairava has been shown in this graph. Starting from the meeting point of the two mountains towards the top right of Lord Śiva, showing the different hues of the rising sun, the phrase begins with 'ṡa' (pink), then 'ġa' (blue of the sky), then 'ṁa' (orange tinge), then 'ṙe' (yellow band), merging with pink (ṡa).

General Description of Rāga Mālkauns

Like Bhairava, Mālkauns is also an ancient established Rāga and its name occurs among the six main Rāgas of the Rāga-Rāginî system according to most of the mats. Earlier it was called 'Mālava-Kaishik' or 'Mālava-Kaushik' which changed to

'Mālkauns' or 'Mālkons' with the passage of time. Śārṅgadeva has attributed its origin to the Kaiśiki Jātî and associated it with the supposedly masculine Vira, Raudra and Adbhuta rasas.[2] In modern times, even if a composition of the Rāga is predominently of Karuna ethos or leans towards the devotional, there is an inherent solemnity in the Rāga. The ancient heptatonic (Sampoorna) structure gave way to the pentatonic (Auḍava) structure wherein the notes 're' and 'pa' were omitted. The sonant is madhyama (ma) and consonant is ṣaḍja (sa), which was the prominent note (aṁśa) in the ancient variety. In the present Mālkauns, the main thrust of the Rāga is on the note madhyama, which also lends the Rāga its solemnity. There is some division of opinion regarding the *ṭhāṭ* (genus) of this Rāga. Some ascribe it to the Bhairavi *ṭhāṭ* while others include it in the Āsāvari *ṭhāṭ*. In both cases, the notes 'ga', 'dha' and 'ni' are flat and in the case of Bhairavi *ṭhāṭ*, the note 're' being flat is of no consequence in Mālkauns since it is omitted. Bhātkhanḍe has included Mālkauns in the Bhairavi ṭhāṭ because of similarity in structure particularly in Uttarāng (ga ma <u>dha</u> <u>ni</u> ṡa etc.). Some people also regard 're' as a *vivādi* note in Mālkauns therefore it is usually included in Bhairavi *ṭhāṭ*. Its time of singing is midnight and the season attributed to it is autumn/winter. Some characteristic phrases of Mālkauns are—

<u>ṇi</u> sa, <u>ḍha</u> <u>ṇi</u> sa <u>ga</u> ma, sa ma <u>ga</u> ma <u>ga</u> sa <u>ṇi</u>
<u>ga</u> sa <u>ga</u> ma, <u>ga</u> ma <u>dha</u> ma <u>dha</u> <u>ga</u> ma
<u>ga</u> sa. <u>ga</u> ma <u>dha</u> ni <u>dha</u> ma, <u>dha</u>
<u>ni</u> ṡa <u>ġa</u> <u>ni</u> ṡa <u>ġa</u> ṁa <u>ġa</u> ṡa

Like Bhairava, the nature of Mālkauns is sombre. Thus, there is much use of meend and it is suitable for slower tempo. It is fully elaborated in all three registers.

The iconography of Mālkauns as given in Sangît Darpaṇa of Damodar Miśra is conveyed from the śloka,

Āraktavarṇo dhṛtaraktayaṣṭih/
vîrah suvîreṣu kṛtapravîryyah/
vîrairdhṛto vairikapālamālā/
mālî mato mālavakauśiko'yaṃ//
—*Sangît Darpaṇa of Pt. Damodara,* p. 89

i.e., having a flushed face seeming red in colour and holding a red stick, he is courageous among the courageous whom the courageous respect. He wears the necklace of his enemies' heads. Such is the Rāga Mālavakauśika.

This iconography has been shown in the demonstrative painting of Mālkauns given in Plate B.

Description of Phrases of Notes Depicted in the Painting of Mālkauns (Plate B)

The phrases of notes as depicted in the demonstrated painting of Mālkauns (Plate B) made by the researcher are being described in this sub-section. Each phrasẹ in being taken up according to Graphs 5, 6, 7 and 8.

(1) Graph 5—dḥa ṇi sa ṇi sa ga ma ga sa ṇi dḥa ṃa dḥa ṇi sa

In this graph,the phrase 'dḥa ṇi sa ṇi sa ga ma ga sa ṇi dḥa ṃa dḥa ṇi sa' depicted in the lower portion of the painting is shown. Starting from the bottom right portion of the painting, 'dḥa' begins at the green tuft of grass. Moving upwards towards the brown of the rock comes ni above which is sa (pink). In the brown (light) of the feet of the nāyak is 'ṇi' again above which are the pink anklets showing 'sa'. The blue of the dhoti shows 'ga' while the orange patkā depicts 'ma'. Again, the dhoti, anklet and feet show 'ga', 'sa' and 'ṇi' respectively. The tuft of green grass depicts 'dḥa', below which is an orange tinge of sand showing 'ṃa'. From there, moving upwards comes 'dḥa' (green grass), then 'ṇi' (light brown of rock) and finally sa (pink).

(2) Graph 6—ma ga ma dha ga ma

The left portion of the painting depicting the phrase 'ma ga ma dha ga ma' is shown in this graph. Starting from 'ma' at the orange tinge of the rock (where the earlier phrase ended), towards the blue of the lake (ga), to the orange of the lotus flowers comes 'ma'. The green leaf shows 'dha', after which comes the blue of the lake showing 'ga'. The phrase ends at the shore of orange flowers depicting 'ma'.

(3) Graph 7—ma ga ma dha ma ga sa

This graph shows the phrase 'ma ga ma dha ma ga sa' depicted in the right portion of the painting of Mālkauns. Starting from ma at the orange tinge of the rock towards the right side, rising to the blue of the lake (ga), to the orange tinged lotus (ma), then the green leaf (dha) and again the orange lotus (ma), going towards the blue of the lake (ga), the phrase ends at the pink tinge of the shore (sa).

(4) Graph 8—dha ni ṡa ġa ṁa ġa ṡa

The top left portion of the painting depicts the phrase 'dha ni ṡa ġa ṁa ġa ṡa' shown in this graph. Beginning at the green patch dha following the orange flowers covering the shore, to the brown sashel covering the headgear which shows 'ṡa' (pink), to the blue of the sky (ġa) and subsequent by the orange band (ṁa) followed by blue (ġa), the phrase ends at the pink strip (ṡa) of the sky.

General Description of Rāginî Toḍi

The present day 'Toḍi' is usually understood as 'Miyān ki Toḍi' which was an innovation of Miyān Tānsen (one of the nine gems at Akbar's court). However, the name of Toḍi occurs in as early as Śārngadeva's Sangît Ratnākara (13th cent. A.D.). Śarngadeva has referred to Toḍi among the popular Rāgas with the prominent note being 'ma'. Locana has referred to it as a Rāginî of Kauśika (Mālakauns) with the notes 're' and 'dha' being flat. Since his basic scale was Kāfi, the structure is similar to modern day Bhairavi. Bhātkhande has attributed the origin of modern Toḍi to the ancient 'Varāti todikā' mela in 'Srimallakśyasamgitaṁ'. In its present form, Toḍi is heptatonic (Sampoorna) with 'dha' being the sonant and 'ga' the consonant note. It is the generic Rāga of the Toḍi *ṭhāṭ* with the notes 're', 'ga', 'dha' being flat and 'ṁa' sharp (tivra). Toḍi is characterised by the phrase 're, ga, re sa' rendered in a typical manner. The use of note 'pa' gives this Rāginî a unique beauty. During the ascent of Toḍi, 'pa' is usually omitted and then brought in sometimes as in the phrase 'ṁa pa dha ṁa ga re ga'. During descent also, pa is sometimes omitted and then brought in as 'ga ṁa dha pa, ṁa ga'. In Kallināth's commentary on Sārṅgadeva's Sangît Ratnākara, Toḍi has been characterised by a shaking (kampita) of pa. In modern Toḍi also, such a feature is noticed usually as 'papa ṁa ga'. By the total omission of 'pa', the Rāga Gurjari Toḍi comes into being. The appropriate time of singing Toḍi has been given as the second *prahara*[3] of morning. Some characteristic phrases are:

dha ṇi sa, re ga re sa, re ga ṁa ga

re ga re sa, sa re ga ṁa dha pa ṁa ga, ga ṁa dha ni dha pa ṁa
dha ṁa ga re ga, ga ṁa dha ni ṡa ṙe ṡa, ni ṡa ni dha
pa, ṁa dha ṁa ga re ga re sa.

The nature of Toḍi leans towards the erotic, calṁ and pathetic sentiments traditionally linked to the feminine temperament. Despite that, it has a solemn disposition in which work of meenḍ and gamak seems attractive. The iconography of Toḍi has been described as a Rāginî of Mālkauns in Sangît Darpaṇa of Damodara Miśra as given in the śloka,

Tuṣāra kuṅdojjwaladehayaṣṭih/
kāśmirakarpuraviliptadehā/
vinodyantî hariṇuṁ vanānte/
viṇādharā rājati toḍikeyaṁ//
—*Sangît Darpaṇa of Pt. Damodara,* p. 90

i.e., fair like snow and the *kunda* flower, her body is anointed with saffron and kamphor. She is humouring deer in the forest while holding a vîṇā. Such is the enticing Toḍi.

The same iconography has been shown in the demonstrated painting of Toḍi (Plate C).

Description of Phrases of Notes Depicted in the Painting of Toḍi (Plate C)

The phrases of notes as depicted in the demonstrated painting of Toḍi (Plate C) made by the researcher are being described in this sub-section. The pharases have been taken up according to Graphs 9, 10, 11 and 12.

(1) Graph 9—dḥa ṇi sa re ga ṁa re ga re sa re ga ṁa dha pa

The left portion of the painting has been shown in this graph. Starting from below left, the phrase dḥa ṇi sa re ga ṁa re ga re sa re ga ṁa dha pa' begins at 'dha' (green grass). Moving upwards to the deer (ni) to the pink patch of flowers (sa), the light yellow flowers (re) to the blue of the river (ga). The Reddish beaks of the ducks depict the note ma in *kaṇa*[4] form to 're' shown through the light yellow ducks. After that follows 'ga' shown through the light blue river. Then comes 're' (light yellow patch of flowers on the bank of the river) followed by 'sa' (pink bed of flowers). The notes 're', 'ga' and 'ṁa' come in quick succession shown as yellow, blue and red flowers in thin strips. Then comes a light green patch of grass showing 'dha' followed by a bed of violet flowers showing 'pa', where the phrase ends.

(2) Graph 10—ṁa ga ṁa re ga ṁa dha ni ṡa

The noddle right portion of the painting showing the phrase 'ṁa ga ṁa re ga ṁa dha ni ṡa' is shown in this graph. The phrase starts at the red border of the odhni worn by the Nāyikā at 'ṁa'. This is followed by 'ga' shown by light blue colour of the odhni. After that comes 'ṁa' in *kaṇa* form shown by red flowers of the print followed by light yellow (re) of the blouse. Again the blue coloured odhni showing 'ga' is followed by the red flowered print (ṁa) and the phrase continues upto the green leaf of the banana tree (dha) reaching upto the branch (ni), to the rosy bird (ṡa) where it ends.

(3) Graph 11—dhạ ṇi dhạ ṇi sa re sa re͡ ga ṁa ga re ga ṁa dha ni dha pa.

Starting from below right portion of the painting, the green grass denotes 'dhạ' followed by the brown deer (ṇi), the patch of green grass seen from over its head shows (dhạ). Thereafter, the foot of the Nāyikā depicts 'ṇi' which is adorned with an anklet showing 'sa'. After that comes 're' shown by light yellow colour of the sari worn by the Nāyikā followed by 'sa' shown through a pink sashel around the waist. Leaving the hand and Vīṇā in the foreground, the phrase continues in the yellow reflection of the Odhni (re) followed by light blue (ga), characteristic of Toḍi. The red flowered print shows 'ṁa' which is again followed by blue (ga) continuing to the yellow blouse (re). Again the note 'ga' is shown by the blue odhni intermingled with red flowers (ṁa). The phrase continues upto the green leaf of a banana tree (dha) moving to the knobs (dark brown) of the Vīṇā showing 'ni', again followed by the green of the banana leaf (dha) and ending at 'pa' shown by the violet flower.

(4) Graph 12—dha ġa ṙe͡ ġa ṙe ṡa

This graph shows the top left portion of the painting in which the phrase 'dha ġa ṙe͡ ġa ṙe ṡa' has been depicted. Starting from the green row of trees or mound covered by trees (either way) the note 'dha' is shown. This is followed by the note 'ġa' shown by light blue colour of the sky. The light yellow strips in the sky show the note 'ṙe' interspersed with light blue (ġa). The pink band shows 'ṡa' where the phrase ends.

PRESENTATION OF MUSICAL ELEMENTS IN THE PAINTINGS

The elements of music which determine the basic structure of a Rāga or Rāginî are the notes according to a particular *ṭhāṭ* (genus), Jātî (determining which notes are to be deleted), Vādi, Samvādi, Anuvādi, Vivādi and the time of singing (in the context of depiction in the paintings). Care has been taken to present all the various elements of music in the three paintings made by the researcher (as examples). For instance, the notes in their modifications of a particular *ṭhāṭ*, flat (komal) or tivra (sharp) have been presented by the lighter and darker hues respectively. The colour of a deleted note has been omitted according to the particular Jāti. For example in Mālkauns, the colours yellow and violet representating ṛshabha and pancama respectively have been omitted. The vādi notes have been shown prominently. For instance, in Mālkauns, the colour orange denoting madhyama is dominant in the whole painting. Likewise in case of Bhairava, the colour light green denoting the vādi note 'dha' has been given prominence. The Samvādi has been shown as next in importance. Similarly, other notes have been shown according to their importance in the Rāga. An attempt has also been made to present certain features of a Rāga such as meenḍ through shading. For example, in case of Bhairava, the meenḍ from 'ma' to 're', or in Toḍi, the meenḍ from 're' to 'ga' and back are shown by a merging of the colours through shading. The time of the Rāgas has also been shown in the painting accordingly. The late night hour in Mālkauns is shown through the moon and stars, the early morning scene of Bhairava is shown through the varied pink, blue and yellow hues of the rising sun (also showing the phrase 'ṡa, ġa ṁa ṙe ṡa').

The total number of notes present according to the Jātî of a Rāga have also been depicted with the help of certain elements in the painting. For example, the number of skulls in the necklaces of Bhairava and Mālkauns correspond to the number of notes of the Rāgas respectively. Similarly, the number of lotus flowers in the painting of Mālkauns or the combined number of ducks, deer and the bird perched up a tree in the painting of Rāginî Toḍi, gives the total number of notes in these two paintings.

References

1. See Chapter 2, p. 106.
2. atha mālavakaiśikah...etc, ślokas 71 and 72, page 63, Sangît Ratnākara (also see Chapter 2).
3. Refer to Chapter 2, p. 77.
4. Reflection of one note in another note.

Colour and note equivalents of S.V. Vadnerkar

Colour		Note
	Pink	Sa
	Light Yellow	<u>Re</u>
	Dark Yellow	Re
	Light Blue	<u>Ga</u>
	Dark Blue	Ga
	Orange	Ma
	Red	M̍a
	Violet	Pa
	Light Green	<u>Dha</u>
	Dark Green	Dha
	Light Brown	<u>Ni</u>
	Dark Brown	Ni

TABLE 29

Bihag (S.V. Vadnerkar)

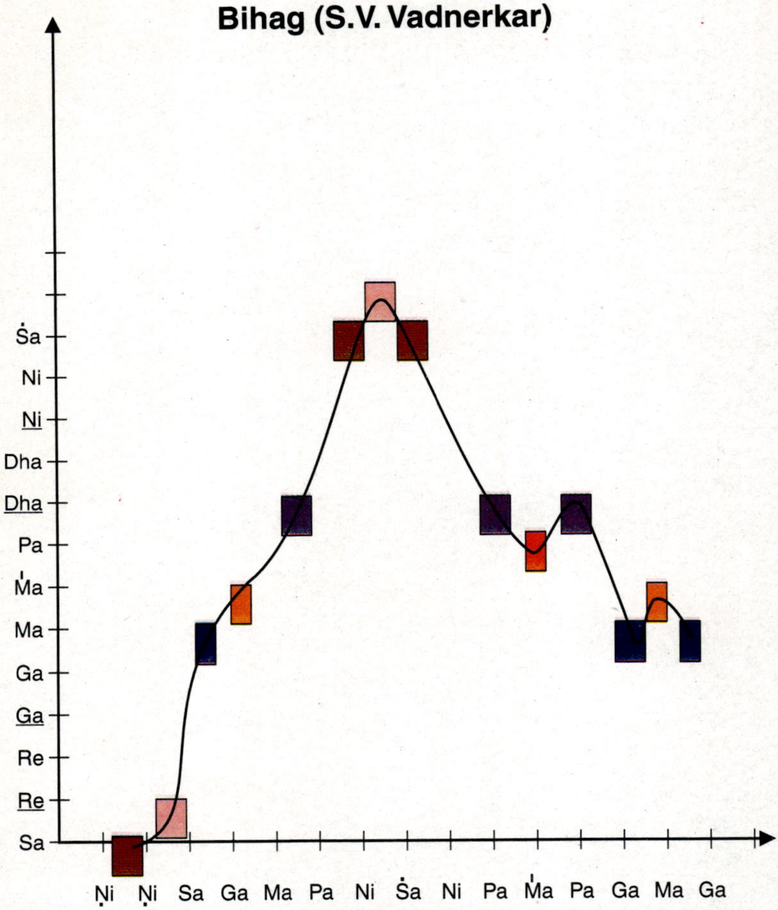

GRAPH 1

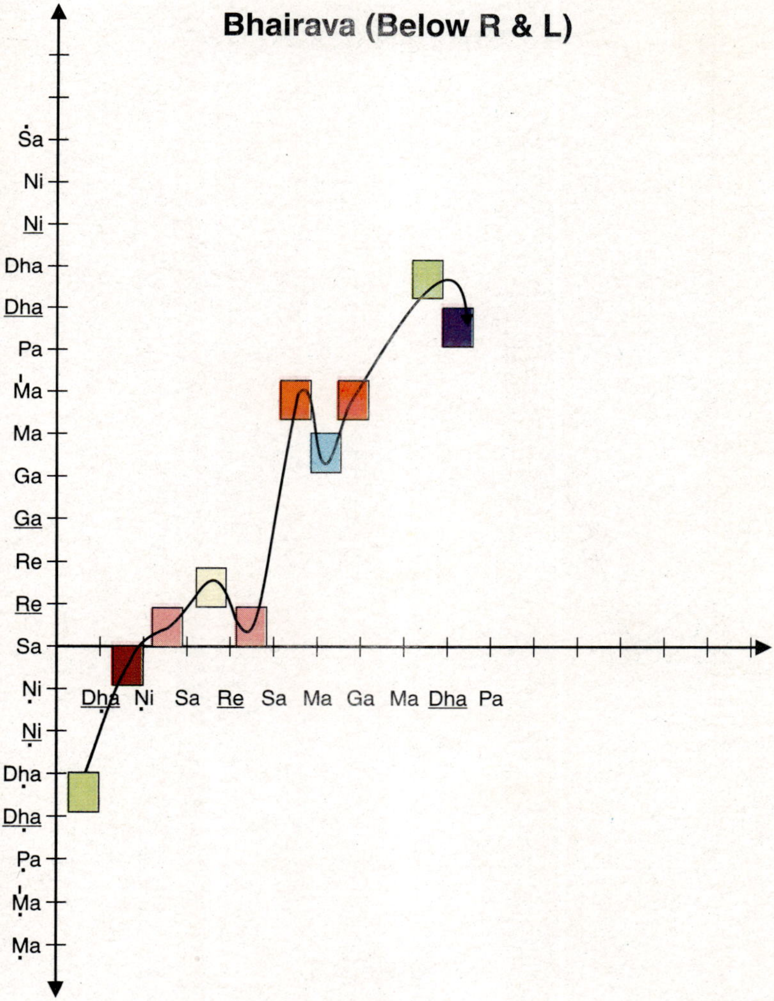

Bhairava (Below R & L)
Ṡa
Ni
Ni
Dha
Dha
Pa
Ma
Ma
Ga
Ga
Re
Re
Sa
Ṇi
Ṇi
Ḍha
Ḍha
P̣a
Ṃa
Ṃa
Ḍha Ṇi Sa Re Sa Ma Ga Ma Dha Pa

GRAPH 2

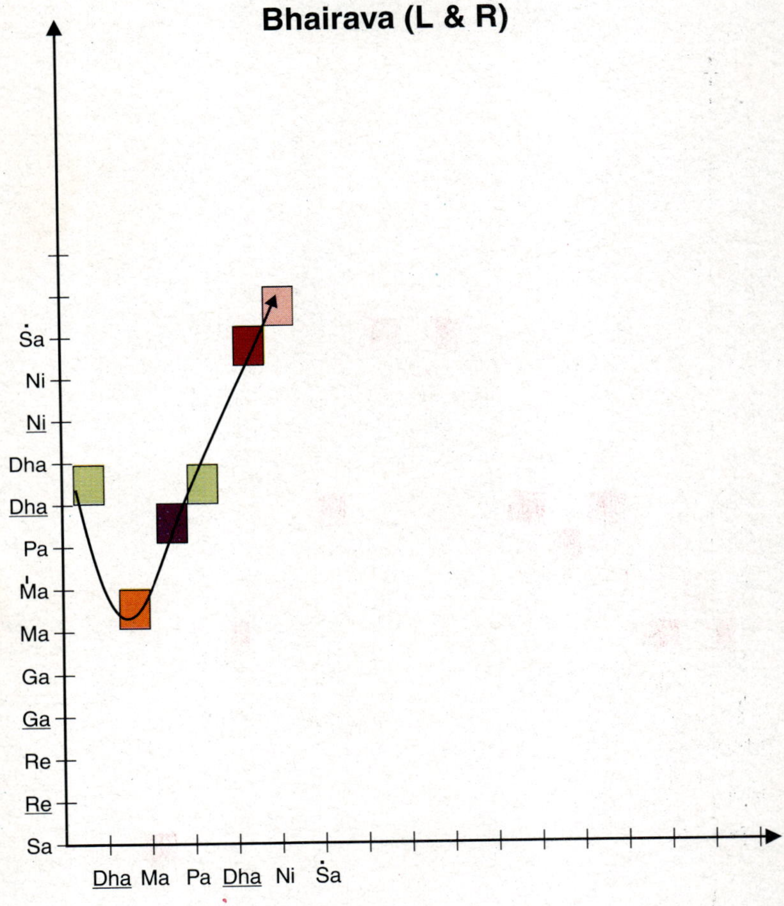
Bhairava (L & R)
Ṡa
Ni
Ni
Dha
Dha
Pa
Ma
Ma
Ga
Ga
Re
Re
Sa
Dha Ma Pa Dha Ni Ṡa

GRAPH 3

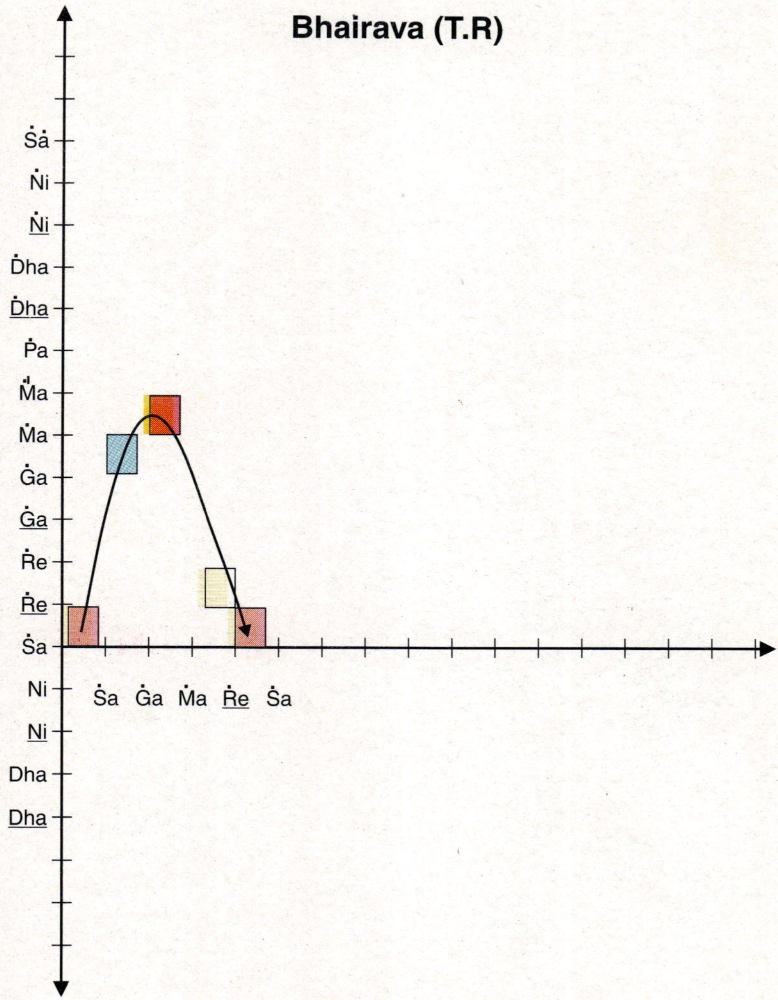
Bhairava (T.R)
Ṡȧ
Ṅi
Ṅi
Ḋha
Ḋha
Ṗa
Ṁa
Ṁa
Ġa
Ġa
Ṙe
Ṙe
Ṡa
Ni
Ni
Dha
Dha
Ṡa Ġa Ṁa Ṙe Ṡa

GRAPH 4

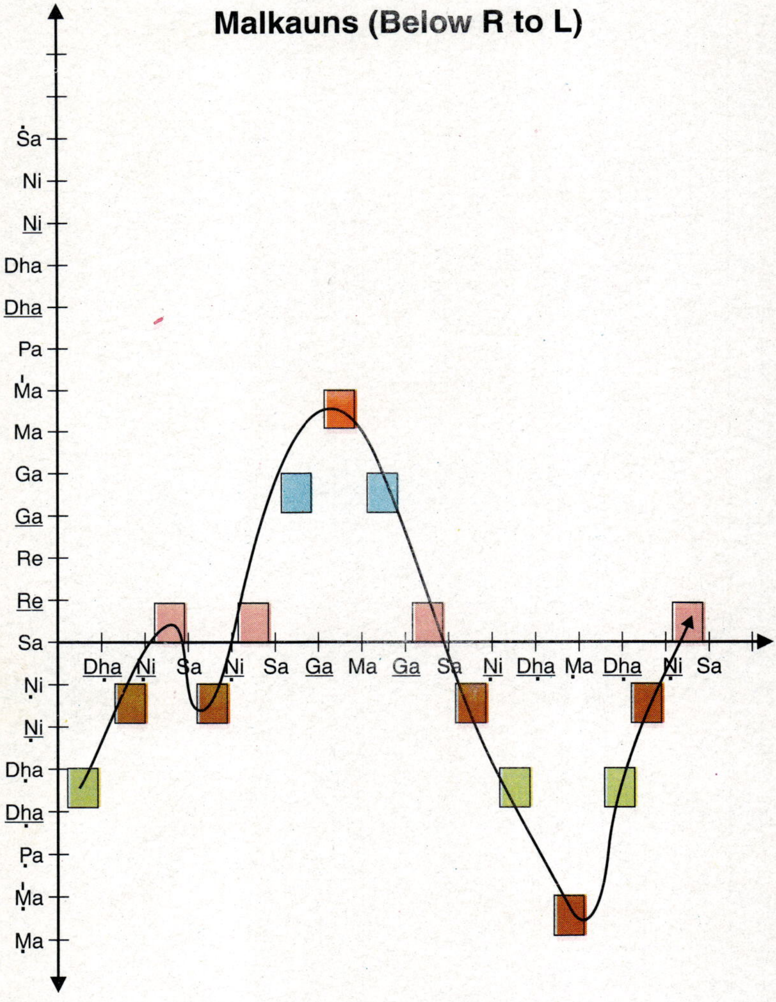
Malkauns (Below R to L)
Ṡa
Ni
Ni
Dha
Dha
Pa
Ma
Ma
Ga
Ga
Re
Re
Sa
Ṇi
Ṇi
Ḍha
Ḍha
P̣a
Ṃa
Ṃa
Dḥa Ṇi Sa Ṇi Sa Ga Ma Ga Sa Ṇi Dḥa Ṃa Dḥa Ṇi Sa

GRAPH 5

Malkauns (L)

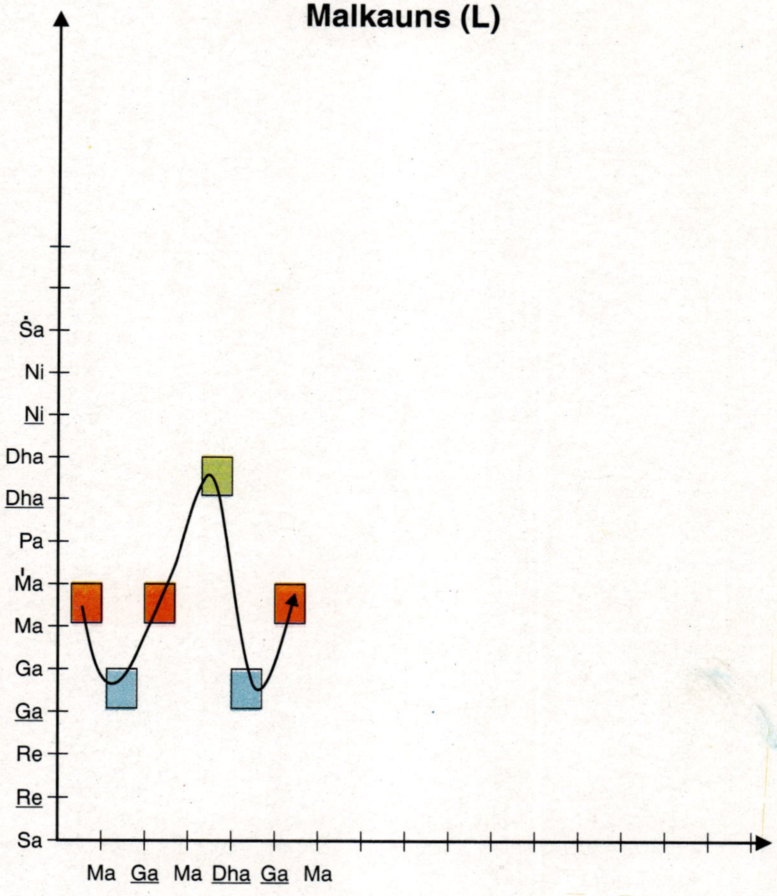

GRAPH 6

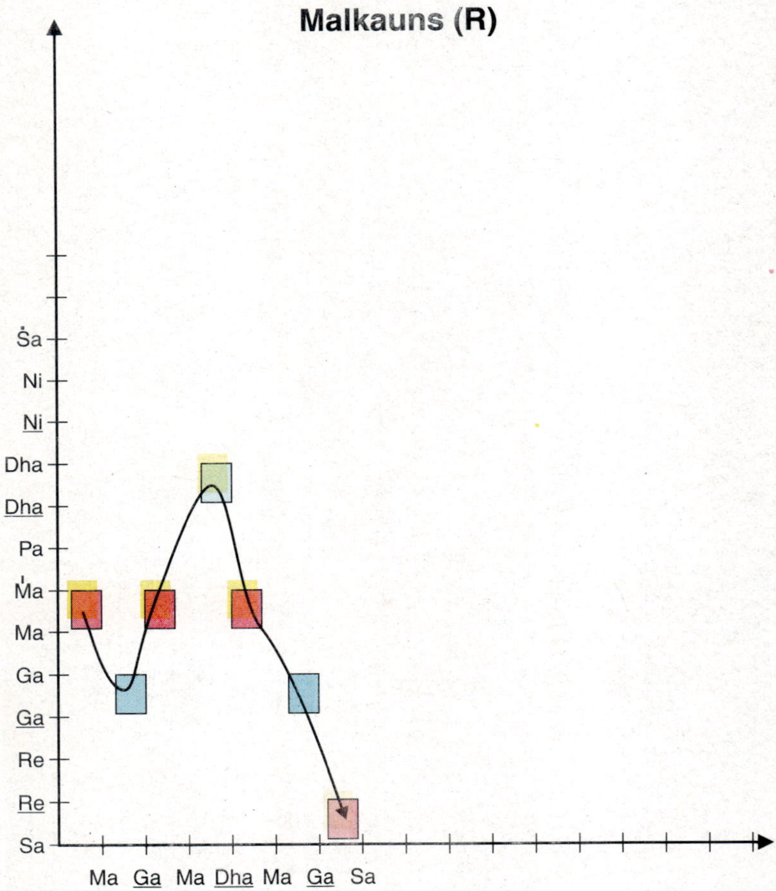
Malkauns (R)
Ṡa
Ni
Ni
Dha
Dha
Pa
Ma
Ma
Ga
Ga
Re
Re
Sa
Ma Ga Ma Dha Ma Ga Sa

GRAPH 7

Malkauns (T.L)

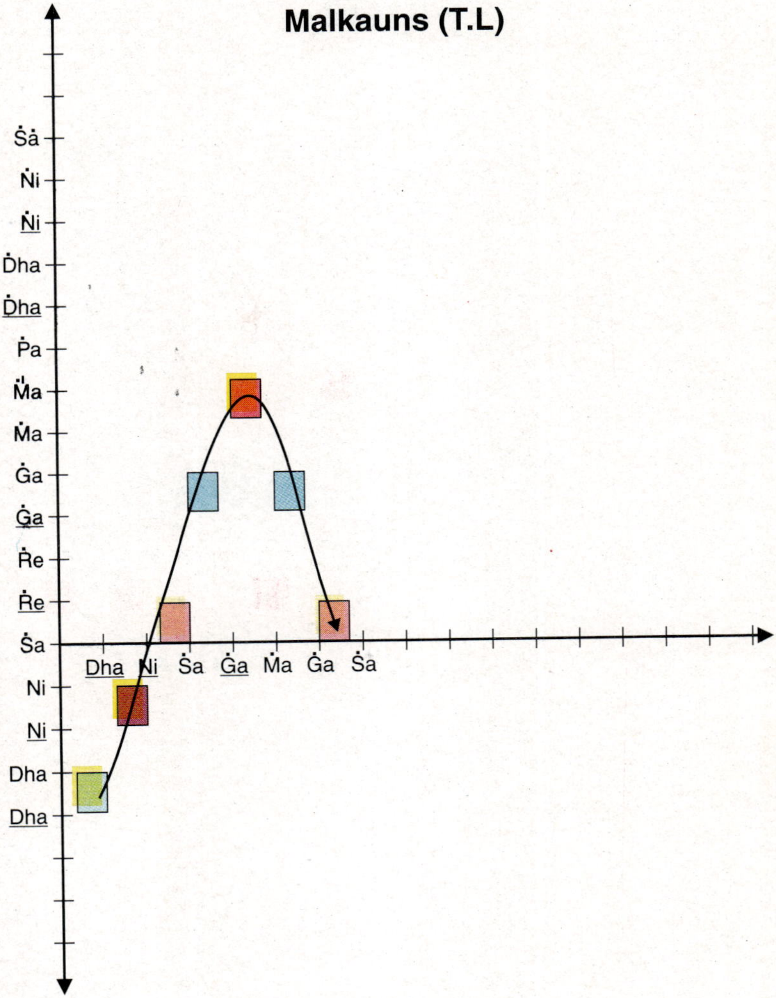

GRAPH 8

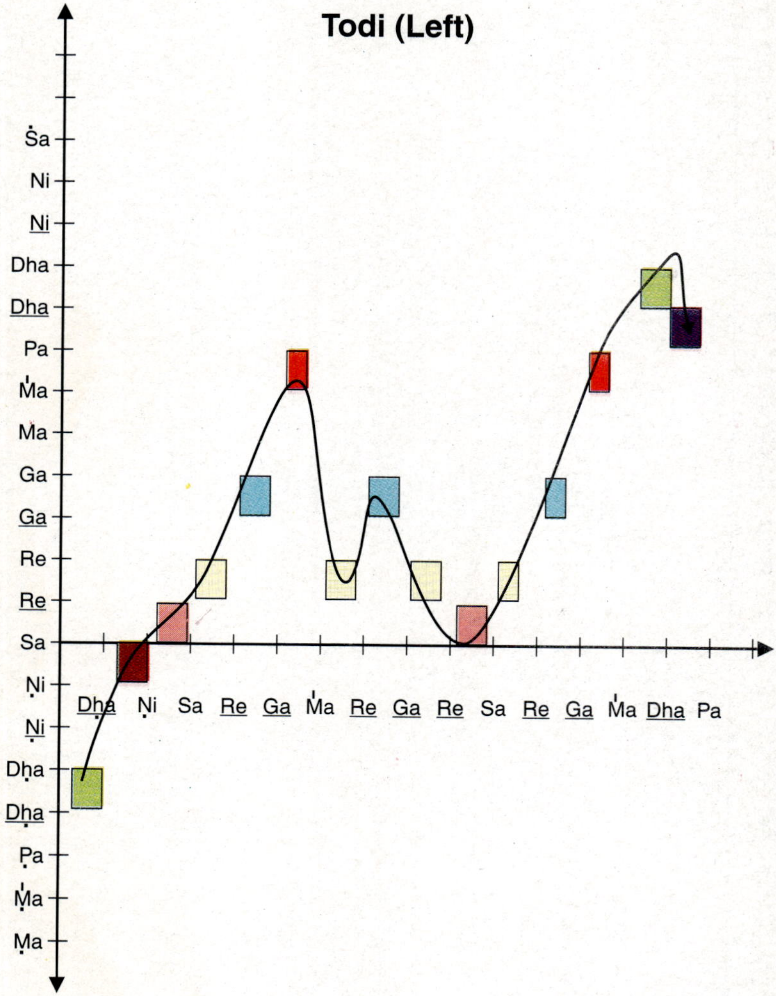
Todi (Left)
Sa
Ni
Ni
Dha
Dha
Pa
Ma
Ma
Ga
Ga
Re
Re
Sa
Ni
Ni
Dha
Dha
Pa
Ma
Ma
Dha Ni Sa Re Ga Ma Re Ga Re Sa Re Ga Ma Dha Pa

GRAPH 9

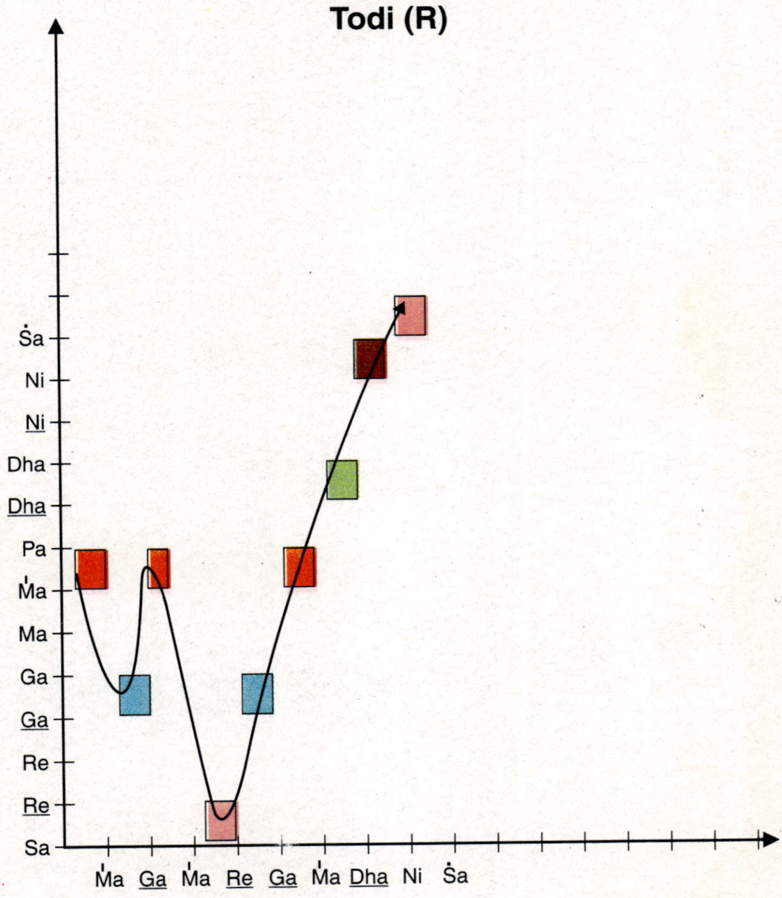
Todi (R)
Ṡa
Ni
Ni
Dha
Dha
Pa
Ma
Ma
Ga
Ga
Re
Re
Sa
Ma Ga Ma Re Ga Ma Dha Ni Ṡa

GRAPH 10

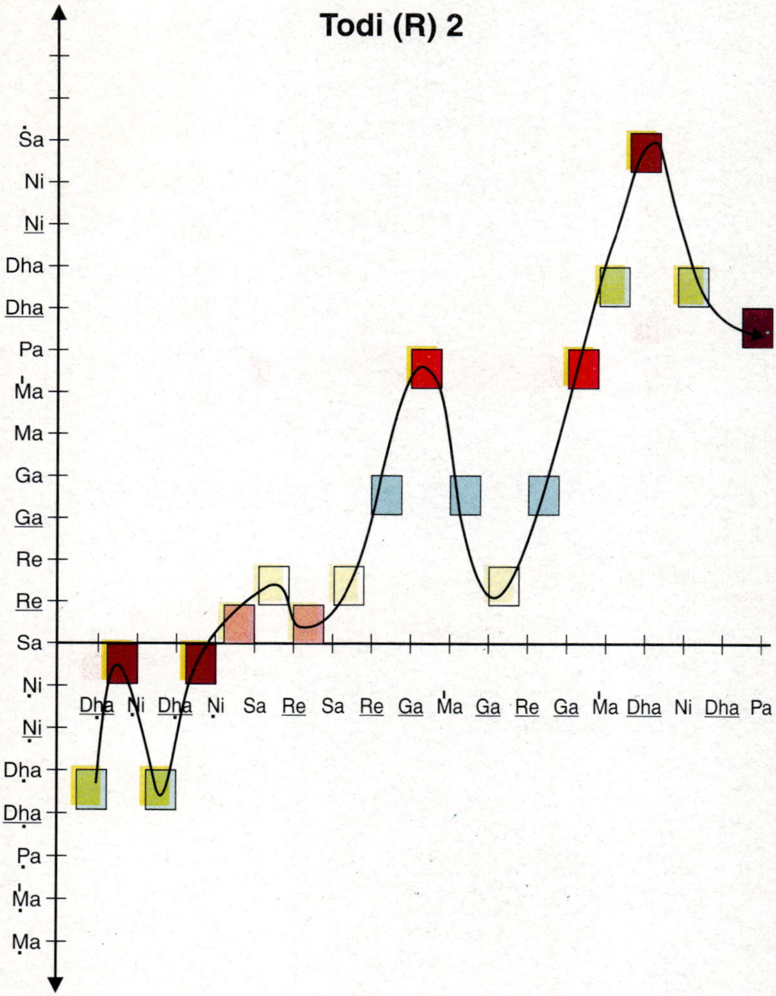
Todi (R) 2
Ṡa
Ni
Ni
Dha
Dha
Pa
Ma
Ma
Ga
Ga
Re
Re
Sa
Ṇi
Ṇi
Dḥa
Dḥa
P̣a
Ṃa
Ṃa
Dḥa Ṇi Dḥa Ṇi Sa Re Sa Re Ga Ma Ga Re Ga Ma Dha Ni Dha Pa

GRAPH 11

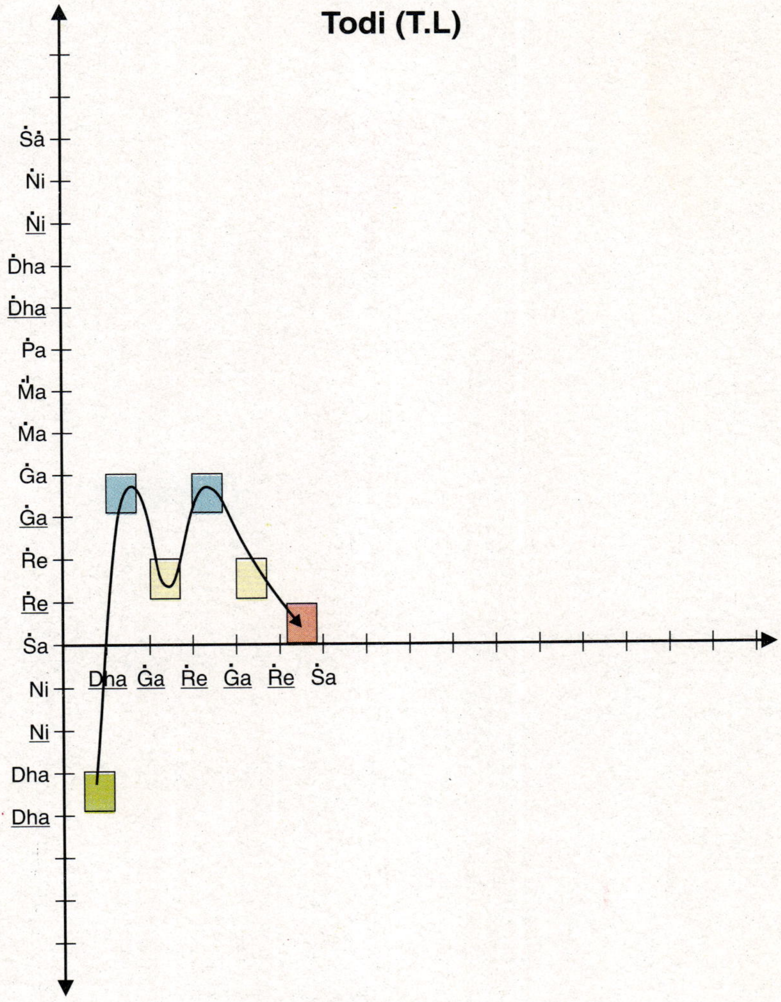
Todi (T.L)
Ṡa
Ṅi
Ṅi
Ḋha
Ḋha
Ṗa
Ṁa
Ṁa
Ġa
Ġa
Ṙe
Ṙe
Ṡa
Ni
Ni
Dha
Dha
Dha Ġa Ṙe Ġa Ṙe Ṡa

GRAPH 12

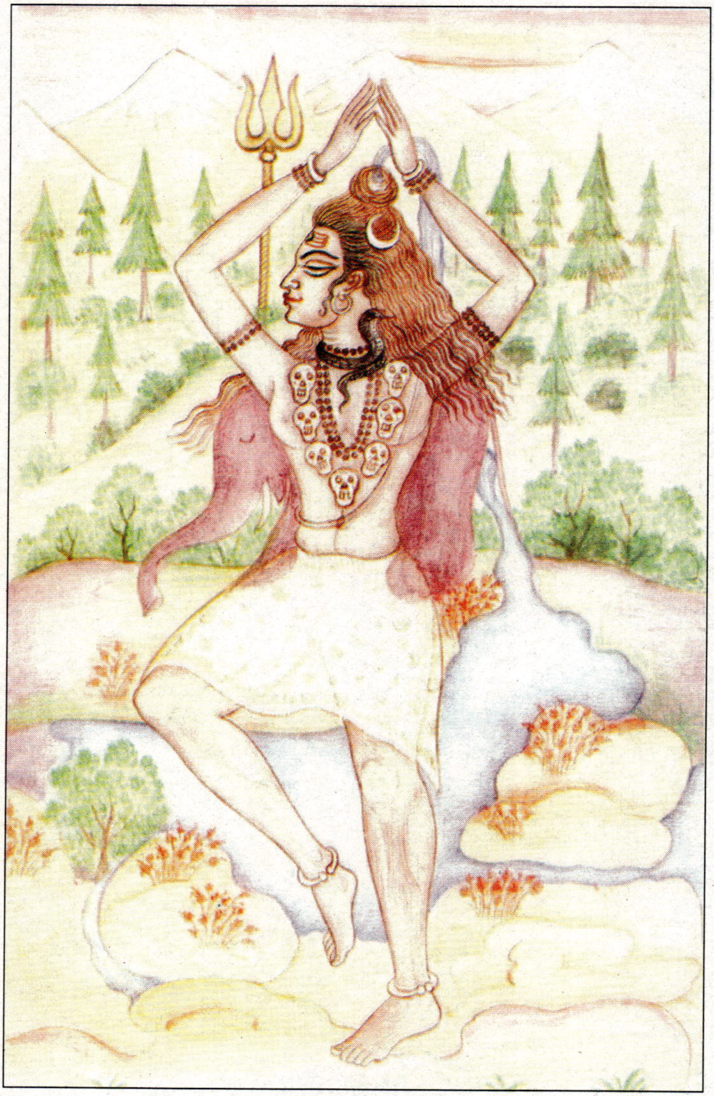

Gaṅgādharah śaśikalātilakastrinetrah
sarpairvi bhuṣitatanurgajakṛttvāsāh /
bhāsvatriśulakara eṣa nṛmuṇḍadhārî
śubhrāṁbarojayāli bhairava ādirāgah //

Bhairava (Pl. A)

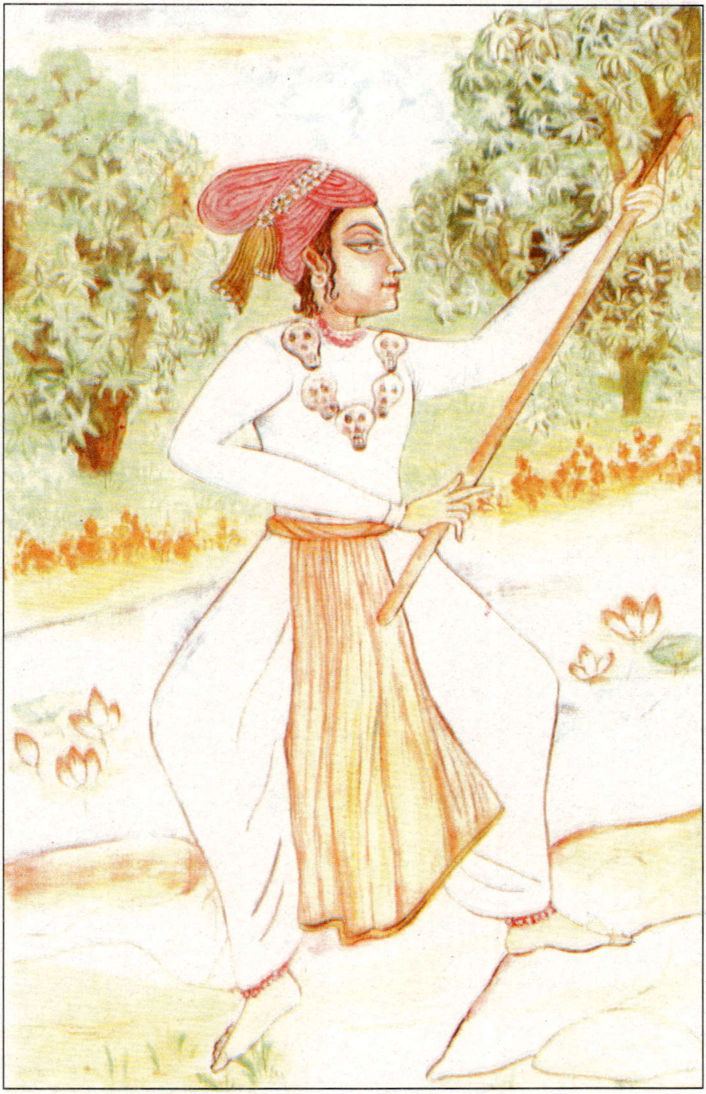

Ārak tavarṇo dhṛtaraktayaṣṭih /
vîrah suvîreṣu kṛtapravîryyah /
vîrairdhṛto vairikapālamālā /
mālî mato mālava kauśiko'yaṁ //

Mālkauns (Pl. B)

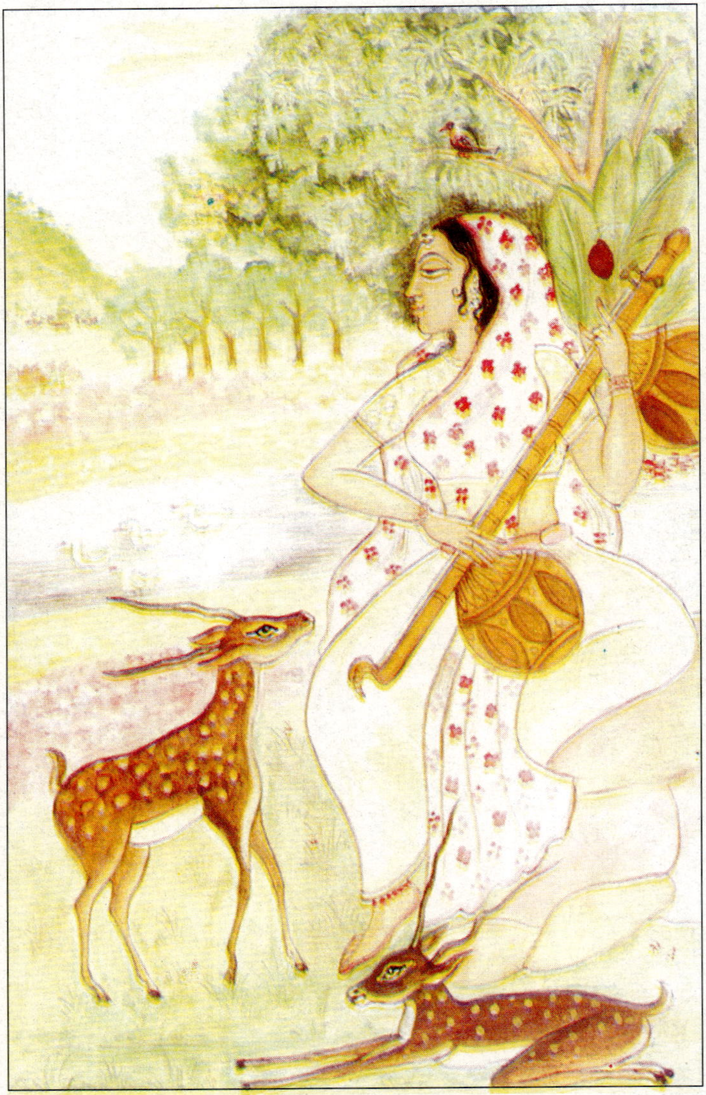

Tuṣāra kuṅdojjwaladehayaṣṭih /
kāśmirakarpuraviliptadehā /
vinodyantî hariṇuṁ vanā ṅte /
viṇādharā rājati toḍikeyaṁ / /

Toḍi (Pl. C)

Conclusion

The Indian traditions of classical music and miniature painting find a common platform for their expression in the form of Rāgamālā paintings. The principle of assimilation of fine arts finds a practical example in these paintings, particularly in the demonstrated paintings given by the researcher. It is not a hybrid art, but the pure art of painting in which music becomes on element. Thus, the primary illusion remains that of virtual space and is not converted into virtual time. The paintings can only be seen and not heard. However, the principle of Synaesthesia comes into play while an attempt is made to grasp the musical phrases depicted in the demonstrated paintings. Therefore, the mutual relationship between the fine arts of music and painting has been established through these paintings. A symbolistic alley has been created for the development of these arts.

To some people, the concept of depicting music through paintings may be farfetched. Say, what is the connection between Lord Śiva with Rāga Bhairava? Here, there is no point in relating any story saying that the Rāga was created by him or any such thing. The connecting factor lies in the sentiments or inherent *rasas* associated with Lord Śiva and Rāga Bhairava. By depicting Lord Śiva in the iconography of Bhairava, the sentiments of *Raudra, Vîra* and *Adbhut* typifying the solemn (traditionally masculine) nature of the Rāga are presented. Similarly, *ṣṛngāric* or erotic ethos is also achieved by the depiction of Kṛṣña and Gopis in the form of Nāyaka and Nāyikās. The arts of music and painting are based largely on imagination. With changing perceptions, the arts are also affected. Thus, the gender based Rāga-Rāginî system gave way to Ṭhāṭ and Rāgānga systems of classification in Indian classical music. Still, in present day classical Indian music, the principle feeling of a particular Rāga should be given due importance. Many Rāgas have similar notes and basic melodic structure but the ethos is different. For instance, Bhairava and Kalingadā, or Kānhḍā and Aḍānā. Here it should also be noted that the ancient structure of the Rāgas has also undergone a sea of change. Some Rāgas which were originally referred to as Rāginîs have achieved a masculine character in modern times. For example, Kānhaḍā has been referred to as a Rāginî of Rāga Deepak according to *Hanumanmat*. However, its present day structure is very solemn and powerful. It is even referred to as a *mardānā* or masculine Rāga. In the demonstrative paintings, the modern structure has been shown which is also compatible with the ancient counter part. Only those Rāgas have been taken into consideration whose iconography has remained constant and the inherent rasa is also the same. The Rāgas Bhairava, Mālkauns and Toḍi continue to have similar ethos as their ancient counter parts as conveyed through paintings. Bhairāva and Mālkauns have a masculine disposition and Toḍi has a feminine delicacy in their practical rendition also in their present form.

In the depiction of notes through paintings, there are certain limits beyond which music cannot be shown. Only certain phrases can be depicted characterstic of the Rāgas. It cannot be called a direct interpretation of concert music. The practical utility of these paintings can be as an aid to the learning process in intial stages. They can be inclucated in the teaching curriculum as a novel and interesting method, particularly to give a glimpse of the generic Rāgas of the ten ṭhāṭs, two of which (Bhairāva and Toḍi) have been given in the present thesis. It is hoped that the researcher has succeeded in bringing the concept of Rāgamālā paintings closer to practical music.

Appendix - I

Table 4
Differentiation of the Fine Arts

(a)

S.No.	*Music*	*Painting*
1.	Illusion of Virtual time	Illusion of Virtual Space (Scene)
2.	Medium (organic) of voice or instrument	Medium (inorganic) of paints or brushes
3.	Audible perception	Visible perception
4.	Element of imagination in greater proportion	Element of symbolic representation in greater proportion
5.	Occurent art (to be perceived during process of creation)	Plastic art (Perceived after process of creation)
6.	Elements peculiar to music-rhythm, notes and words	Elements peculiar to painting — colourful motifs. Also, the six elements — Rupa Bheda etc.

(b)

S.No.	*Music*	*Poesis*
1.	Illusion of Virtual time	Illusion of virtual life or history (also related to time but mostly in the past)
2.	Audible perception	Audible/audio visual perception
3.	Elements peculiar to music apart from words in vocal-rhythm and notes (Images and symbols are expressed through rhythm and notes)	Elements peculiar to poesis-words. (Word bound images and symbols)

(c)

S.No.	*Painting*	*Poesis*
1.	Illusion of Virtual space (scene)	Illusion of Virtual life (history)
2.	Visible perception	Audible, audio visual perception
3.	Plastic art	Occurent art
4.	Medium of paints or brushes	Medium of voice or pen
5.	Elements of symbolic representation in greater proportion	Element of imagination in greater proportion
6.	Elements peculiar to painting—colourful motifs. Also the six elements—Rupa bheda etc.	Elements peculiar to poesis—words (word bound images and symbols) Except three of the six elements of Painting—Bhāva, Pramān and lāvanya Yojanam, the others are absent

(d)

S.No.	*Painting*	*Sculpture*
1.	Illusion of 2-dimensional virtual space (abstraction of scene)	Illusion of 3-dimentional virtual space (abstraction of virtual kinetic volume)
2.	Surrounding environment not related to the painting	The work of sculpture is in harmony with the environment as an actual living form.
3.	Medium—Paints and brushes	Medium-stone, metal, wood etc.

(e)

S.No.	*Painting*	*Architecture*
1.	Illusion of 2-dimensional virtual space (scene)	Illusion of 3-dimensional virtual space (abstraction of virtual domain-place)
2.	Surrounding environment not related to painting	Surrounding environment becomes an extension of the work of architecture
3.	Medium—Paints, burshes	Medium-stone, bricks, cement etc.

(f)

S.No.	*Sculpture*	*Architecture*
1.	Abstraction of virtual kinetic volume in virtual space	Abstraction of virtual domain in virtual space.
2.	Surrounding environment and the work of sculpture are in harmony with each other	Surrounding environment becomes an extension of the work of architecture

(g)

S.No.	*Poesis*	*Sculpture*
1.	Illusion of Virtual life (history)	Illusion of Virtual space (abstraction of virtual kinetic volume)
2.	Audible/Audio-visual perception	Visible perception
3.	Occurrent art	Plastic art
4.	Medium-voice or pen	Medium-stone, wood, metal
5.	Element of imagination in greater proportion	Element of symbloic represetation in greater proportion.
6.	Image in an element—the words are image bound	The total form acts as an image

(h)

S.No.	*Poesis*	*Architecture*
1.	Illusion of Virtual life (history)	Illusion of Virtual space (abstraction of virtual kinetic volume)
2.	Audible/audio-visual perception	Visible perception
3.	Occurrent art	Plastic art
4.	Medium-voice or pen	Medium-stone, bricks, cement etc.
5.	Element of imagination in greater proportion	Element of symbolic representation in greater proportion.
6.	Image is an element—the words are image bound	The total form acts as an image

(i)

S.No.	*Music*	*Sculpture*
1.	Illusion of Virtual time	Illusion of Virtual space (Abstraction of virtual kinetic volume)
2.	Audible perception	Visible perception
3.	Occurent art	Plastic art
4.	Medium-voice or instrument	Medium-stone, wood, metal
5.	Element of imagination in greater proportion	Element of symbolic representation in greater proportion.

(j)

S.No.	*Music*	*Architecture*
1.	Illusion of Virtual time	Illusion of Virtual 3-dimensional space
2.	Medium (organic) of voice or instrument	stone, bricks or cement
3.	Audible perception	Visible perception
4.	Element of imagination in greater proportion	Element of symbolic representation in greater proportion
5.	Occurent art (to be perceived during process of creation)	Plastic art (Perceived after process of creation)
6.	Elements peculiar to music-rhythm, notes and words	Elements peculiar to painting—colourful motifs. Also, the six elements —Rupa Bheda etc.

Table 5
Murchanās in Nāṭya Śāstra

(a) Sa Scale

S.No.	*Murchanā*	*Order of Notes*
1.	Uttaramandrā	Sa ni dha pa ma ga ri
2.	Rajani	Ni dha pa ma ga ri sa
3.	Uttarāyatā	Dha pa ma ga ri sa ni
4.	Śuddha Ṣadja	Pa ma ga ri sa ni dha
5.	Aśvakrāntā	Ga ri sa ni dha pa ma
6.	Abhirudgatā	Ri sa ni dha pa ma ga

(b) Ma Scale

S.No.	Murchanā	Order of Notes
1.	Sauvîrî	Ma ga ri sa ni dha pa
2.	Harināśva	Ga ri sa ni dha pa ma
3.	Kalopanatā	Ri sa ni dha pa ma ga
4.	Śuddha madhyamā	Sa ni dha pa ma ga ri
5.	Mārgî	Ni dha pa ma ga ri sa
6.	Pauravî	Dha pa ma ga ri sa ni
7.	Hṛṣyakā	Pa ma ga ri sa ni dha

Table 6
Modified Notes (svara sādhāraṇa) of Bharata

No. of Śruti	Pure Note	Modified Note
1		
2		Kākalî niṣāda
3		
4	ṣadja	
5		
6		
7	ṛṣabha	
8		
9	gāndhār	
10		
11		antara gāndhār
12		
13	madhyama	
14		
15		
16		
17	pancama	
18		
19		
20	dhaivata	
21		
22	niṣāda	

Table 7
Grāma Rāgas of Mataṅga and their Bhāṣās—Vibhāṣās

Grāma Rāga	*Bhāṣā*	*Vibhāṣā*
1. Ṭakka Rāga	Travaṇā, travaṇodhabhavā, veranjikā, chevāṭi, mālavesarikā, gurjarî, saurāṣṭri, saindhavi, vesarî pancamî, ravicandrā. ambāharî lalitā, kolāhalî, madyamagrāmadehā, gāndhārpancamî (16)	Pota (1)
2. Mālavakaiśika	Śuddhā, ardhavesarikā, harṣapuri, māngālî, saindhavi (?) ābhirî, khanjari, gurjarî(?) (8)	
3. Kakubha	Kāmbojā madhyamagrāmikā śatavāhanikā, bhogavardhani, muharî, śakamiśritā, bhinnapancami (7)	
4. Hindolaka	Vesari, manjari, chevāṭi (?) ṣaḍjamadhyamā, madhurî (5)	
5. Pañcama	Ābhîrî, bhāvinî, māṅgalî (?) tānodbhavā, trāvanî, kaiśiki (6)	Saindhavi, gujarî dakṣinātyā āndhāli (4)
6. Bhinnaṣaḍja	Viśuddha, dāksinātyā (?) gāndhārî paurālî, māngālî (?), saindhavî (?) Kālingî (77)	śrikaṇṭhi, pulindi (2) (antara bhāṣā)
7. Samvîraka	Sauvîrî, vega-madhyamā, sādhāritā gāndhāri (?) (4)	
8. Bhinnapancama-	Śuddha bhinnā, vārāṭî, viśālā (3)	dhaivatabhu-ṣitā (1)
9. Boṭṭa rāga	māngāli (Bāngāli) (?) (1)	
10. Mālavapancama	Bhāvinî (1)	
11. Takkakaiśika	Mālava, ḅhinnavālikā, drāviḍi (3)	
12. Vesaraṣāḍava	Bāhyaṣāḍavā, nādākhyā (2)	
13. Bhinnatāna	Tānodbhavā (1)	
14. Gāndhāra--pancama	Gānadhārikā (1)	
15. Pancamaṣāḍava	Śakākhyā (1)	

Table 8
Classification of Rāgas in Sangît Makaranda

(a) Musculine, Feminine and Neuter Rāgas

S.No.	*Masculine (20)*	*Feminine (24)*	*Neuter (13)*
1.	Bangāla	Tuṅḍi	Kaiśiki
2.	Soma	Turuṣka tunḍi	Lalita
3.	Shri	Malvāri	Dhannāśî
4.	Bhupāli	Māhuri	Kurañjikā
5.	Chāyā Gouḍa	Pourāliki	Sourāṣṭri
6.	Śuddha Hindolikā	Kāmbhāri	Drāvaḍi
7.	Āndolî	Bhallāti	Nāga Varātikā
8.	Dombulî	Saindhavi	Kāmodiki
9.	Gouḍa	Sālaṅga	Rāmakri
10.	Karṅātaka	Gāndhāri	Sāveri
11.	Phada mañjî	Devakri	Balhansa
12.	Śuddha Nātî	Deshinî	Sāmvedi
13.	Mālava gaulaka	Velāvali	Śaṅkarā bharaṇa
14.	Chāyā Nāṭî	Bahuli	
15.	Kolāhala	Gunḍakri	
16.	Sourāṣṭrî	Ghurjari	
17.	Vasaṅta	Varāti	
18.	Śuddha Sāraṅga	Drāvaḍi	
19.	Bhairavi	Haṅsi	
20.	Rāga dhvani	Gouḍi	
21.		Nārāyaṇî	
22.		Aharî	
23.		Megharañjî	
24.		Mishra Nāṭa	

(b) 8 Main, 23 Yośita or Stri Rāgas

S.No.	*Main Rāga*	*Yosita Rāga*
1.	Bhupāla	Velāvāli, Malhari, Bahuli
2.	Bhairava	Devakriya, Pourāli, Kāmbhāri
3.	Śri	Kāmbhoji, Bhallāti, Kuranjikā
4.	Phaḍmañjari	Deshi, Manohari, Tunḍi
5.	Nāṭa	Sāraṅganāṭā, Ahari
6.	Bangāla	Nārāyaṇî, Gāndhāri, Rañjî
7.	Vasanta	Parātî, Dravaḍî, Haṅsî
8.	Mālava	Guṅḍakriya, Ghurjarî, Gouḍi

(c) 6 Main, 36 Uparāgas

S.No.	*Main Rāga*	*Uparāga*
1.	Sri	Kolāhali, Drāvali, Āndoliki, Mādhavi, Devagāndhāri
2.	Pañcama	Śuddha Nāta, Sāveri, Saindhavi, Mālati, Troti, Kāmodiki
3.	Megha	Sourashtrî, Kāmbhāri, bangāli, Madhumādhavi, Devakri Bhupāli
4.	Nāṭanārāyaṇa	Vallabhā, Mādhavi, Vidigdhā, Abhisārikā, Triveni, Megharñji
5.	Vasanta	(79 sl. missing)
6.	Bhairava	

(d) Classification of Rāgas According to Time of Singing

	Suryānsa Rāgas	*Noon Rāgas*	*Candramaṅśa Rāgas*
1.	Gandhāra	Śankarābharaṇa	Śuddha Nāṭa
2.	Deva Gandhāra	Poorva	Sālag Nāṭā
3.	Dhannasi	Balahaṁsa	Śuddha Varātikā
4.	Saindhavi	Deśî	Goula
5.	Nārāyaṇî	Manohari	Mālava Gouḍâ
6.	Gurjari	Sāveri	Śri
7.	Bangāla	Dombuli	Ahari
8.	Pala (ta) Manjari	Kāmbhoji	Rāmakriti
9.	Lalita	Gopi Kāmbhoji	Ranji
10.	Andola Srika	Kaiśiki	Cāya
11.	Souraṣtreya	Madhu Mādhavi	Sarva Varātikā
12.	Jayasākṣika	Bahuli	Varātikā
13.	Malhāra	Mukhāri	Drāvatikā
14.	Sāmavedi	Mangala Kauśikā	Deśî
15.	Vasanta		Nāga Varātikā
16.	Śuddha Bhairava		Karnāta
17.	Velāvali		Gouḍî
18.	Bhupāla		
19.	Soma		

Table 9
Twelve Modified or 'Vikrita' Notes of Śārṅgadeva

S.No.	*Śruti*	*Pure Note*	*Modified Note*	*(extent)*
1.	Tîvrā			
2.	Kumudvatî			
3.	Mandā		cyuta ṣadja (sādhāraṇa)	(2-3)
4.	Chan dovati	ṣadja	acyuta ṣadja	(3-4)
5.	Dayāvatî			
6.	Rañjani			
7.	Raktikā	ṛṣabha	catuhśruti ṛṣabha	(4-7)
8.	Raudrî			
9.	Krodhā	gāndhāra		
10.	Vajrikā		triśruti gāndhāra	(8-10)
11.	Prasārinî		catuhśruti (antara gāndhara)	(8-11)
12.	Prîti		cyuta madhyama	(11-12)
13.	Mārjanî	madhyama	acyuta madhyama	(12-13)
14.	Kṣiti			
15.	Raktā			
16.	Sandîpanî		triśruti (kaiśika) pañcama	(14-16)
			catuhśruti pañcama (madhyama sādhāraṇa)	(13-16)
17.	Ālāpinî	pañcama		
18.	Madantî			
19.	Rohinî			
20.	Ramyā	dhaivata	catuhśruti dhiavata	(17-20)
21.	Ugrā			
22.	Kṣobhinî	niṣāda		
1.	Tîvrā		triśruti (kaiśika) niṣāda	(21-1)
2.	Kumudvatî		catuhśruti (kākali) niṣāda	(21-2)

Table 10
The Śruti Classes and Distribution of Śrutis among Notes According to Śārngadeva

Svara or	*Śruti Class*				
Notes	*Dîptā*	*Ayatā*	*Mṛdu*	*Madhyā*	*Karuṇā*
Ṣadja	tîvrā (1)	kumudvatî (2)	mandā (3)	chandovati (4)	
Ṛṣabha			raktikā (3)	ranjani (2)	dayāvati (1)
Gāndhāra	raudrî (1)	krodhā (2)			
Madhyama	vajrikā (1)	prasāriṇi (2)	prîti (3)	mārjanî (4)	
Pañcama		sandîpanî (3)	kṣiti (1)	rakta (2)	ālāpinî (4)
Dhaivata		rohinî (2)		ramyā (3)	Madantî (1)
Niṣāda	ugrā (1)			kṣobhinî (2)	

Table 11
Murchanās of the Two Grāmas According to Śārṅgadeva

Ṣadja			*Madhyama*		
No.	*Name*	*Order of Notes*	*No.*	*Name*	*Order of Notes*
1.	Uttaramandrā	sa ri ga ma pa dha ni sa ni dha pa ma ga ri	1	Sauvirî	ma pa dha ni sa ri ga ma ga ri sa ni dha pa
2.	Rajani	ni sa ri ga ma pa dha ni dha pa ma ga ri sa	2.	Hariṇāśvā	ga ma pa dha ni sa ri ga ri sa ni dha pa ma
3.	Uttarāyatā	dha ni sa ri ga ma pa dha pa ma ga re sa ni	3.	Kalopnatā	ri ga ma pa dha ni sa ri sa ni dha pa ma ga
4.	Śuddha ṣaḍjā	pa dha ni sa ri ga ma pa ma ga ri sa ni dha	4.	Śuddha madhyā	sa ri ga ma pa dha ni sa ni dha pa ma ga ri
5.	Matsarikṛtā	ma pa dha ni sa ri ga ma ga ri sa ni dha pa	5.	Mārgî	ni sa ri ga ma pa dha ni dha pa ma ga re sa
6.	Aśvakrāntā	ga ma pa dha ni sa ri ga ri sa ni dha pa ma	6.	Pauravî	dha ni sa ri ga ma pa dha pa ma ga ri sa ni
7.	Abhirudgatā	ri ga ma pa dha ni sa ri sa ni dha pa ma ga	7.	Hṛṣyakā	pa dha ni sa ri ga ma pa ma ga ri sa ni dha

Table 12
Lineage, Caste, Colour, Tones of Birds or Animals, Deity, Rasa, Sages and Metre of Notes as Given by Śārṅgadeva

S.No.	*Note*	*Relative Tone of Bird or Animal*	*Sentiment*	*Colour*	*Caste*	*Family*	*Deity*	*Sage*	*Chanda*
1.	Ṣaḍja	Peacock	Herosm,	Red	Brāhmin	Devtā	Agni	Agni	Anuṣṭupa
2.	Ṛṣabha	Ox or chātaka	Herosm,	Plae Yellow	Kṣatriya	Ṛṣi	Brahma	Brahma	Gāyātri
3.	Gāndhāra	Goat	Compassion	Golden Yellow	Vaiśya	Devta	Saraswati	Candramā	Triṣṭupa
4.	Madhyama	Crane	Humour & Love	Sparkling White	Brāhmin	Devta	Mahādeva	Viṣṇu	Bṛhati
5.	Pañcama	Nightingale	Humour & Love	black	Brāhmin	Pitṛ	Lakṣmipati	Nārada	Pañkti
6.	Dhaivata	Frog	Disgust, Alaram	Plain Yellow	Kṣatriya	Ṛṣi	Gaṇesha	Tumburu	Uṣṇika
7.	Niṣāda	Elephant	Compassion	Variegated	Vaiśya	Asura	Surya	Tumburu	Jagati

Table 13
The Grāma Rāgas of Śārṅgadeva

S.No.	*Svarāśrita Gîti*	*Number of Constituent Rāgas*	*Grāma Rāgas*
1.	Śuddhā	(7)	Śuddha kaiśika madhyama, śuddha sādhārita, ṣaḍja grāma (from S.G.*), *pañcama,* madhyama grāma, ṣāḍeva and śuddha kaishika (from M.G.**)
2.	Bhinna	(5)	Kaiśika madhyama, *bhinna ṣaḍja* (from S.G.) *tāna,* kaiśika and *bhinna pañcama* (from M.G.)
3.	Gauḍi	(3)	Gouḍa kaiśika madhyama, gauḍapañcama gauḍa kaiśika (from M.G.)
4.	Vesarā	(8)	*Takka, Vesara ṣāḍava, sauvira* (S.G.), *boṭṭa, mālavā kaiśika, mālava pañcama* (M.G.), *ṭakka kaiśika* & *hinḍola* (B.Gs).***
5.	Sādhāraṇî	(7)	Rupa sādhāra, śaka, bhammāṇa pañcama (S.G.), narta, *gāndhārapañcama,* ṣaḍja kaiśika (M.G.), *kakubha* (B.Gs).

Note: (Underlined are parent Rāgas of bhāṣās, vibhāsas and antara bhāṣās. Two other parent Rāgas are uparāgas—revagupta and ṣāḍava pañcama)

* S.G. — Ṣaḍja Grāma
** M.G. — Madhyama Grāma
*** B.Gs — Bodh Grāmas

Table 14
The Tenfold Classification of Rāgas by Śārṅgadeva

S.No.	*Category*	*No.*			
1.	Grāmarāgas	30	(in first section) 178		
2.	Uparāgas	8			
3.	Rāgas 20				
4.	Bhāṣā rāgas	96			
5.	Vibhāṣa rāgas	20			
6.	Antrabhāṣās	4			
Popular in Ancient Period				Popular in Śārṅgadeva's Period	
7.	Rāgāṅgas	8	34 (in 2nd section)	13	52
8.	Bhāṣāṅgas	11		9	
9.	Kriyāṅgas	12		3	
10.	Upāṅgas	3		27	
	Total 264				

Table 15
Rāgas and Rāginîs According to Saṅgîtopaniṣatsāroddhāra of Sudhākalaśa (14th Century A.D.)

S.No.	*Rāga*	*Bhāṣā*
1.	Śri	Gauḍi, Kolāhala, Āndhālî, *Dravaḍi*, Mālavakaiśiki, Devagandhāri
2.	Vasant	Āndola, Kauśiki, Prathama manjarî, Gunḍagiri, Devaśākhā, *Rāmgri*
3.	Bhairava	Bhairavi, Gurjari, *Bhāṣā*, Velāvali, Karnāti, Raktahansā
4.	Pañcama	Triguṇā Stambhātîrthî, *Ābhirî*, *Kukubhā*, Vairādî, Sābherî
5.	Megha	Bangālā, Madhurā, Kāmodā, Cokśasāṭikā Devagiri, *Devālā*
6.	Naṭnārāyaṇa	Toṭikā, Moṭikā, Naṭa, Dumbi, Malhārî, Sindhu Malhāri

Table 16
Rāgas Derived from Twelve Samsthānas of Locana

S.No.	*Samsthāna*	*Derived Rāgas*
1.	Bhairavi	Bhairavi, nilāmbari
2.	Todî	Toḍî
3.	Gaurî	Malava, śrigaurî, caitîgaurî, pahāḍi gaurî, deśi toṭî, deśakārî, gaurā, trivaṇa, multāni, dhanāśri, basanta, bhairava, vibhāsa, rāmakali, gurjari, bahulî, revā, bhātiyāra, khaṭa, mālavapañcama, jayataśrî, āsāvarî, devagāndhāra, sindhiāsāvari, guṇakri.
4.	Karṇāṭa	Karṇāṭa, bāgîśvari, khammāca, soraṭha, paraja, māru, jaijaivantî, kukubha, kāmoda, kedāra, mālavakauśika, hinḍola, sugharai, aḍānā, gāra, kānharā, śri rāga.
5.	Kedāra	Kedāra nāṭa, ābhiranāṭa, khambāvati, śaṅkarābharaṇa, bihāgaḍa, hammira, śyāma, chhāyānaṭa, bhupāli, bhimapalāsi, kauśika, māru.
6.	Îman	Îman, śuddha kalyāṇa, puriyā, jayata kalyāṇa.
7.	Sāraṅga	Sāraṅga, paṭamanjari, brindāvani, sāmantasāraṅga, badhansa.
8.	Dhanāśri	Lalita
9.	Purvā	Purvā
10.	Mukhāri	Mukhāri
11.	Megha	Megha mallāra, gauḍa sāranga, bilāvala, alhayyā, śuddha suhava, desa, śuddha nāḍa
12.	Dipaka	None

Table 17
Rāga-Rāginîs of Locana

	Masculine Rāga	*Rāginîs*
1.	Bhairava	Bangāli, Madhumādhavi, Varāḍi, Bhairavi, Sindhu
2.	Kauśika	Toḍi, Khambāvati, Gauri, Kakubha, Guṇkarî
3.	Hinḍol	Velāvali, Deṣākha, Rāmakari, Lalitā, Paṭamanjari
4.	Dîpaka	Kedāra, Kānharā, Deśi, Kāmoda, Bihāgara
5.	Śrî	Vasanta, Mālava, Mālasiri, Dhanāsiri, Asāvari
6.	Megha	Malāri, Deśikā, Bhupāli, Taka, Dakṣiṅagurjari.

Table 18
Modified Notes of Locana

S.No.		Pure Note	Modified Note
1.			
2.			
3.			
4.	Chandovati	Sa	
5.			
6.			Komal Re
7.	Rattika	Re	
8.			
9.	Krodhi	Ga	
10.			Tivra ga
11.			Tivaratara Ga
12.			Tivratama Ga
13.	Mārjani	Ma	Atitivratama Ga
14.			
15.			Tivratara ma
16.			
17.	Ālāpini	Pa	
18.			
19.			Komal Dha
20.	Ramyā	Dha	
21.			
22.	Kṣobhini	Ni	
1.	Tivra Ni		
2.	Tivratara Ni = Kākali Ni		
3.	Tivratama Ni		

Table 19
Rāmāmātyas Notes

S.No.	*Pure Note*	*Modified Note*	
1.		Kaiśika ni (ṣaṭśruti dha)	
2.		Kākali ni	Pratinidhitva
3.		Cyuta ṣaḍja ni	
4.	Ṣaḍja		
5.			
6.			
7.	Ṛṣabha		
8.			
9.	Gāndhāra		
10.		Sādhāraṇa ga (ṣaṭśruti re)	
11.		Antara ga	Partinidhitva
12.		Cyuta ma ga	
13.	Madhyama		
14.			
15.			
16.		Cyuta pañcama ma	
17.	Pañcama		
18.			
19.			
20.	Dhaivata		
21.			
22.	Niṣāda		

(Thus, he has omitted acyuta sȧ, vikrit re, acyuta ma, vikrit pa and vikrit dha of Śārṅgadeva).

Table 20
Rāgamālā of Punḍarîka Viṭṭhala

S.No.	*Rāga*	*Rāginîs*	*Putras*
1.	Śuddha Bhairava	Dhannāsî Bhairavî Saindhavî Māravî, Āsāvarî	Bhairava, Śuddha Lalita Pañcama, Paraj Bangāla
2.	Hinḍol	Bhupālî, Basantî Toḍî, Prathama Manjarî, Turuṣka Toḍî	Basanta Śuddha Bangāla, Śyāma, Sāmanta, Kāmoda
3.	Deśakāra	Rāmakrî, Bahulî Deśi, Jaitśrî, Gurjarî	Lalita, Vibhāsa Sāranga, Trivaṇa, Kalyāṇa
4.	Śrî	Gaunḍî, Pāḍî, Guṇakarî Śuddha Rāmakri, Nāda Rāmakrî, Gunḍakrî	Taṅkka Devagāndhāra Mālava, Śuddha Gauḍa, Karṇātā Bangāla
5.	Śuddha Nāṭa	Mālavaśrî, Deśākśî Devakrî, Madhumādhavî Ahîrî	Jijāvantî Sālaṅganāṭa Karnāta, Chhāyānāṭa Hamîranāṭa
6.	Naṭanārāyaṇa	Belāvalî, Kāmbojî Sāverî, Suhavî Saurāṣṭrî	Malhāra Gauḍa, Kedāra Śaṅkarābharaṇa Vihāgaḍā

Table 21
The Modified Notes of Puṇḍarîka Viṭṭhala

S.No.	*Puṇḍarîka*	*Viṭṭhala's Notes*	*Hindustāni*	*Notes*
1.	Śuddha	Re	Komal	Re
2.	Catuhśrutika	Re	Tîvra	Re
3.	Śuddha	Ga	Tîvra	Re
4.	Sādhāraṇa	Ga	Komal	Ga
5.	Laghu	Ma	Tîvra	Ga
6.	Laghu	Pa	Tîvra	Ma
7.	Śuddha	Dha	Komal	Dha
8.	Catuhśrutika	Dha	Tîvra	Dha
9.	Śuddha	Ni	Tivra	Dha
10.	Kaiśika	Ni	Komal	Ni
11.	Laghu	Sa	Tîvra	Ni

Table 22
Modified Notes of Somnāth

S.No.	Pure Note	Modified Note
1.		Kaiśika Ni
2.		Kākali Ni
3.		Mṛdu Sa
4.	Sa	
5.		
6.		
7.	Re	
8.		Tivra Re (catuhśruti)
9.	Ga	
10.		Sādhāraṇa Ga
11.		Antara Ga
12.		Mṛdu Ma
13.	Ma	
14.		
15.		Tîvratama Ma
16.		Mṛdu Pa
17.	Pa	
18.		
19.		
20.	Dha	
21.		Tîvra Dha (catuhśruti)
22.	Ni	

Table 23
Rāgas and Rāginîs of Usulun Naghmāt-e Āsifi

S.No.	Rāga	Rāginîs
1.	Bhairava	Bhairavî, Rāmakalî, Gujarî, Khaṭa, Gandhāri, Āsāvarî
2.	Mālkauns	Bāgeśwarî, Deśî, Suha, Sugharai, Multānî
3.	Hinḍola	Puriyā, Basanta, Lalita, Pañcama, Dhanāsrî, Mārwā
4.	Śrî	Gaurî, Purvî, Gaurā, Trivin, Mālśrî, Jaitśrî
5.	Megha	Madhmad, Gaud, Śuddha Sāraṅga, Baḍhans, Sāmant, Soraṭh.
6.	Naṭa	Chāyānaṭa, Hamîra, Kalyāṇa, Kedāra, Bihāgaḍā, Yaman.

Table 24
Bharat Mata (6 Rāgas, 30 Rāginîs)

S.No.	*Rāga*	*Rāginîs*
1.	Bhairava	Madhumadhavî, Lalita, Berārî, Bhairavi, Bahuli
2.	Mālkauns	Gaurî, Dayavati*, Toḍî, Khambāvatî, Kukubha
3.	Hindola	Rāmkalî, Mayavati/Mālavî, Āsāvarî, Devarî, Guṇkalî**
4.	Dîpaka	Kedāra, Gaurî, Gauḍa,*** Gurjari, Rudravatî
5.	Śrî	Saindhavî, Kāfî, Thumrî, Vicitra, Sirhati/Sohnî
6.	Megha	Malhara, Sāranga, Desî, Rati Ballabha, Kāverî/ Kānhrā

Each Rāga has eight Putras each and their 8 Bhāryās.
* Vidyavati at some places
** Keki at some places
*** Kāmoda at some places

Table 25
Kallinātha Mata (15th Century A.D.)
(6 Rāgas and 36 Rāginîs)

S.No.	*Rāga*	*Rāginîs*
1.	Śrî	Gaurî, Kolāhal, Dhol/Dhawala, Rudrāni*, Mālkauns Deva Gandhāra.
2.	Basanta	Andoli/Andhyālî, Gamkî, Paṭamajarî, Gauḍkrî, Dhāmkî Devasākha
3.	Bhairava	Bhairavi, Gurjarî, Bhāshā, Bilawalî, Karnāta or Kanhṛā, Raktahansa.
4.	Megha	Bengāli, Madhurā, Kāmod, Dhanāśri, Devatirtha, Devālî
5.	Nata Nārāyana	Tirotki**, Tilangî, Purvî, Rāma, Gāndharî, Sindh Mallerî.
6.	Pāncama	Trivenî, Haṁstantaretahā, Ahîrî, Kokabha, Berārî, Āsāvari

Putras mostly similar to Hanuman Mata (given in table 28B)
* Varirājî at many places
** Trivaṅki at many places

Table 26
Rāgārṇava Mata (14th Century A.D.)
(6 Rāgas and 30 Rāginîs)

S.No.	*Rāga*	*Rāginîs*
1.	Bhairava	Bangālî, Guṇākrî, Madhyamādi, Basanta, Dhanāśrî
2.	Pañcama	Lalita, Gurjarî, Deśî, Varāḍî, Rāmakṛta
3.	Nāṭā	Naṭanāryaṇa, Gāndhāra, Sālaga, Kedāra, Karṅāṭa
4.	Mallāra	Megha, Mallārî, Mālakauśika, Patamañjarî, Āsāvarî
5.	Gauḍa	Hinḍola, Trivaṇa, Āndhārî, Gaurî, Paṭahamsikā
6.	Deśākhya	Bhupālî, Kuḍāî, Kāmodî, Nātikā, Velāvalî

Table 27
Someśvara (or Śiva) Mata (12th Century A.D.)
(6 Rāgas and 36 Raginîs)

S.No.	*Rāga*	*Rāginîs*
1.	Śrî	Malawi,Trivenî, Gaurî, Kedādra, Madhumādhavî, Pahāḍikā
2.	Basanta	Deśî, Devagirî, Varaṭî, Toḍikā, Lalita, Hinḍolî
3.	Pañcama	Vibhāsa, Bhopālî, Karnāṭî,Baḍhans, Mālaśrî, Patmanjarî
4.	Bhairava	Bhairavî, Gurjarî, Rewā*, Guṇakrî, Bengālî, Bahulî.**
5.	Megha	Malhāra, Soraṭha, Sāverî, Kauśikî or Mālkauns, Gāndhāri, Harsingār.
6.	Nata Nārāyana	Kāmod, Kalyāṇa, Ābherî, Natkî, Sāranga, Naṭa Hamîra

Putras mostly similar to Hanuman Mata
* Rāmkalî at some places
** Saindhavî at some places

Table 28
Hanuman Mata

(a) 6 Rāgas and 30 Rāginîs

S.No.	*Rāga*	*Rāginîs*
1.	Bhairava	Madhyamāda, Bhairavî, Barārî, Saindhavî, Bangāla
2.	Mālkauns	Toḍî, Gaurî, Guṇakrî, Khambāvatî, Kakubha
3.	Hinḍola	Verāvara/Velāvalî, Rāmakrî, Deśākhya, Patamanjarî, Lalita
4.	Dîpaka	Kedāra, Kāmoda, Deśî, Naṭa, Kanharā/Karnātî
5.	Śrî	Malaśrî, Marwa/Mālavî, Dhanāśrî, Basanta, Āsāvarî
6.	Megha	Ṭanka, Malhāra, Gurjarî, Bhopālî, Deshkāra.

(b) Rāga and Putras According to Hanuman Mata

S.No.	*Rāga*	*Putras*
1.	Bhairava	Harṣa, Tilaka, Puriyā, Mādhava, Suhu, Balneha, Madha, Pañcama
2.	Mālkauns	Māru, Mewāḍa, Barhansa, Prabal, Candraka, Nanda, Bhanwara, Khokhara/Niṣtanga/Vidhwansa
3.	Hinḍola	Candrabimba, Mangala, Shobha, Ānanda, Vinoda, Pradhāna, Gaura, Vibhasa/Śukra
4.	Dîpaka	Kuntala, Kanwala/Kamala, Kalinga/Kalindra, Campaka, Kusumbha/kusuma, Rāma, Lāhila, Himala.
5.	Śrî	Sindhu, Mālava, Gaunḍa/Kalyāṇa or Hamira, Guṇasāgara, Kumbha, Gambhîra, Śankara/Angada/Angata, Bhagra/Bigad//Vikaṭa
6.	Megha	Jālandhara, Sāranga, Naṭa Nārāyaṇa, Śaṅarābharaṇa, Kalyāṇa, Gajadhara, Gandhāra, Śahānā.

Table 30(a)
A.K. Coomarswamy's Classification of Indian Paintings

	Painting	*Region*		
1.	Hindu	Rājput	Rājasthānî	
			Pahāri	Jammu (now given place to Basohli style) Kangra, Garhwal
			Sikh	
		Dravidian (Deccan)		
2.	Buddhist*	Nepalese (also Indian Tibet)		
		Sin Halese (Kandy)		
3.	Jain	Gujarat, Kathiawar, Sravana Belgola		
4.	Eclectic	Mughal	Lahore, Agra, Delhi, Oudh, Patna	

* The author has included Ajantā and Pāla schools in this category.

Table 30(b)
Modified Version of Coomarswamy's Classification (with emphasis on Rāgamālā Schools)

Painting	*School*	*Style*	*Sub-school*
1. Hindu	Rājput	Rājasthānî	Mewār, Mārwār, Ḍhunḍhāda, Hāḍauti
		Pahāri	Basohli and Kullu Kangra and Guler
	Deccan		Bijapur, Ahmadnagar, Golconda
2. Buddhist	Ajantā Pāla		
3. Jain	Western India		
4. Eclectic	Mughal Modern		

Appendix-II

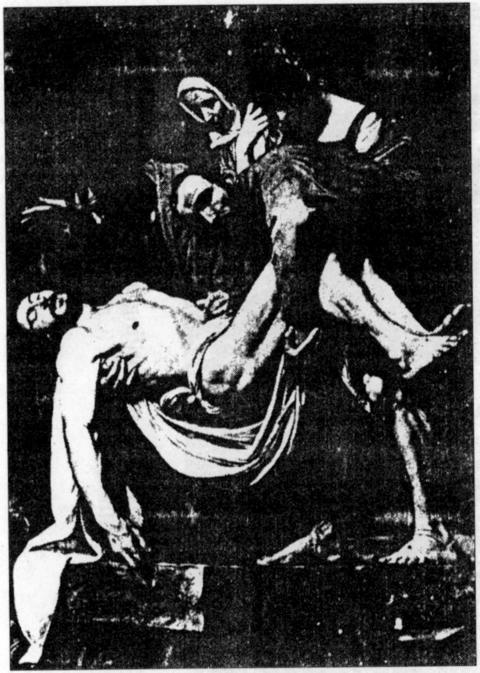

Painting by Italian Artist Michelangelo da Caravaggio (1573-1610) showing the Burial of Christ.

Plate 1(a)

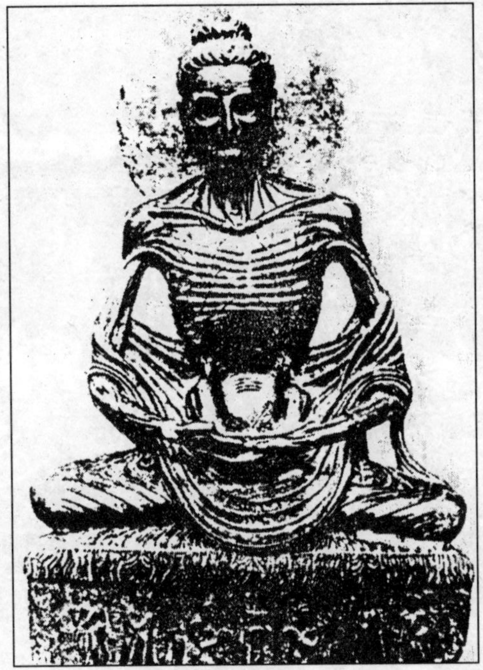

Sculpture from Gandhar showing the Shriveled Body of an Ascetic.

Plate 1(b)

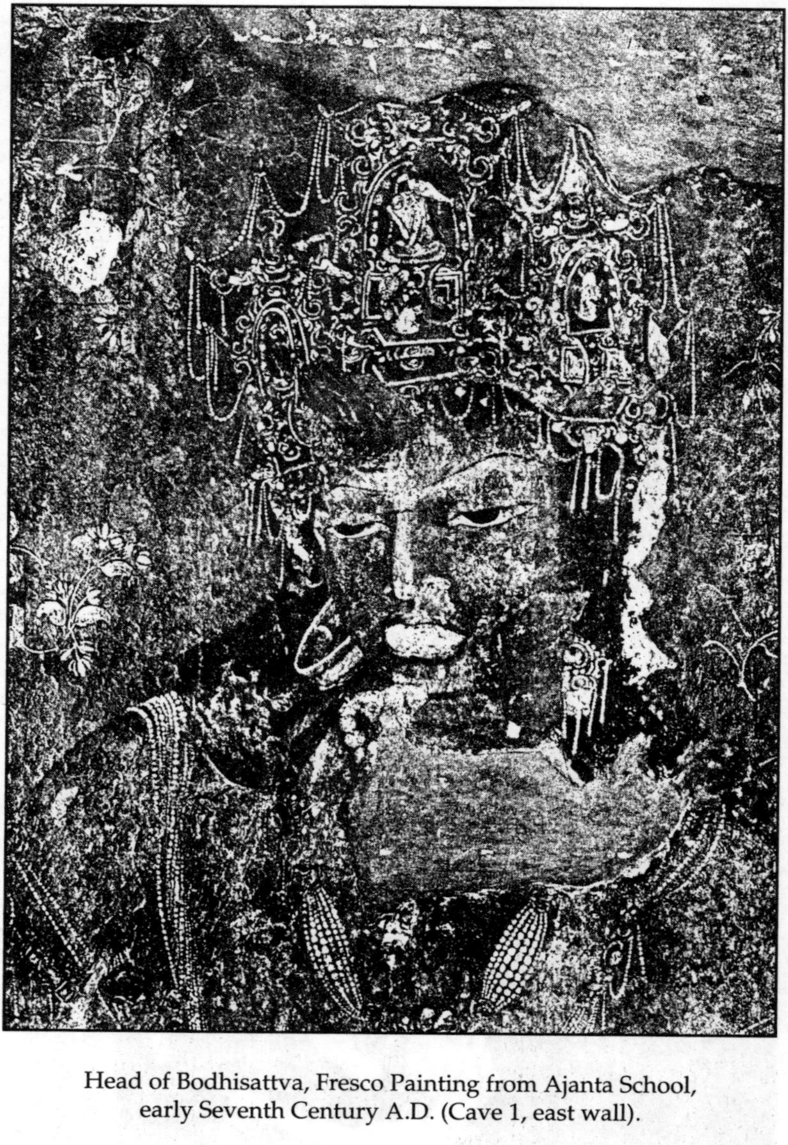

Head of Bodhisattva, Fresco Painting from Ajanta School, early Seventh Century A.D. (Cave 1, east wall).

Plate 2

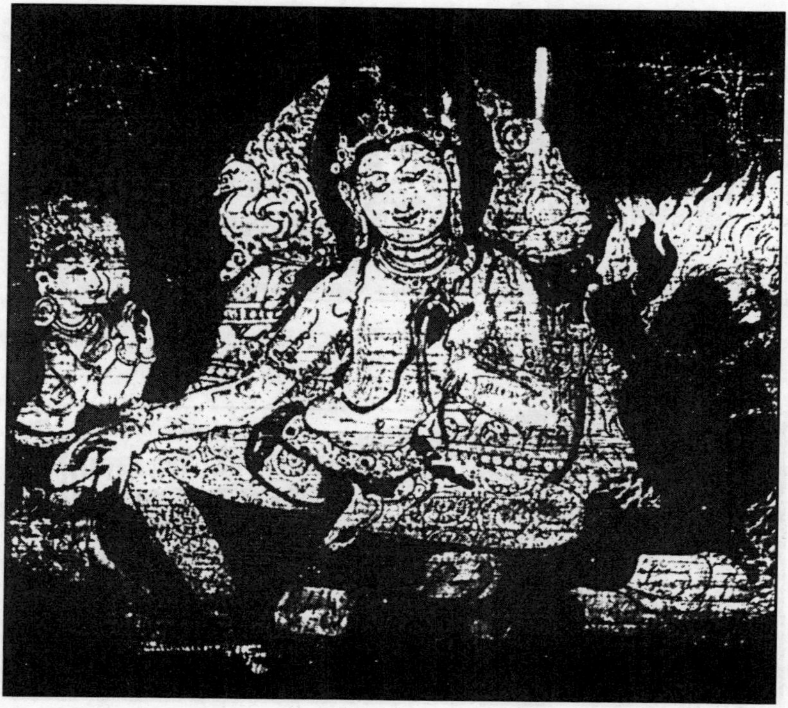

Illustration from a Bengali palm leaf Buddhist Manuscript dated 1087 A.D., Pāla School (Victoria and Albert Museum, London).

Plate 3

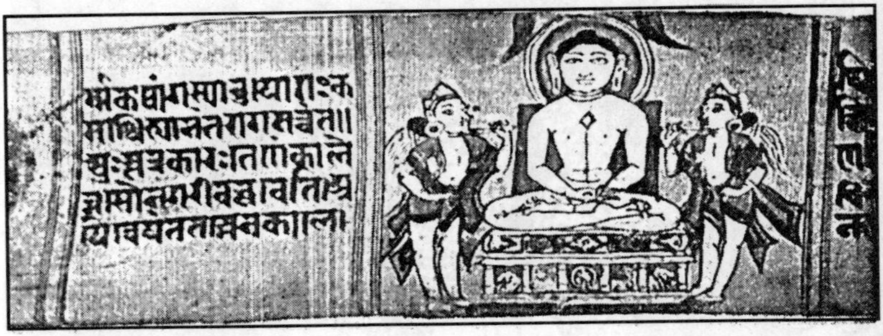

Figure 1

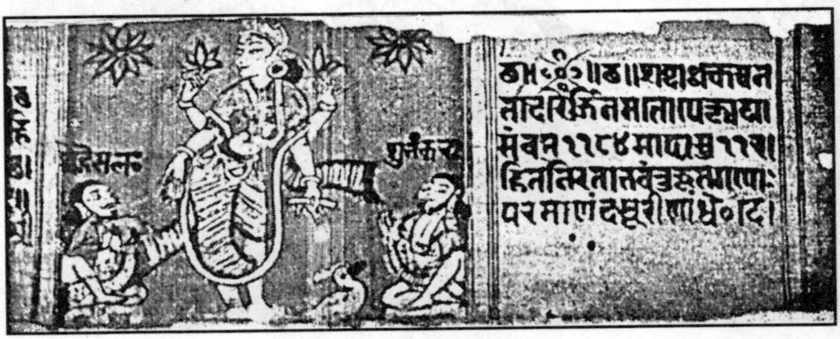

Figure 2

Illustrations from Jain palm leaf Manuscript *Niśitha Curni* dated 11-12 Century A.D., Western Indian School.

Plate 4

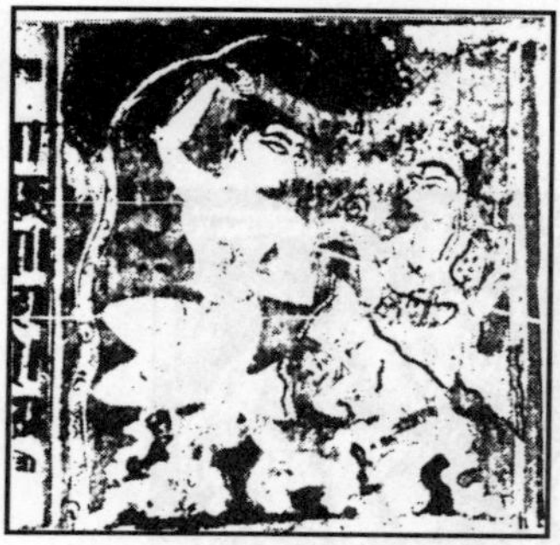

Figure 1

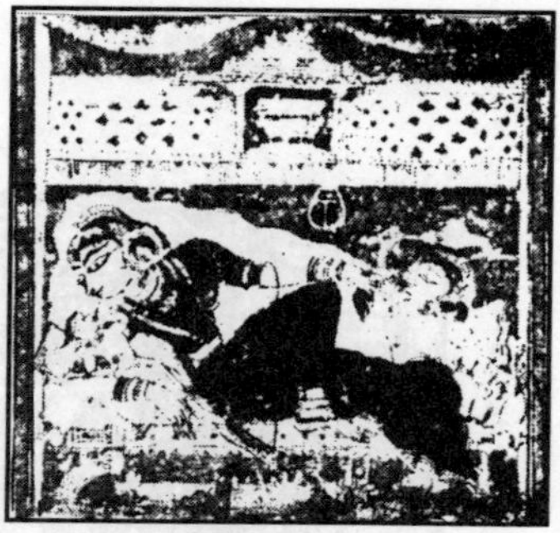

Figure 2

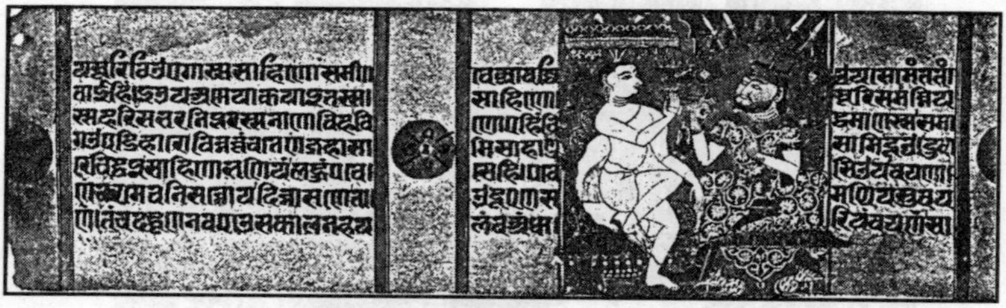

Figure 3

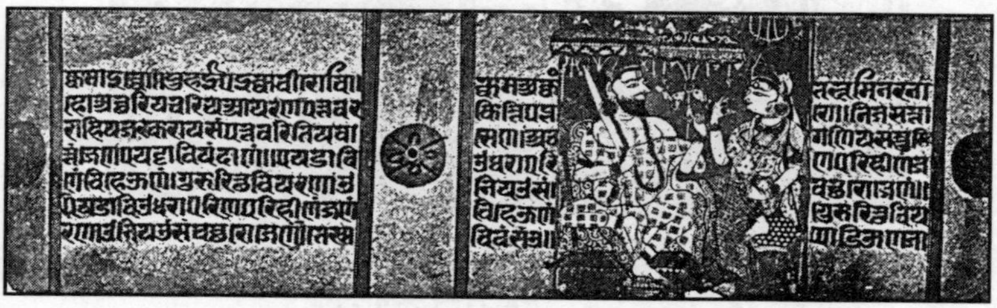

Figure 4

Illustrations from Jain Manuscript *Kalpasutra* and *Kalākāchārya Kathā* of Pa›an on Paper dated late 14th Century A.D. (Figs. 1 & 2) and 1400 A.D. (Figs. 3 & 4) Western Indian School.

Plate 5

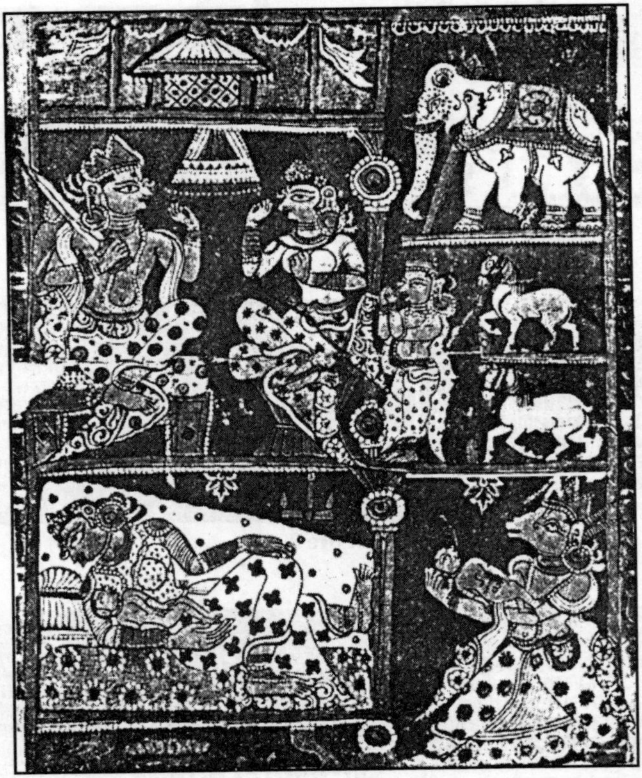

Illustration from *Kalpasutra* of Mandu
dated 1439 A.D., Western Indian School (Pre-Rajasthani Style),
National Museum of India, New Delhi.

Plate 6

(Rāgas)
SRI VASANT BHAIRAV PANCHAM MEGHA

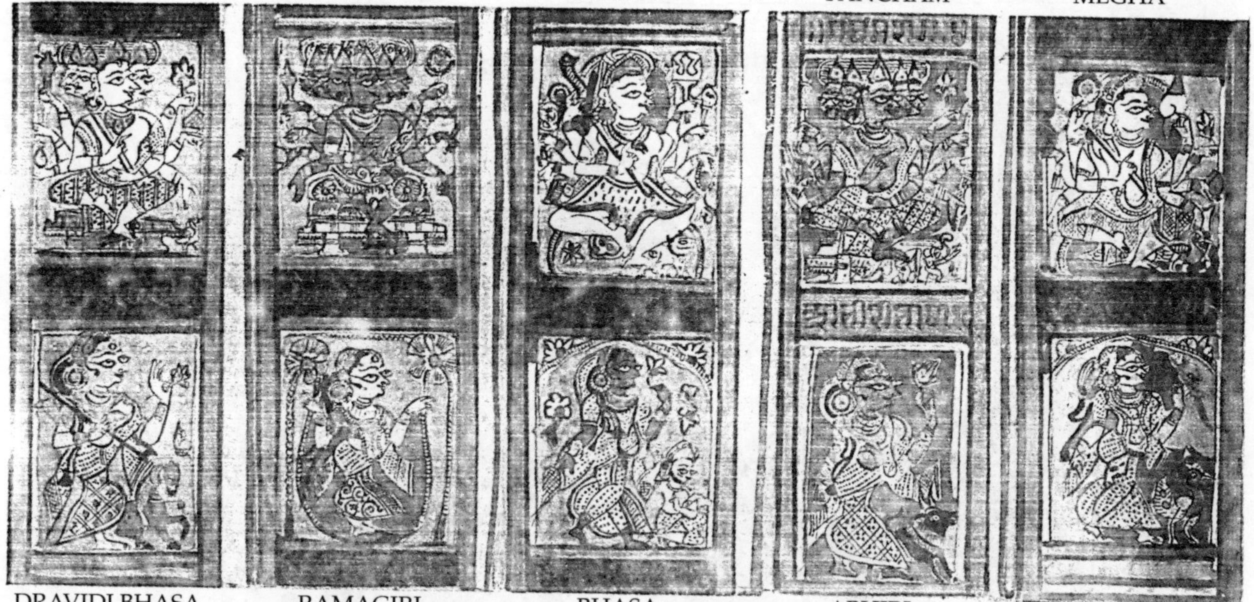

DRAVIDI BHASA RAMAGIRI BHASA ABHIRI DEBALA
(Raginis)

Earliest example of Rāgamālā Paintings—Illustrations of *Kalpasutra* Manuscript dated 1475 A.D., Western Indian School/Pre-Rajasthani Style (corr. to Rāgas and Bhāsās of Sudhā Kalaśa).

Plate 7

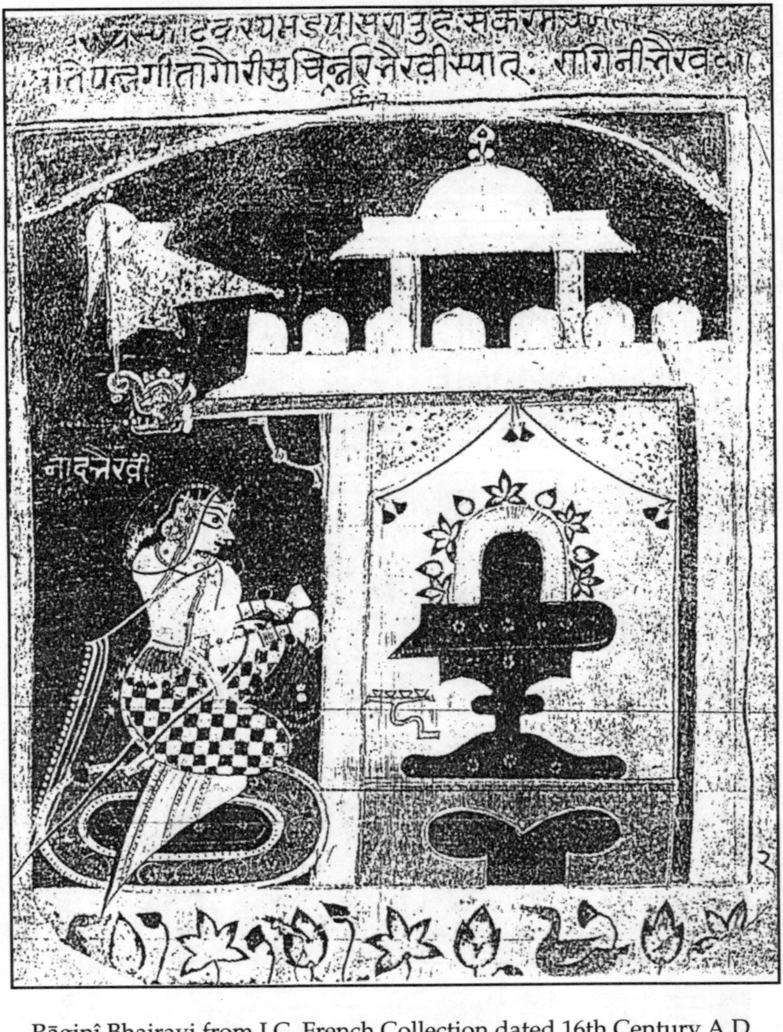

Rāginî Bhairavi from J.C. French Collection dated 16th Century A.D., Rajasthani Style.

Plate 8

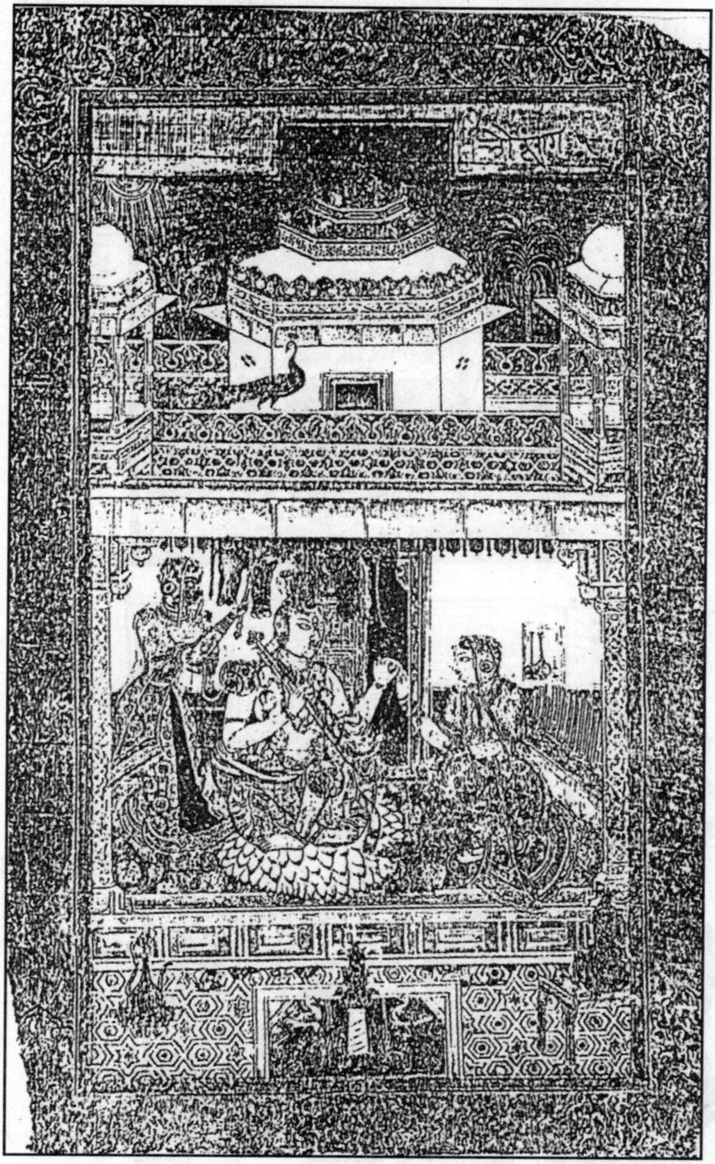

Rāga Bhairava, Chunār Rāgamālā (1591 A.D.), Rajasthani Style.

Plate 9

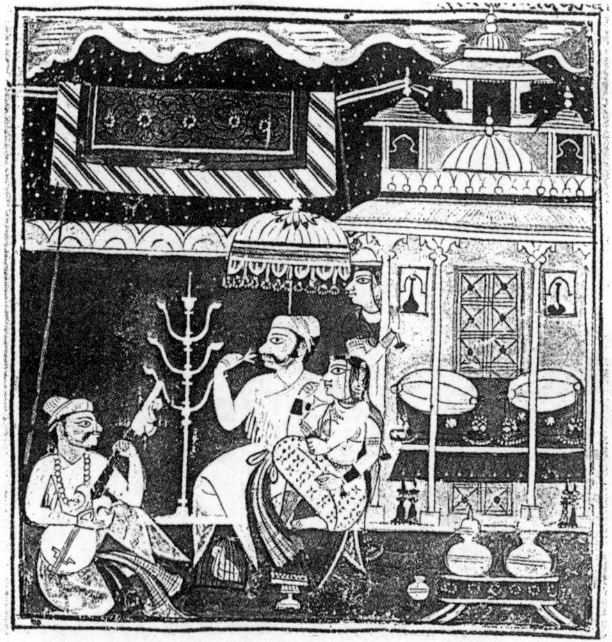

Dîpak Rāga (from a Rāgamālā), Painted by Nisaradi, Mewar School, Chawand 1605 A.D., (Miniature 6 3/8 x 6 1/8")
G.K. Kanoria Collection, Calcutta.

Plate 10

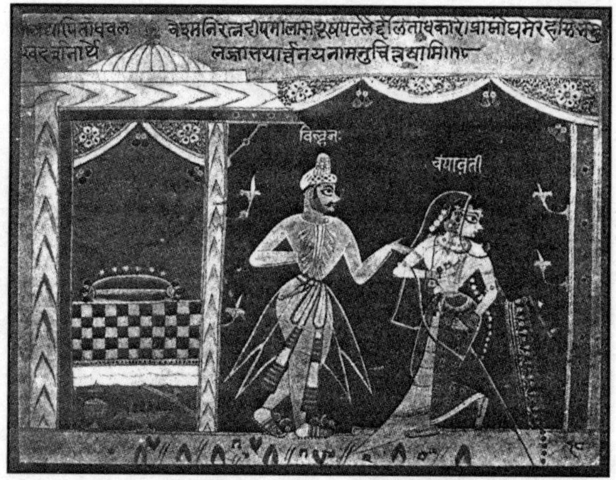

Chaurapanchasika Painting (16th Century A.D.),
Pre-Rajasthani Style Culture
Century, Ahmedabad.

Plate 11

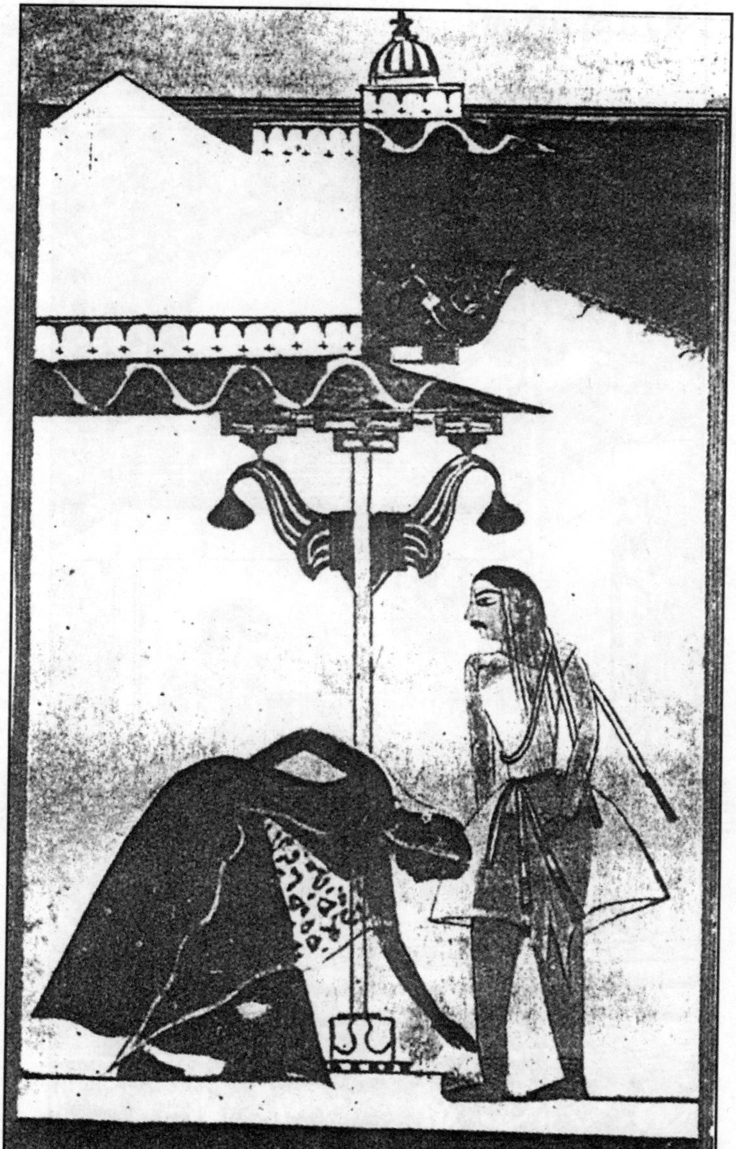

Laurchanda Painting, 1560 A.D. from Manchester Rylands Library
Fish Eye takes Place of Jain 'further eye'.

Plate 12

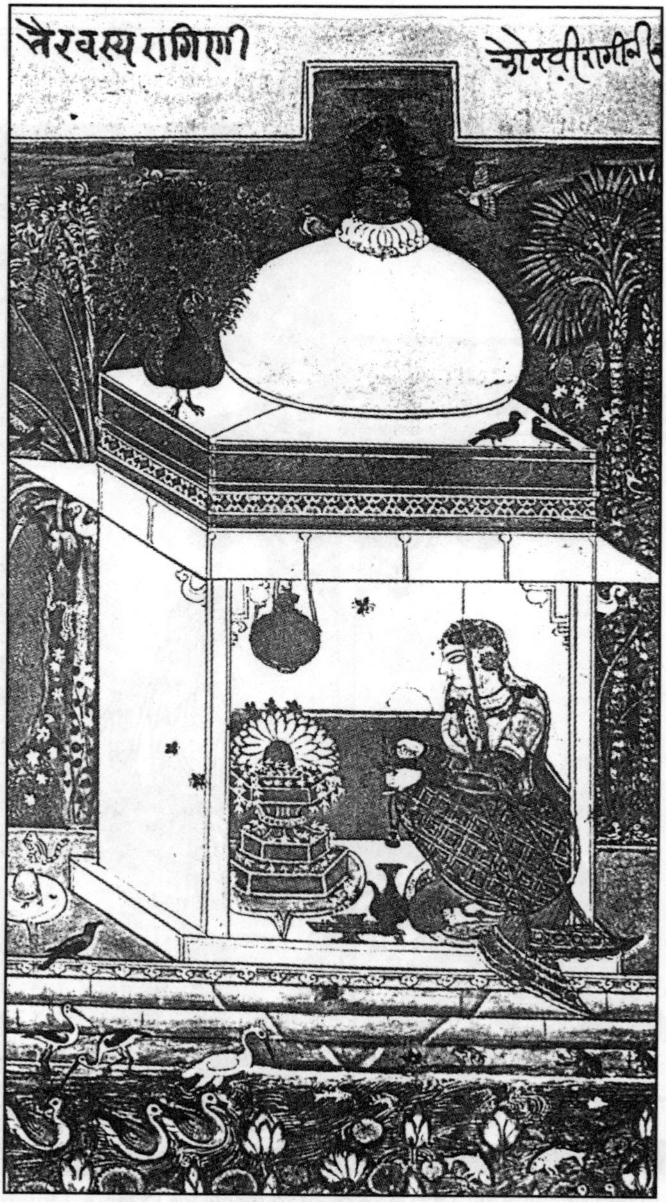

Bhairavi Rāginî (from a Rāgamālā), Bundi School, about 1625 A.D., (8 x ½") Allahabad Museum.

Plate 13

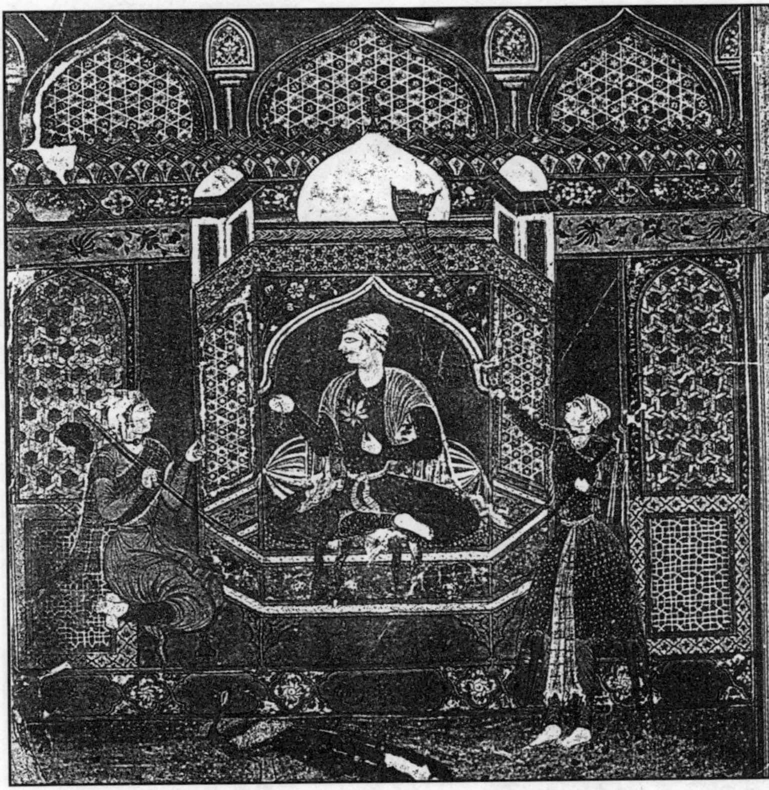

Rāgamālā Series: Rāga Śri, Bijapur, 1590-1600 A.D., (7⅞ x 6⅞")
Khajanchi Collection, Bikaner.

Plate 14

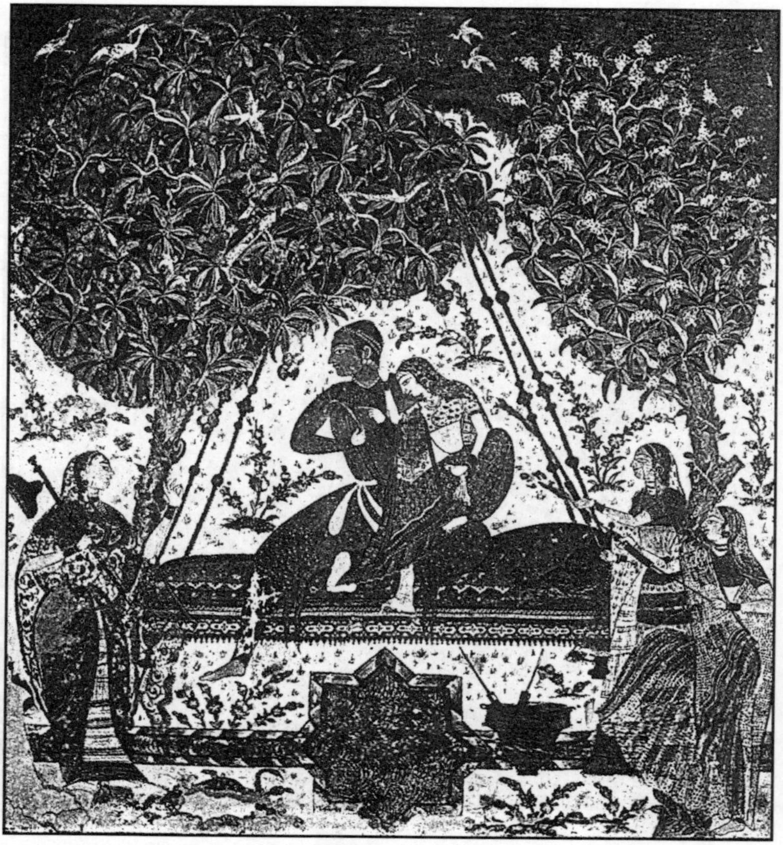

Rāgamālā Series: Hindola Rāga, Ahmadnagar, late Sixteenth Century (7 5/8 x 7")
National Museum, New Delhi.

Plate 15

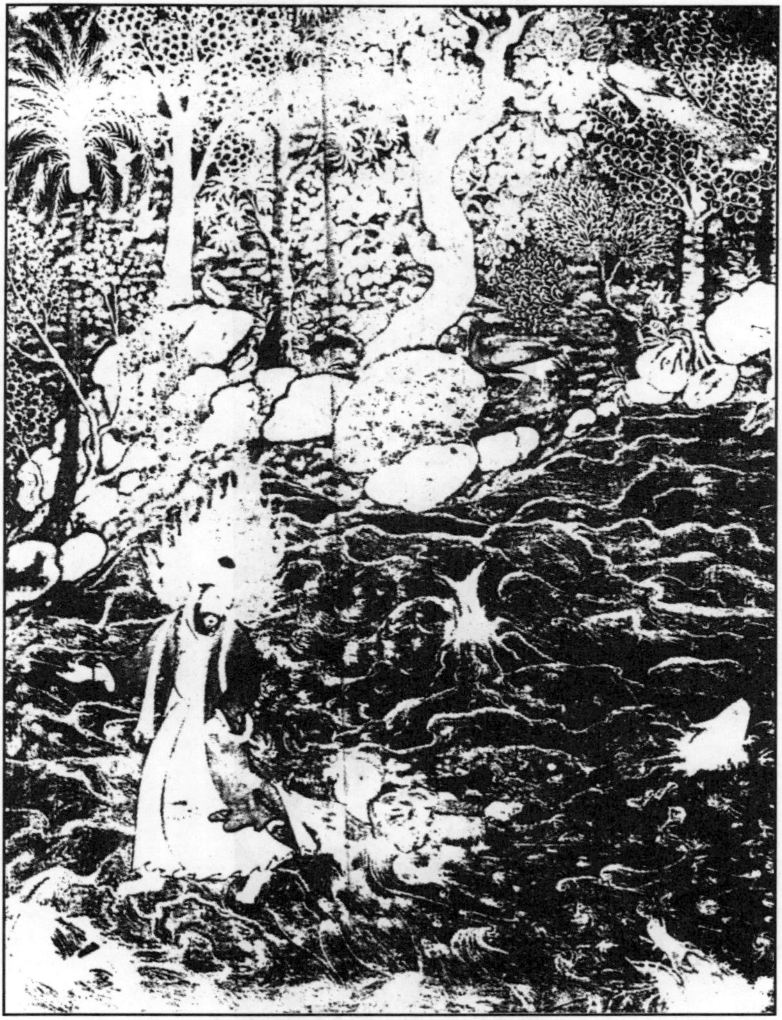

Episode from *Hamzāhnāmā*, 1564 A.D., Mughal School, British Museum, London.

Plate 16

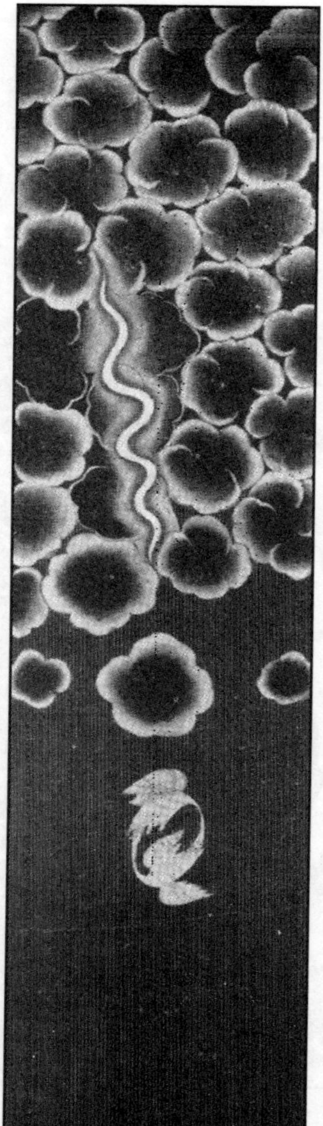

Rāga Megh Mallār (17th Century A.D.), Abstract Fresco with Chinese Influence, Jaipur City Palace.

Plate 17

Bibliography

1. *Aesthetic, Benedetto Croce*, translation by Douglas Ainslie, Pub. Rupa & Co., Calcutta, 4th Edition, 1911.
2. *Aesthetical Essays*, S.K. Saxena, Pub. Chanakya Publication, Delhi, 1981.
3. *Aesthetic Theory and Art,* R.K. Ghosh, Pub. Ajanta Publications, Delhi, 1979.
4. *Aesthetic Education and the Grammar of Art,* H.L. Sharma, Pub. Mansi Prakashan, Meerut, 1991.
5. *Aristotle's Theory of Poetry and Fine Art*, S.H. Butcher, Pub. Dover Publications Inc., 4th edition, 1951.
6. *Art and Philosophy*, S.K. Saxena, Pub. Chanakya Publication, Delhi.
7. *A Critical Study of Sangîta Makaranda of Nārada,* M. Vijay Lakshmi, Pub. Gyan Publishing House, New Delhi, 1996.
8. *A History of Indian Painting,* Krishna Chaitanya, Pub. Abhinav Publication, 1982.
9. *Bhāratiya kalā ke āyām,* Nihar Ranjan Ray, translation by Suresh Uniyal, Pub. Purvodaya Prakashan, New Delhi, 1984.
10. *Bhāratiya Sangît kā itihāsa,* Dr. Saracchandra Shridhar Paranjpe, Pub. Chowkhamba Vidya Bhawan, Varansai, 2nd edition, 1975.
11. *Bhāratiya saundarya śāstra kā tātlvika vivecan evam lalita kalāyen,* Dr. Ram Lakhan Shukla, Pub. National Publishing House, New Delhi, 1978.
12. *Bharat Bhāṣyaṁ of Nanya Bhupal,* Parts 1 and 2, ed. Chaitanya P. Desai, Pub. Indira Kala Sangit Vishwavidyalaya, Khairagarh, M.P., 1st edition, 1961.
13. *Bhārat ki citrakalā*, Rai Krishna Das, Pub. Bharati Bhandar, Allahabad.
14. *Bhātkhande Smriti Granth,* Commemoration volume, Pub. Indira Kala Sangit Vishwavidyalaya, Khairagarh, M.P., 1966.

15. *Bhavanon par citrit Rāga*, S.V. Vadnerkar, in Sangeet Kala Vihar, monthly journal, pub. V.R. Athvale, Jan. 1979.
16. *Bṛhaddeśî of Mataṅga muni, Kalāmula Śāstra granthmālā*, general editor — Kapila Vatsyayan, ed. Premlata Sharma, Pub. Indira Kala National Centre for the Arts and Motilal Banarasidass Publishers.
17. *Catalogue of the Indian Collections in the Museum of Fine Arts*, Boston, Part IV, Jaina Paintings, A.K. Coomarswamy.
18. *Comparative Aesthetics*, Vol. 1, Indian Aesthetics, Dr. K.C. Pandey, Pub. Chowkhamba Sanskrit Series Office, Varanasi, 2nd edition, 1959.
19. *Comparative Aesthetics*, Vol. 2, Western Aesthetics, Dr. K.C. Pandey., Pub. Chowkhamba Sanskrit Series Office, Varanasi, 2nd edition, 1972.
20. *Deccani Painting*, Mark Zebrowski, Pub. Roli Books International, 1983.
21. *Earliest Indian Miniatures*, B.N. Mukherjee, Pub. Arts India Publication, Calcutta, 1992.
22. *Elements of Indian Aesthetics*, Vol. II, *Elements of Fine Arts, Crafts and Gesture, Part 1, History and Thoughts of Indian Arts*, S.N. Ghoshal Shāshtri, Pub. Chaukhamba Orientalia, Varanasi, Delhi, 1983.
23. *Encyclopaedia Britannica*, Vol. 2 and 12, Pub. William Benton, Encyclopaedia Britannica Ltd., London, Chicago, Geneva, Sydney, Toronto, 1964.
24. *Feeling and Form*, Susanne K. Langer, Pub. Routledge and Kegan Paul Ltd., London, 1953.
25. *Hindustani Music—A study of its Development in Seventeenth and Eighteenth Centuries*, Dr. Najma Parveen Ahmed, Pub. Manohar Publications, New Delhi, 1984.
26. *Indian Aesthetics and Aesthetic Perspectives*, H.L. Sharma, Pub. Mansi Prakashan, Meerut, 1990.
27. *Indian Miniatures*, Mario Bussagli, Pub. Paul Hamlyn, The Hamlyn Publishing Group Ltd., Middlesex, 1969.
28. *Indian Music*, Dr. Thakur Jaidev Singh, Pub. Sangeet Research Academy, Calcutta, 1995.
29. *Indian Painting*, Percy Brown, the Heritage of India series, Pub. Y.M.C.A. Publishing House, Calcutta, 5th edition, 1947 (1st edition 1917).

30. *Indian Painting, the Scene, Themes and Legends,* Mohinder Singh Randhawa and John Kenneth Galbraith, Pub. Oxford and IBH Publishing Co., Calcutta, Bombay, New Delhi, 1968.
31. *'Kalidasa on the Arts',* Dr. T. Bhaskaran and *'Painting and Allied Arts as Revealed in Banāś Works'*, C. Sivaramamurti, *Gleanings of Indian Music and Art,* ed. Leela Omcherry and Deepti Bhalla, Pub. Sundeep Prakashan, Delhi, 1991.
32. *Kangra Rāgamālā Paintings,* M.S. Randhawa, Pub. National Museum, New Delhi, 1971.
33. *Madhyakāleen Bhāratiya katayen evaṁ unkā vikās.* Dr. Ramnath, Pub. Rajasthan Hindi Granth Academy, Jaipur, 1973.
34. *Nāṭya Śāstra of Bharatmuni*, ed. Manmohan Ghosh, Pub. Maneesha Granthalaya Pvt. Ltd., 1967.
35. *Pahari Miniature Painting,* Karl Khandalavala, Pub. The New Book Company Pvt. Ltd., Bombay, 1958.
36. *Paintings of India,* Douglas Barett and Basil Gray, Treasures of Asia Series, Pub. Albert Skira, Editions d' Art, 1963.
37. *Philosophy in a New Key*, S.K. langer, Pub. Harvard University Press, Cambridge, Massachusetts, 3rd edition, 1976.
38. *Radha Govind Sangît Sār*, Sawai Pratap Singh Dev, Pub. Balwant Triyamvak Sahasrabuddhe, Gayan Samaj, Pune, 1912.
39. *Rāga Vibodha of Somanatha,* ed. Pt. S. Subrahmanya Sastri, Pub. Adyar Library, Madras, 1945.
40. *'Ragamala-Indiaś Visible Music'*, article by Klaus Ebeling in Span, Dec. 1973.
41. *Rāgamālā—The Mussing Link*, Tilak Gitai, Pub. Shashi Agarwal, Jaipur, 1997.
42. *Ragmala Painting*, Klaus Ebeling, Pub. Ravi Kumar, Basel, Paris, New Delhi, 1973.
43. *Rāgas aṇd Rāginîs,* O.C. Gangoly, Vol. 1, Pub. Munshi Ram Manohar Lal, 1935.
44. *Rajasthani Rāgamālā Citra Paramgara,* Dr. Mahendra Kumar Sharma 'Sumahendra', Pub. Publication Scheme Jaipur.
45. *Rajasthan ki Sānskritik Parampara.* Dr. Jai Singh Neeraj, Dr. B.L. Sharma, Pub. Rajasthan Hindi Granth Academy, Jaipur, 1989.
46. *Rajput Painting*, A.K. Cooṃarswamy, Vol. 1, Pub. Motilal Banarsidass, 1916.
47. *'Ranga aur sangît'* by Hirendra Kumar' Basu in Sangeet Journal, Pub. Sangeet Karyalaya, Hathras, Nov. 1993 issue.

48. Review of W.G. Archer's '*Indian Painting in the Punjab Hills*', by J.C. French in '*Art and Letters;* Vol. XXVI, No. 1, 1952.
49. *Ṛgveda, Vishweshwaranand Bharatabharati granthmālā 23,* Vishweshwaranand Vaidic shodh samsthāna parakāshan 312, pt. V ed. Vishwabandhu.
50. *Sangît Darpaṇa of Damodar Mishra*, translation & edited by Vishwambharnath Bhatt, Pub. Sangeet Karyalaya, Hathras, 2nd edition 1962.
51. *Sangît Ratnakara of Pt. Śārṅgadgva*, part 1, 1st chapter, ed. Pt. S. Subramanya Sastri, Adyar Library, Pub. Chowkhamba Sanskrit Series part 2, 2nd chapter, translation by Shringy and Sharma, Pub. Munshi Ram Manohar Lal Publishers, 1989.
52. *Saundarya—Aesthetics, Philosophy of Beauty and Art,* Dr. Rajendra Bajpai, Pub. Madhya Pradesh Hindi Granth Academy, Bhopal, 1998.
53. *Saundarya Śāstra ke tattva* Dr. Kumar Vimal, Pub. Raj Kamal Prakashan, New Delhi, 2nd edition, 1981.
54. *Saundarya tattva mimansa*, Dr. Syamala Gupta, Pub. Seema Sahitya Bhavan, 1992.
55. *South Indian Music,* Book IV, Prof. P. Sambamoorthy, Pub. The Indian Music Publishing House, G.T. Madras, 1963.
56. *Studies in Jaina Art,* Umakant P. Shah, Pub. Jaina Cultural Research Society, Banaras, 1955.
57. *Studies in the Nātya Śāstra,* G.H. Tarlekar, Pub. Motilal Banarsidass, 1975.
58. 'Tara Nath's chapter on Buddhist Art, Indian Antiquary', W.L. Healey, 1975 from *'Marg'* Vol. IX, No. 2, 1956.
59. *Tarjuma-i-Mānakutuhala and Risālā-i-Rāga Darpana,* ed. Shahab Sarmadee, general ed. Kapila Vatsyayan, Pub. Indira Gandhi National Centre for the Arts, New Delhi, 1996.
60. *The Canons of Indian Art,* Tarapada Bhattacharya, Pub. Firma. K.L. Mukhopadhyaya, Calcutta, 2nd edition, 1963.
61. *The Historical Development of Indian Music*, Swami Prajnananda, Pub. Firma K.L. Mukhopadhyaya, Calcutta, 1960.
62. *'The Philosophy of Fine Art'*, G.W.F. Hegel in *Aesthetic Theories — Studies in the Philosophy of Art*, ed. Karl Aschen Brenner and Arnold Isenberg.
63. *The Practical Sanskrit-English Dictionary*, V.S. Apte, Vol. 1, Pub. Prasad Prakashan, Poona, 1957.

64. *The Music of India*, H.A. Popley, Pub. Award Publishing House, New Delhi, 1986.
65. *The Structure of Aesthetics*, F.E. Sparshott, Pub-University of Toronto Press (Toronto) and Routledge and Kegan Paul, London, 1963.
66. *Vastu Shastra*, Vol. II, D.N. Shukla, Bharatiya Vāstu Śastra series, Vol. IX, Pub. Vastu Vanmaya Prakashanshala, Lucknow, 1958.
67. *Viṣṇu Purāṇa, A System of Hindu Mythology and Tradition*, translation from Sanskrit, H.H. Wilson, Pub. Punthi Pustak, Calcutta, 1961.

Index